The American Church that Might Have Been

The
American Church
that Might Have Been

A History of the
Consultation on Church Union

Keith Watkins

Foreword by Michael Kinnamon

☙PICKWICK *Publications* · Eugene, Oregon

THE AMERICAN CHURCH THAT MIGHT HAVE BEEN
A History of the Consultation on Church Union

Pickwick Publications
An Imprint of Wipf and Stock Publishers
199 W. 8th Ave., Suite 3
Eugene, OR 97401

www.wipfandstock.com

ISBN 13: 978-1-62564-431-2

Cataloging-in-Publication data:

Watkins, Keith.

    The American church that might have been : a history of the Consultation on Church Union / Keith Watkins ; foreword by Michael Kinnamon.

        xviii + 244 p. ; 23 cm. —Includes bibliographical references and index.

        ISBN 13: 978-1-62564-431-2

        1. Consultation on Church Union. 2. Christian union—United States. I. Kinnamon, Michael K., 1949–. II. Title.

BR516.5 .W38 2014

Manufactured in the U.S.A.

Remembering with love,
Billie Lee Caton Watkins
Now singing alto in the
Choir of Angels
July 19, 1931 – August 12, 2014

Contents

Foreword

THE CONSULTATION ON CHURCH Union, COCU as it was commonly called, was the most ambitious effort ever undertaken to unite Protestant churches in the United States. It began in 1960 with a focus on addressing divisions inherited from the Reformation; but once three Black Methodist churches joined the Consultation in the late 1960s, it began to deal as well with the most divisive of all issues in the American context—race. The Christian community has needed a careful, engaging history of this forty-year effort, and I celebrate the fact that Dr. Keith Watkins has now provided it.

This book will certainly be of interest to those who lived through the ecumenical excitement of the 1960s or who remember when COCU shifted gears in the 1970s and 1980s, moving from a plan of union to one of Covenant Communion. It should also be of interest, however, to all persons who care about the church and its wholeness and want to know what can be learned from the history of this Consultation.

In the end, COCU did not result in a union of the participating denominations, did not lead to a Protestant church that, in the language of the Consultation, was truly catholic, truly evangelical, and truly reformed. I share Watkins' judgment, however, that COCU should not be evaluated solely on the basis of this failure. There can be little doubt that the churches were changed—renewed—through their engagement with one another in the Consultation. For example, COCU helped stimulate and shape a consensus on the renewal of Protestant worship and helped sensitize the churches to the ecclesiological implications of discrimination with regard to race, gender, class, and physical or mental disability. Four decades of shared Bible study and theological reflection, shared mission and common prayer, enabled the churches to know one another more intimately and to think more deeply about the unity they have in Christ.

All of this is set forth with great clarity, with sympathy that does not shy away from critique, in *The American Church that Might Have Been*. Watkins obviously believes that COCU was a missed opportunity to move beyond a denominational system that has become sociologically obsolete to a pattern of church life better adapted to present realities. But his tone is one of appreciation for what was accomplished as well as lamentation for what might have been. And, through a careful reading of COCU's theological and political dynamics, he distills from this history an ongoing agenda for churches that are concerned for how the gospel relates to American culture.

I, personally, was deeply involved in COCU, serving as its final General Secretary from 1999 to 2002. Watkins' treatment strikes me as thorough and balanced. Reading his account, I was impressed, as I suspect many readers will be, by the tenacity of so many Christian leaders to the vision of a united American church, by the sheer amount of work that went into this forty-year journey, and by the number of church leaders and theologians who contributed to it. This volume also reminds us just how much the church is shaped by, and is a shaper of, its social, historical context.

Some may argue that a post-mortem of COCU is premature; in 2002, COCU morphed into Churches Uniting in Christ (CUIC), an ecumenical initiative that, while foundering, still exists. It is hard to deny, however, the thesis of this book: that COCU ended without accomplishing its primary goal—the creation of a new, integrated Protestant church in the United States. Whatever CUIC becomes in the future, it will not be what the COCU pioneers envisioned. And, as Watkins emphasizes, we are not likely to see such an effort again.

But that is not the end of the story. In the sermon that gave rise to COCU in 1960, Eugene Carson Blake declared that "our separate [church] organizations, however much we sincerely try to cooperate in councils, present a tragically divided church to a tragically divided world. Our divided state makes almost unbelievable our common Christian claim that Christ is Lord and that he is the Prince of Peace." *The American Church that Might Have Been* reminds us that this remains as true in the early decades of the twenty-first century as it was in the middle decades of the twentieth. The challenge is to find new forms of faithful response.

Michael Kinnamon
School of Theology and Ministry
Seattle University

Acknowledgments

As a member of COCU's Commission on Worship from 1968 to 1988, I participated in semi-annual gatherings of this working group, nine plenary assemblies of the Consultation on Church Union, and the 2002 assembly during which the Consultation bequeathed its mission to the Churches Uniting in Christ. The remembrance of innumerable conversations, debates, drafting activities, addresses, and periods of worship provided the context within which my rereading of the literature by and about COCU took place. Gratefully I acknowledge my indebtedness to the men and women, many of whom are named in this narrative, who influenced my understanding of the church and its life in the world.

The two persons who served as COCU's general secretaries throughout its most active years—Paul A. Crow Jr. and Gerald F. Moede—have been especially helpful as I have written this history. Michael Kinnamon, a colleague for a quarter of a century whose career of scholarly ecumenical leadership included serving as COCU's final general secretary, has provided insights related to the Consultation's final period. I am grateful that he has been willing to write the foreword to this book. Others who have read portions or all of this manuscript and have given me their responses include Harold M. Daniels, Thomas E. Dipko, James O. Duke, Raymond R. Sommerville Jr., John H. Thomas, Robert K. Welsh, and W. Clyde Williams. I thank them for their assistance in preparing this history.

Although I have carefully considered the many comments about the Consultation on Church Union that have come to me, I take full responsibility for the narrative, especially the concluding chapters in which I assess this movement and the ongoing challenge of manifesting the unity of Christ's Ecclesial Body in an historically recognizable way.

Most of my research has used the Consultation's published records and reports and other materials published in scholarly journals, newspapers, and journals of opinion. In addition, I used a small collection of Paul Crow's personal files, which subsequently were transferred to the archives of the Consultation on Church Union at the Library of Princeton Theological Seminary in Princeton, New Jersey.

The Cole Library of the Disciples Seminary Foundation in Claremont, California, provided the long-term loan of volumes of *Mid-Stream* and other hard-to-access COCU materials, and served as a hospitable location for periods of research. The library and staff of Christian Theological Seminary in Indianapolis, Indiana, on whose faculty I served during my COCU years, continued to assist me with print materials, personal assistance, and access to online data resources. The Fort Vancouver Regional Library in Vancouver, Washington, assisted with interlibrary loan services and access to electronic data banks, and the Kellenberger Library at Northwest Christian University in Eugene, Oregon, provided access to periodical literature. To this network of institutions and their dedicated staffs, I express my sincere appreciation.

Introduction

"Protestant plan for unity hailed." Under this headline on December 5, 1960, *New York Times* reporter George Dugan wrote that a proposal "to unite four of this country's major Protestant denominations has captured the imagination of churchgoers."[1] The chief executive officer of the United Presbyterian Church, Eugene Carson Blake, had proposed the plan in a sermon the previous day at Grace Cathedral in San Francisco. Host pastor James A. Pike, bishop of the Protestant Episcopal Diocese of California, had seconded the proposal and during the next few days other church leaders who had been in the church when the sermon was preached declared their interest in the idea. In addition to the Presbyterian and Episcopal churches, the plan initially included The Methodist Church and the United Church of Christ.

The four churches accepted Blake's proposal. At their organizational meeting April 9–10, 1962, their representatives named the new venture the Consultation on Church Union (COCU) and invited other churches to join them. During COCU's active years, nine churches, with a combined membership of 25 million, were full participants. Had this new Protestant church at the center of American life come into being, it would have been second only to the Roman Catholic Church in its size and distribution throughout the nation.

The comprehensive character of this vision was suggested by the formula that soon developed to describe the new church the members hoped to establish: it would be *truly catholic, truly evangelical, and truly reformed,* and thereby more inclusive in its theological and missional character than any other church in the nation. This new church would bridge one of the major cleavages that for 450 years had separated Catholic and Protestant variants of western Christianity. It would increase significantly the possibilities for intercommunion among Christians who for generations had been

1. Dugan, "Protestant Plan for Church Union Hailed," *New York Times,* December 6, 1960.

denied "communion in sacred things." It would provide a way for Protestant churches in America to move beyond the denominational system, a structural pattern born in this country that was rapidly becoming dysfunctional. In what may have been its most important contribution, this new church would focus attention upon and move toward resolving, as no other public institution had done, the systemic fractures in American life defined by race, gender, and social class, which from earliest years had compromised the American dream of liberty and justice for all.

From the outset of this effort, there were misgivings among the churches. Some people declared that their separate traditions and patterns of life were so important that the existing denominations needed to be preserved. Because the new church would be so large, others claimed, it would be administratively top-heavy and bureaucratically clumsy. Some were convinced that the ideas in Blake's proposal did not go far enough and that the American church needed more radical and faster action than COCU could deliver. Some questioned whether this kind of church was appropriate in the United States because it seemed too much like an established church. Some critics argued that the union could come about only by means of coercion or compromise. These and other misgivings could arise, in part, because the plan failed to give details about the process by which the merger of these churches could be achieved.

Despite these and other objections, the churches moved forward vigorously, with leaders from their highest echelons taking the lead. Executives, scholars, pastors, and lay leaders of the participating churches wrote a significant body of theological literature, attended meetings, participated in deliberative assemblies, and in other ways labored diligently for the cause. Other churches and church organizations—Roman Catholic, Orthodox, Lutheran, Baptist, Brethren, Pentecostal, from North America and abroad—sent observer participants to COCU meetings, and contributed significantly to this effort to reshape American Christianity.

During the first decade of its work, the COCU churches worked through a series of deeply rooted theological challenges dealing with the relationship of Scripture and Tradition, the central themes of the Christian faith, patterns of worship, and the forms of ministry. Their progress was so promising that the Consultation prepared a comprehensive plan of union that was intended to be the basis on which the participating churches would unite and other churches would be attracted to join the new ecclesial body.

The importance of the COCU venture to churches everywhere was summarized in the evaluation offered by one of the Roman Catholic Church's observer-consultants, John F. Hotchkin, who was his church's principal American officer dealing with ecumenical and interreligious affairs. "The

Church of Christ Uniting," the name that had been given the new church, "will not only change the religious topography of the United States, it will undoubtedly occupy a position of central importance in the new situation that is created by its emergence." Hotchkin focused his evaluation upon two aspects of COCU's vision: its "recovered sense of communion among all Christians" and its emphasis upon the gospel's requirement that this communion would "bring together men and women, blacks and whites, persons who have achieved wisdom through simplicity and persons of sophisticated intelligence." Hotchkin concluded his essay by stating that the Consultation on Church Union "has become the most advanced and most concrete endeavor attempted in the ecumenical history of this country."[2]

Hotchkin wrote at a time when his church, reenergized by the Second Vatican Council, was increasingly active in ecumenical discussions and actions around the world. Scholars everywhere were becoming conversation partners in ways that previously had hardly seemed possible. The work of existing ecumenical agencies, such as the Commission on Faith and Order of the World Council of Churches, was becoming more comprehensive than had previously been possible. Some Protestant scholars were finding that the journal *Worship* published by the monks of St. John's Abbey in Collegeville, Minnesota, was an attractive venue in which they could publish their work dealing with theological and pastoral dimensions of Christian worship. In local communities around the world, and certainly in the United States, Protestant and Catholic Christians were discovering a new kind of communion with one another.

COCU's determined effort to create a comprehensive union of American churches stretched out for four decades, from its founding in 1962 until its conclusion in 2002. During these decades of interaction, the COCU churches came to understand one another in a far deeper way than at any previous time and increased significantly their modes of shared life and ministry. They resolved some of the church dividing issues and made constructive progress in overcoming others. They developed constructive liturgies of the Eucharist, Baptism, and other rites of the church. COCU served its churches as one means of participating in and shaping the cultural and religious transformation that was taking place in this nation and around the world.

In 2002, the Consultation on Church Union bequeathed its legacy to an organization shaped by a different vision of churchly communion—Churches Uniting in Christ (CUIC)—without accomplishing the goal for which the churches had labored so diligently. A new kind of American

2. Hotchkin, "COCU and the Wider Reality of Ecumenism," 214–21.

church—fully catholic, fully evangelical, and fully reformed—had not yet come into being. These years of close interrelationship demonstrated that although the yearning for unity was strong, the established ways of life, systems of belief, modes of liturgical practice, and organizational processes were even stronger and more deeply ingrained than anyone wanted to admit. As the churches dealt openly with issues of power, prestige, and precedent, both in church life and in the broader society, they came to realize how intractable these issues really were. When the times to make binding decisions arrived, the churches—white and black—were unwilling to yield their sovereignties so that they could "be dissolved and sink into union with the body of Christ at large."[3]

Despite a significant degree of theological rapprochement, the central issues of ecclesiology, sacramental practice, and Christian identity in the nation would remain unresolved. At a time when the participating churches were experiencing significant organizational challenges, they insisted on maintaining their denominational system of separated life instead of entering into a new pattern better adapted to the social realities of their generation. During a generation in which the people of the United States were facing the enduring legacy of racism, the churches made serious and partially successful efforts to include all people regardless of race and culture, but continued to exist as denominations distinguished in large part by race. Rather than developing new spiritual resources to address the human needs of the nation, these churches found themselves losing their grip on America's centers of power and realized that they were increasingly becoming marginalized in the very nation they had intended to heal and renew.

The question has to be addressed: If the Consultation on Church Union failed to create the new church it had struggled so valiantly to establish, why should we, a generation later, pay attention to this episode of American religious history?

Short answers can be given. *The first is that these ecumenical Protestant churches were culture changers, and the Consultation on Church Union was one of the instrumentalities they used to reshape American life.* From the 1940s onward, and especially in the 1960s, the leaders of these churches took an increasingly active role in public affairs, asking their constituencies "to follow them in antiracist, anti-imperialistic, feminist and multicultural directions that were understandably resisted by large segments of the white

---

3. The phrase comes from *The Last Will and Testament of the Springfield Presbytery,* a document written by Barton W. Stone and others in 1804. The Christian movement that emerged from Stone's work was later embodied in the Christian Church (Disciples of Christ) and the Christian Connection, which was one of the constituent bodies, in the United Church of Christ.

public, especially in the Protestant-intensive southern states."[4] It is clear to historian David Hollinger that the dramatic shift in American religious life since the 1960s, away from the ecumenical denominations and to the evangelical churches, which defended the old ways, is in large part the result of the culture-changing actions by leaders of the formerly dominant denominations. What these church leaders dared to do needs to be recognized and honored.

The second reason for paying attention to the Consultation on Church Union is that this venture was the most comprehensive effort to create a united Protestant church in American history. Why the venture was undertaken, how it did its work, how it succeeded and where it failed, and who participated in this multi-phased process deserve to be remembered. A remarkable body of scholarly work about the Christian tradition, the life and work of the churches, and the new challenges of Christian mission in the late-twentieth century was generated because of COCU and this deposit of information and wisdom needs to be kept alive and used in years to come.

A third answer is that the Consultation on Church Union provided an especially intense environment for communication, collaboration, and confrontation that changed the nature of the relationship of the high-ranking leaders of some of the nation's most prominent churches. Following COCU's organizational meeting in 1962, historian Martin E. Marty wrote that when they came together in church councils, these church leaders operated "from guarded centers, from behind facades, from within protecting walls." In this new relationship they were becoming acquainted "not as a present cousin but as a future brother in the confessional life of the church."[5] During their COCU years, these churches came to understand one another more fully than they ever had before, and as a result their on-going relations continued with a new sense of realism and acceptance, despite the decision to maintain the cousinly role rather than entering into a closer relationship as siblings in a blended family. As cousins, however, they are connected with bonds of affection and loyalty greater than they possessed in the years prior to the Consultation on Church Union.

A fourth reason for remembering the Consultation on Church Union is that it was the last effort by American churches to establish a comprehensive union in order to be faithful to the gospel. Last can mean *most recent*, but with respect to COCU the word has a second and more important sense. If

4. David Hollinger, Interview with Amy Frykholm, *Christian Century,* July 11, 2012. This interview was prompted by Hollinger's presidential address at the 2011 annual meeting of the Organization of American Historians. See Hollinger, *After Cloven Tongues of Fire.*

5. Martin E. Marty, *Christian Century,* April 25, 1962, 514–15.

one conclusion can be drawn from the Consultation's history, it is that the century-long pursuit of multilateral church mergers can no longer be regarded as a viable way to manifest Christian unity in the United States. It is hard to imagine any combination of theological and social factors, save the virtual collapse of existing ecclesial systems, that could inspire a new effort to achieve a comprehensive American plan of Christian unity in the decades immediately before us. For this reason, it is especially important to reflect upon what can be learned from the forty-year history of the Consultation on Church Union.

The fifth and most important reason for keeping COCU alive in current memory is that the nation still needs the kind of ecclesial community that the churches in the Consultation sought to become—a church truly catholic, truly evangelical, truly reformed—and a church where faith in Christ brings the people of the nation together in a way that unites the cultures, classes, and ethnicities that so often separate us from one another.

Despite their differences in worship patterns, organizational systems, racial composition, and congregational cultures, the ecumenical Protestant churches are very much alike. They hold the classic theological tradition based on Scripture and the church's lived experience in a continuing relationship with the larger intellectual heritage that shapes much of American life. These churches are committed to an ecclesial life in which people are bound together in God's love and commissioned to share that love in constructive ways in the communities where they live. Their convictions and habits keep them seriously engaged in public affairs but in ways that maintain strong distinctions between religious and political institutions. They are open to dialogue with people of different faith traditions and of no faith.

At a time when the nation and the world are in turmoil, with religious differences often at the center of the struggles, the nation needs, perhaps now more than ever before, a church very much like *A Church of Christ Uniting*, the new form of ecumenical Protestantism that the Consultation on Church Union almost became.

PART ONE

Moving from Vision to Plan (1960–1970)

1

The Bold Proposal

Jesus Christ, whom all of us confess as our divine
Lord and Savior, wills that his church be one.

—EUGENE CARSON BLAKE

IN THE FALL OF 1960, Presbyterian minister Eugene Carson Blake was fifty-four years old and a dominant figure in American church life. The people of his own church were well aware of his career, which included eleven years as pastor of First Presbyterian Church in Pasadena, California, one of the largest churches of the denomination and nine years as Stated Clerk of its General Assembly—the highest-ranking executive post in the church's national office. People in other churches would have heard of this articulate Presbyterian because of his five-year stint, beginning in 1953, as host of the Protestant portion of the nationally broadcast television program "Frontiers of Faith."

Largely because of Blake's opposition to the anti-Communism campaign of Senator Joseph McCarthy, the United Presbyterian Church in the United States of America was the first Protestant church to take a stand "against the possible loss of individual freedom and constitutional rights in the name of patriotism and anti-Communism."[1] Blake was a central figure in the nine-person American delegation, sponsored by the National Council of Churches in 1956, which traveled to the Soviet Union and met with leaders of Russian and Armenian Orthodox, Baptist, and Lutheran Churches.

1. Brackenridge, *Eugene Carson Blake*, 66.

3

As a result of his involvement in a wide range of ecumenical activities, he had become a prominent leader of the World Council of Churches based in Geneva and the National Council of Churches of Christ in the United States, headquartered in New York City.

A few weeks before the National Council's triennial General Assembly, scheduled to meet in San Francisco in December of 1960, Blake received an invitation from James A. Pike, Episcopal Bishop of California, to preach at the Eucharist in Grace Cathedral on the Sunday that the Assembly would begin.[2] This would dramatize for the community, Pike proposed, "the unity we hold in Christ." Accepting the invitation, Blake began work on a sermon designed for this occasion, conferring with his friend about the message. The moment was especially challenging because the Kennedy-Nixon presidential campaign (especially the debate on November 8, 1960, less than a month before the National Council assembly) had focused public attention upon the church's role in American life. Blake was convinced that the churches were perceived "as competing social groups pulling and hauling, propagandizing and pressuring for their own organizational advantages." He hoped that his sermon could break new ground for the churches and their ministry to a world, which he and many others believed was in deep distress.[3]

Bishop Pike was also well known and prominent in the American religious scene. His education and early professional career were in the law. He was reared as a Roman Catholic and in early adult years described himself as agnostic. Following their marriage, Pike and his wife entered the Episcopal Church and soon thereafter he enrolled in seminary. He was ordained priest in 1946, and following pastoral service in two parishes he became head of the Department of Religion and chaplain at Columbia University. In 1952, Pike was appointed dean of the nearby Episcopal Cathedral of St. John the Divine. In 1955, he launched a successful national TV series that continued for six years.

Pike's sermons, television presence, and books on ethical, political, and theological topics had thrust him into the public arena, especially since he dealt with controversial topics such as birth control, abortion laws, racism, and capital punishment.[4] He challenged McCarthyism and helped

---

2. In personal correspondence, Paul A. Crow Jr., reported a conversation with Blake in which Blake said that he had asked Pike for the privilege of preaching that Sunday at Grace Cathedral. The invitation came in response to that request.

3. Brackenridge, *Eugene Carson Blake*, 129.

4 By the time of Blake's sermon, Pike had already published nine books, among them: *Beyond Anxiety* (1953); *The Church, Politics and Society* (1955); *Doing the Truth* (1955); *If You Marry Outside Your Faith* (1954); *Roadblocks to Faith* (with John M.

President Dwight D. Eisenhower undermine Senator Joseph McCarthy's influence over Americans. As one of the leaders of Protestants and Other Americans United for Separation of Church and State, he had opposed the 1960 presidential bid of John F. Kennedy.

In 1958, Pike was elected bishop coadjutor and then bishop of the Diocese of California, centered at Grace Cathedral in San Francisco. By that time, says his biographer David M. Robertson, he had refocused his energies away from political or social prophesy to ecumenism and secularism. Soon after coming to San Francisco, the new bishop commissioned a market survey of his diocese and concluded that he would devote his energies to helping his church attract "to his diocese the expanding market of what he personalized to other Episcopalians as 'the lapsed Methodist or [the] secularist seeker.'"[5] He instructed rectors (pastors) of the churches of the diocese "to provide communion to any confessing Christian who attended services, rather than limiting the participants to confirmed Episcopalians."[6]

Among the members of his diocese were Goodwin J. Knight, the Republican governor of California, William W. Crocker, a San Francisco banker, and Casper Weinberger, a prominent lawyer who would later become Ronald Reagan's Secretary of Defense.[7] Two signs of Pike's practical effectiveness were significant growth in the membership of his diocese and a financial campaign that made it possible to complete Grace Cathedral, which had existed unfinished since 1929.

It is hard to imagine a more dramatic or storied setting for Blake's precedent-setting sermon than this grand church that had begun early in San Francisco's history (December 30, 1849) as Grace Chapel, with gold miners as worshipers and members. In 1862 a more substantial building was constructed at Stockton and California Streets on what was to become

---

Krumm; 1954); and *A Roman Catholic in the White House* (with Richard Byfield; 1960). They demonstrated the reach of his interest in theology, ethics, politics, and interchurch relations. He had been co-author of an adult study book, *The Holy Bible* (1949), which was volume one of a series published by the Episcopal Church under the general title *The Church's Teaching*. He collaborated with Norman Pittenger, a noted Episcopal theologian, in a 1951 book entitled *The Faith of the Church* (revised and republished in 1961).

5. Robertson, *A Passionate Pilgrim,* 100.

6. During this period, I was a doctoral candidate at Pacific School of Religion in Berkeley and occasionally attended the Eucharist at Grace Cathedral. Guided by the explanation and invitation printed every Sunday in the worship folder, I received communion at the altar in that church even though I was not an Episcopalian.

7. Robertson also reports a scornful criticism of some of Pike's activities by "a Methodist professor of the Old Testament at Pacific School of Religion" and Pike's annoyed rejoinder, both published in the *Christian Century*. See Pike, "That They May Be One," and Nelson, "Pike, Hedley and Otwell."

known as Nob Hill. This building was gutted by the fire that swept over the city following the earthquake in 1906 (the year of Blake's birth). A dramatic site at the top of the hill was given to the church by the family of William H. Crocker, and in 1914 the Founders Crypt was opened, which served as the church for more than a decade. In 1927, a seismically safe concrete and steel structure was erected—the nave and sanctuary of the French Gothic church that was envisioned—and in 1929 this partially completed building was occupied as the cathedral's place of worship. In 1960, even though the building was still incomplete, Grace Cathedral's lively connection with California history and its preeminent clergy, commanding location, imposing architecture, and cultural preeminence made it one of grandest ecclesial spaces in the country.[8]

A Sermon to Transform the American Church

The sermon matched the occasion. A few lines into his message, Blake made a startling proposal: "Led, I pray by the Holy Spirit, I propose to the Protestant Episcopal Church that it together with the United Presbyterian Church in the United States of America invite the Methodist Church and the United Church of Christ to form with us a plan of union both catholic and reformed on the basis of principles I shall later in this sermon suggest." Other churches ready to "accept both the principles and the plan would also be warmly invited to unite with us." Among reasons for making this proposal was the conviction that "Jesus Christ, whom all of us confess as our divine Lord and Saviour, wills that his church be one."[9]

Blake was persuaded that "our separate organizations, however much we sincerely try to cooperate in councils, present a tragically divided church to a tragically divided world." Referring to the acrimonious debate during the just concluded Nixon-Kennedy election, he stated that "never before have so many Americans agreed that the Christian churches, divided as they are, cannot be trusted to bring to the American people an objective and authentic word of God on a political issue. Americans more than ever see the churches of Jesus Christ as competing social groups pulling and hauling, propagandizing and pressuring for their own organizational advantages."

Blake devoted most of this long sermon to outlining the principles for the reunited church he envisioned. His central point was "that a reunited

8. The cathedral was completed in 1964 and the first Holy Communion was celebrated at the high altar on November 22, 1964.

9. The sermon and Pike's response were published in several formats and are appended to this book.

church must be both reformed and catholic. If at this time we are to begin to bridge over the chasm of the Reformation, those of us who are of the Reformation tradition must recapture an appreciation of all that has been preserved by the catholic parts of the church; and equally those of the catholic tradition must be willing to accept and take to themselves as of God all that nearly five hundred years of Reformation has contributed to the renewal of the church."

Then came Blake's outline of three catholic principles that would mark the church he envisioned. The reunited church "must have visible and historical continuity with the Church of all ages before and after the Reformation." It "must clearly confess the historic Trinitarian faith received from the Apostles and set forth in the Apostles' and Nicene Creeds." The reunited Church "must administer the two sacraments, instituted by Christ, the Lord's Supper (or Holy Communion, or Eucharist) and Baptism."

In his discussion of the catholic qualities, Blake gave special attention to the ministry because this was the point of deepest separation and disagreement between churches. "I propose that, without adopting any particular theology of historical succession, the reunited church shall provide at its inception for the consecration of all its bishops by bishops and presbyters both in the apostolic succession and out of it from all over the world, from all Christian churches which would authorize or permit them to take part." They would "cut the Gordian knot of hundreds of years of controversy by establishing in the united church an historic ministry recognized by all without doubt or scruple."

Blake also outlined four reformed principles that would be present in the reunited church and that would provide the necessary safeguards and controls of the ministry he had proposed. This church "must accept the principle of continuing reformation under the Word of God by the guidance of the Holy Spirit." It must be "truly democratic in its government, recognizing . . . that all Christians are Christ's ministers even though some in the church are separated and ordained to the ministry of word and sacrament." This reunited Church "must seek in a new way to recapture the brotherhood and sense of fellowship of all its members and ministers." It must find a way "to include within its catholicity (and because of it) a wide diversity of theological formulations of the faith and a variety of worship and liturgy including worship that is non-liturgical." While affirming the value of retaining familiar ways of worship, Blake warned against imposing worship against peoples' will and he urged the reunited church to develop "freshly inspired" ways of worship.

As soon as Blake finished, Pike spoke to the congregation, endorsing the ideas that his guest had proposed. Pike's ideas were stated more fully in an essay that he contributed to the *Christian Century* for its series "How My Mind Has Changed," which was published two weeks later along with the report by Harold E. Fey, the *Century's* editor, of Blake's sermon and the National Council assembly. Pike commented upon issues related to ministry and worship, illustrating his ideas by describing changes in organization and liturgical practice that he had instituted in his diocese. He defended the idea of bishop because of "something existential" in his experience of the office. "I just know that there is something different about the relationship I have to my job and to my mission and to my clergy than a transferable and re-electable executive secretary has."

Perhaps most important, was his determination that the life of the church, including worship at altars in his diocese would no longer be bound by denominational restrictions. "I shall go on doing the best I can to affirm the fact that all baptized Christians who believe in Jesus Christ as Lord and Savior are members of the holy catholic church; and if our national bodies can't grasp this fact, we will still do our best in the diocese of California to operate on that principle."[10]

News that something special was going to happen that Sunday morning had begun to spread as delegates to the National Council's assembly made their way to San Francisco. Denominational leaders were "taken by surprise when Blake and Pike alerted folk at the last minute about the sermon to take place the next day.[11] George G. Beazley Jr., who had just begun his work as ecumenical officer for the Christian Church (Disciples of Christ), learned about it from his Presbyterian seatmate as they flew to the city on December 2, 1960. On the plane he read the *New York Times* interview with Blake that had taken place at a New York airport before he had made his own departure for the Bay Area city.[12] Blake had told George W. Cornell, religion reporter for the Associated Press, that he intended to speak an important word. Cornell had alerted other journalists, and the church was filled, its regular communicants augmented by delegates to the NCC General Assembly and media representatives.[13] Describing the responses

10. Pike, "Three-Pronged Synthesis," 1499.

11. Thomas E. Dipko, personal communication.

12. Beazley, "A Personal View of the Consultation on Church Union," 13–14. An electronic search (October 2012) of the *New York Times* archives for this period brought up several news reports about Blake's intention to make this overture and the initial responses by several church groups. The two news releases published prior to the sermon, however, had been removed from the electronic database and were not available for my research.

13. In his *Christian Century* review of the National Council gathering, Harold E. Fey reported that there had been 120 reporters, 531 voting delegates from the 34 N.C.C. churches and 3,712 people brought together for the assembly. The number of persons

in the secular and religious press, Blake's biographer, states that "probably no single sermon in modern times prompted such a widespread reaction and exchange of opinion" as this San Francisco address.[14] Three of the most widely read national news magazines—*Time, Newsweek,* and *Life*—featured the sermon, one providing a detailed analysis of its contents and another praising it in an editorial.

Even if they did not understand the precedent-shattering ecclesial principles in the sermon, reporters recognized the significance of the proposed new church that would embrace the dominant religious core of American life. Protestantism, historically divided into denominations, would for the first time have one corporate presence that would be large enough to counter the increasingly active Roman Catholic Church. It was not just the numbers that counted. Together, Episcopalians and Presbyterians represented the corridors of influence and power while Methodists and Congregationalists (in the United Church of Christ) represented the broad middle class all across the country. Although Lutherans, Baptists, and Pentecostals would be noticeably absent, by their own choice, from COCU, the church that Blake proposed held the possibility of radically changing the religious and cultural balance in the United States.

One reporter who did understand what was being proposed was Harold E. Fey, editor of the *Christian Century,* the leading journal of opinion in American Protestantism. Two weeks following the close of the National Council meeting, he devoted two pages to the dual San Francisco event (the sermon and the National Council's assembly) under the title "Unity at the Golden Gate." Blake's bold proposal dominated talk during the early part of the assembly and references were so numerous "that on the final day Mr. Blake expressed regret that his sermon on Sunday had seemed to detract attention from the assembly."

Among church leaders speaking in favor of the idea of creating this new church were G. Bromley Oxnam, retired Methodist bishop who had achieved national acclaim from his opposition to Senator Joseph McCarthy; Baptist pastor E. T. Dahlberg, outgoing president of the National Council of Churches; and Lesslie Newbigin, renowned bishop of the Church of South India. Speaking out against Blake's proposal were Methodist bishop Gerald Kennedy of the Los Angeles area; the two presidents of the United Church of Christ and UCC theologian and church activist Robert Spike; and prominent Episcopal layman Charles P. Taft. Later in its meeting, the

---

present to hear Blake's sermon was not reported (Fey, "Unity at the Golden Gate," *Christian Century,* December 21, 1960, 1503–4).

14. Brackenridge, *Eugene Carson Blake,* 137.

National Council for the first time in its history, elected a layman to serve as president: J. Irwin Miller, a national leader in industry, education, religion, and the arts. Although Miller's church, the Christian Church (Disciples of Christ) was not included in Blake's initial proposal, it soon became one of the six churches that comprised the Consultation on Church Union during its most hopeful years.[15]

Principles and Patterns for a United Church

It is difficult to know whether the Presbyterian pastor-church executive and Episcopal priest-bishop had clear ideas of how this new church would look and act. Its central feature, however, was foreshadowed by a little-known action early the morning after Blake's sermon. On Sunday afternoon following the Cathedral Eucharist, during the opening session of the National Council of Churches' assembly, someone passed word to John H. Burt, an Episcopal priest from Pasadena, California, that the the next morning, in the cathedral chapel, Bishop Newbigin would celebrate the Eucharist according to his church's liturgy.[16] Early Monday morning, while it was still dark, Burt hiked up Nob Hill to the chapel in order to be one of the worshipers. To his delight, Ganse Little, the pastor of the Pasadena Presbyterian Church and his close colleague in ministry, was also there. Although the disciplines of the Episcopal Church at that time did not permit them to receive the Eucharist in each other's churches, they could on this occasion because both of their churches were in communion with the Church of South India.

When Newbigin entered the chapel, he was accompanied by the president of the United Church of Christ, the elected head of the Methodist bishops in the United States, the presiding bishop of the Episcopal Church, and Blake, the chief executive office of the United Presbyterian Church. These four church leaders would serve as "assisting ministers." "Together, for the first time in my own experience," Burt reported, "all of us shared Christ in the Eucharist. It was an unforgettable moment for Ganse and me—a foretaste, we hoped, of the unity we believed God intends for his church in America. Our life together as pastors in adjacent local congregations was forever changed after that service."[17]

Although the initial reports of this spectacular San Francisco Sunday say little about the shape and functioning of the new church that Blake had proposed, one characteristic was at the center: the mutual recognition of

15. *Christian Century,* December 21, 1960, 1503–4.

16. Church of South India, *The Book of Common Worship,* 1–20.

17. Burt, "Adventures in Mending the Seamless Robe of Christ," 4–5.

one another's churches as equally members of the one Church of Christ, of one another's ministries as authentic and authorized ministers of Word and Sacrament, and of one another's members as full members of the one church. The most dramatic sign of this radical mutuality would be a new acceptance of one another's sacraments with the result that the eucharistic table would be open to all members irrespective of their former church affiliations.

Beyond this central conviction, however, it is not clear that the authors of this proposal had developed ideas about how this new church would be organized and do its work. Their assumption seems to have been that once the central assertions about church, ministry, and sacraments had been publicly affirmed by participating churches, other matters of polity and procedures could be cared for relatively expeditiously. The proposal came at a time when Christian unity was very much in the air. The people gathered in San Francisco, because of their mutual engagement in the National Council of Churches, would surely have been aware of significant efforts during the previous quarter of a century to overcome the divided state of the church in its historical form.

Among these unity movements were some that would later become known as *bilateral mergers*. The United Church of Christ, one of the churches Blake had included in his proposal, had come into being only three years earlier, in 1957, by this process and the two uniting denominations were still in the process of working out the details of their new relationships.[18] The Methodist Church was itself the merger in 1939 of the Methodist Episcopal Church, the Methodist Episcopal Church, South, and the Methodist Protestant Church. In 1960, The Methodist Church and the Evangelical United Church were engaged in discussions pointing toward union. For more than a generation, Presbyterians and Episcopalians had tried unsuccessfully, both in Britain and the United States, to forge agreements that would allow exchange of members and ministers and full access to sacramental life among the churches of their communions. During the 1950s, the Methodist Commission on Church Union and the Episcopal Church's Commission on Approaches to Unity met to explore the possibilities of organic union of these two American branches of "the same mother church."[19] At the same time as the Blake-Pike proposal was announced, the Episcopal Church was beginning new bilateral discussions with Lutheran Churches and Orthodox Churches.

18. The two denominations were the Congregational Christian Churches and the Evangelical and Reformed Church. The union was consummated in 1957.

19. Holt and Keeler, *Approaches Toward Unity,* 7.

Beginning in the 1930s, E. Stanley Jones began promoting what he and others described as a federal plan of Christian unity. Jones, a missionary to India and popular Christian writer and lecturer, developed his plan in a 1944 book, *The Christ of the American Road*, in which he coupled a wide-ranging critique of American religion with a statement of his conviction that Christianity properly practiced and the central genius of American democracy were tightly intertwined.[20] Central to Jones's vision was the idea of *E pluribus unum*, one out of many, which avoids two pitfalls: having complete sovereignty in each state and having complete sovereignty in the union. Jones believed that the application of *E pluribus unum* to the full range of human affairs in economic and political matters around the world would solve the problems that war could never solve. If this "principle of federal union—a new man out of both parties—is inherent both in American democracy and in Christianity," Jones asked, "then what about applying it to the churches themselves?"

His federal union of the churches would begin with "the great renunciation" by which the separate churches would cease to exist. The new church would have branches, such as the Baptist branch and the Episcopal branch, each retaining "local self-government" with respect to church practices such as baptism and ordination, thus allowing Baptists to continue immersion and Episcopalians to have bishops. Jones had worked out an organizational pattern, which included a General Assembly of the Church of Christ in America with state, county, and local assemblies. There would be a parallel church in each nation of the world, and reigning over them would be "The World Assembly of the Church of Christ."

The grandiose character of Jones' proposal becomes clear in his assertion that by forming this federal union, the churches would be "fitted to lead in something that is emerging inevitably in the world situation—a federal union of the nations . . . If federal union of the nations is our collective destiny, then it is the national destiny of America to help form that federal union, for it is but the flowering of something inherent in our central genius. And if that is our American destiny, it is the destiny of the churches of America to lead America to fulfill her world destiny of helping create the world federal union." A divided church, however, cannot do this, for "a divided church in a divided world has no moral authority. Christians of America, unite!"[21]

As interest in Jones' federal union was winding down, another union effort was coming forward: the *Conference on Church Union*, usually referred

---

20. Jones, *The Christ of the American Road*, 107.
21. Ibid., 200.

to as the *Greenwich Plan*, named for the Connecticut city where meetings took place. Early in the Conference's life, Christian unity advocate Charles Clayton Morrison reported in *The Ecumenical Review* that the Conference came into being as a result of the request (in 1946) of the General Council of Congregational Christian Churches[22] that the Federal Council of Churches invite denominations that recognized one another's ministries and sacraments "to send official representatives to a plenary conference where the possibility of their union would be explored." [23] Nine churches expressed sufficient interest to send delegations: Methodist, Presbyterian U.S.A., Presbyterian U.S., Congregational Christian, Disciples of Christ, Evangelical and Reformed, African Methodist Episcopal, Colored Methodist Episcopal, and the National Council of Community Churches, representing a total membership of over 16 million. Their goal was defined as "an organic union, a fellowship and organization of the church which will enable it to act as one body under Jesus Christ who is the head of the church." Conferees were confident that major problems had already been met by previous mergers and by the United Church of Canada.

Non-participating churches included the Episcopal Church, because it did not "recognize the full validity of ministries and sacraments of other communions"; Lutherans, some because they practiced close communion and others because they were so intent on intra-Lutheran unity; and Baptists, probably because of their "non-recognition of the sacrament of baptism administered by any other mode than immersion." While recognizing that final details would emerge out of the discussions, participants also believed that "the discussion of the ecumenical imperative must come down from the cloud-land of abstraction and vagueness to the solid ground of practical action. This requires as clear an envisionment of the end or goal as it is possible to conceive, in order that appropriate means may be adopted for its attainment." The plan envisioned four levels, which they initially referred to as local church, presbytery, regional synod, and national council "in which the regional synods would be integrated as a federal union." The presupposition underlying "this conception of the general structure of a united church is that the differences among the nine participating denominations are matters of degree rather than of principle, and are greatly exaggerated by the diversity of nomenclature."

By the meeting in May 1953, Presbyterians had lost interest and neither Presbyterian Church sent delegates. A letter from the United Presbyterian

---

22. This denomination was the larger of the two churches that later formed the United Church of Christ.

23. Morrison, "The Ecumenical Trend in American Protestantism," 10–13.

Church U.S.A. stated its intention to withdraw. The AME Zion Church had joined, which kept the list at nine. No major changes were made to the Plan of Union, which began with a statement of faith patterned after the Apostles' Creed. It did not deal with the sacraments, either doctrines or modes of administration. The existing ministries of participating churches would be considered the ministry of the church universal; and there would be bishops. A general council of 1,000 would be the highest governing authority. Ironically, one of Eugene Carson Blake's first actions after becoming the national executive of his church was to discontinue its participation in the Greenwich Plan.

Two multi-lateral church unions, *The United Church of Canada* and *The Church of South India* were undoubtedly on the minds of church leaders interested in ecumenism. The United Church of Canada was founded in 1925 as a merger of the Methodist Church of Canada, the Congregational Union of Ontario and Quebec, two-thirds of the congregations of the Presbyterian Church in Canada, and the Association of Local Union Churches. When Blake delivered his sermon, the Canadian church had had 35 years of history, long enough that its legitimacy and effectiveness could be evaluated. One person who did so was Claris Edwin Silcox who called attention to two types of church, the Erastian and the Evangelical. "An Erastian church is essentially one based upon a conception of the community or nation at prayer; an evangelical church, strictly speaking, is rooted in a particular gospel, or in a particular interpretation of a particular gospel . . . Strictly speaking, national and community churches are Erastian while among the evangelical churches one might designate such widely-differing communions as Roman Catholicism, Methodist and Christian Science."[24] Clearly, the United Church of Canada was Erastian, and although Blake and Pike did not use this term, the united church they envisioned would be similar in character.

More recent, and more important as a potential trendsetter because it included Anglicans, was the Church of South India, inaugurated in 1947, which united churches of Congregational, Presbyterian, Methodist, and Anglican traditions. This was the first union in the world that was successful in uniting Anglican and non-Anglican churches. One of its first bishops, Lesslie Newbigin, had come to India as a missionary of the Church of Scotland, a church ardently committed to government by councils of presbyters rather than by individual bishops exercising oversight. The Church of South India created a polity that recognized Episcopal, Presbyterian, and Congregational elements and developed a book of worship that bridged the

24. Silcox, "Ten Years of Church Union in Canada," 356–57.

liturgical traditions that came into this new church. It set up a plan by which existing ministries were accepted while including processes which would lead to the time, a generation later, when all ministers would have been ordained by bishops in apostolic succession. The Church of South India was important as a prototype for a new American church because two factors had come together: the cross-confessional nature of its constituent parts and the intention to be, in effect, the Protestant Christian presence in communities all across the southern territories of its nation.

Plans for the organic union of churches in various countries, including the United States, received a boost from the definition of unity offered by the World Council of Church's assembly in 1961: "We believe that the unity which is both God's will and his gift to his Church is being made visible as all in each place who are baptized into Jesus Christ and confess him as Lord and Saviour are brought by the Holy Spirit into one fully committed fellowship, holding the one apostolic faith, preaching the one Gospel, breaking the one bread, joining in common prayer, and having a corporate life reaching out in witness and service to all." Between 1965 and 1972, united churches, based on such a model and involving two or more confessions, were born in Zambia, Jamaica and Grand Cayman, Madagascar, Ecuador, Papua New Guinea and the Solomon Islands, Belgium, North India, Pakistan (and Bangladesh), Zaire (now the Congo), and Great Britain. These churches were by no means uniform, but they all affirmed that unity involves the costly death of previous identities, and that "it is dying in order to receive fuller life."[25]

When Eugene Carson Blake preached his sermon on December 4, 1960, this activist Presbyterian at the center of the religious affairs understood, perhaps better than any other church leader in America, what it would take to bring about a significant reunion of Christians and their churches. Even he, however, had not yet come to realize how difficult the task would be. His conviction was strong, and he was determined to make full use of his personal skills and the powers of his office to achieve this the goal he had announced. The integrity of the church in America, he believed, and the renewal of American life in a time of growing turmoil depended upon what he and others, blessed by the Holy Spirit, would soon set out to do.

25. Paton, *Breaking Barriers,* 60.

2

The Challenge to Reunion
in Concrete Terms

If the churches are unwilling to give this proposal full seriousness,
they are "abdicating their ecumenical responsibility."

—ROBERT MCAFEE BROWN

THE FIRST STEP IN implementing Eugene Carson Blake's proposal came
later in that same month (December 1960) when the Detroit Presbytery,
representing 110 United Presbyterian congregations, voted 218 to 4 to en-
dorse the idea and recommend that their church move forward according
to the plan.[1] During the next few weeks, approximately 60 other presbyteries (from a total of 213) sent overtures to the United Presbyterian Church's
general assembly scheduled for May 17–24, 1961. All but one favored
Blake's proposal, although the Chicago Presbytery had recommended that
they include conditions "insisting upon explicit Episcopal recognition of
Presbyterian ordination before conversations should begin." The General
Assembly's resolution did not include that limitation. After sharp debate, the
assembly approved the resolution overwhelmingly. The resolution included
an element that had been suggested in conversations with The Methodist
Church, that the words "truly evangelical" be added to "truly catholic and
truly reformed," the terms that Blake had originally proposed.[2]

---

1. "Church Merger Backed," *New York Times,* December 30, 1960.
2. Blake, "An Interim Report," 83.

While preparing the sermon, Blake had conferred not only with Bishop Pike but also with a second friend and colleague in the Episcopal Church, Robert F. Gibson Jr., bishop of the diocese of Virginia and an active participant in the Episcopal Church's ecumenical activities. During the early 1950s, Gibson had been a member of the Joint Commission on Approaches to Unity of the Protestant Episcopal Church and the Commission on Unity of The Methodist Church, contributing a paper entitled "The Christian Ministry."[3] Gibson affirmed the ideas that Blake had presented, as did the presiding bishop of the Episcopal Church (Blake's counterpart as head of communion) who had been at San Francisco when Blake had preached. The Episcopal Church's General Convention approved the proposal in its regular meeting in September 1961, four months following the Presbyterian action. The two churches extended their invitation to The Methodist Church and the United Church of Christ, which were well aware of the movement, and these two churches accepted the invitation.

Each church appointed a nine-member commission to begin the discussion. With a combination of excitement and uncertainty, the commissions and invited guests gathered the following spring (April 9-10, 1962) in facilities on the grounds of the National Cathedral in Washington, D.C. Like Grace Cathedral in San Francisco, this imposing Episcopal Church had not yet been completed, but its setting, architecture, self-understanding, and history made it another one of the prestigious religious locations in the United States. On this fifty-seven acre campus at the highest elevation in the nation's capitol, it was easy to imagine that the new church would embrace and confirm the sense of the cultural and political centrality that the historic Protestant denominations had long occupied in American life.

Although there had been other interdenominational meetings of American Christians to discuss Christian unity, this gathering on Mount St. Alban was unique: rather than being the coming together of individuals acting as individuals, these four delegations came as official representatives of churches that had voted to participate in this new venture. This point became even clearer when the churches provided financial support from their central treasuries. Here Robert Gibson was especially significant because he understood the need for reliable support as a way of maintaining the seriousness of participation and was adept at discovering who in each church could unlock purse strings. Year by year, he was able to persuade the churches to provide the necessary funds.[4] The composition of the four delegations— high-ranking church officials and prominent theologians—underscored the

---

3. Gibson, "The Christian Ministry," 63–74.
4. Paul A. Crow Jr., pers. comm.

serious attention that these four churches were giving to the proposal that they create a new church.

Creating the Consultation on Church Union

The people who planned this first meeting understood that in order to develop a practical plan for uniting their churches they would have to work their way through a series of theological questions. They picked two of these issues and arranged for the presentation of scholarly papers to focus discussion. Church historian Ronald E. Osborn later wrote, that the "Genius of the Consultation [was] its deliberately theological approach to the practical problems of church union. [This] corporate venture in doing ecclesiology distinguishes it from every other large-scale attempt in the twentieth century to bring the American churches together."[5]

The first issue to be addressed was why the existing denominational system should be set side in favor of a new, more comprehensive American church. Commissioned to discuss this issue was John Dillenberger, a theologian in the United Church of Christ and professor at Drew University, whose publications included books on Martin Luther and the relation of science and theology. Dillenberger stated his thesis in two sentences: "From the Reformation into the nineteenth century, churches came into being out of an earnest concern for theological integrity and cultural relevance. Today, the same regard for theological integrity and meaningful witness demands the union of the churches." Each denomination had been formed to call attention to an aspect of the gospel that seemed to be inadequately manifested in the church of the time and therefore in its division still "assumed that a greater wholeness of the church resulted, that is the wholeness of its truth." Gradually, these churches "began to live out of their distinctiveness rather than out of their previous concern for the wholeness of the church."

Over time, however, the ethos of American life had been transformed so that the denominational pattern had become sociologically obsolete. Dillenberger stated clearly that church union would be more than "patching together our respective heritages. In fact, church union will not genuinely advance unless we are willing to face the possibility and necessity of our own death in the hope that a new resurrection will not only include what we have treasured but provide for it in new settings and with new riches."[6]

The second theological issue put forward at this organizing meeting was the one that many people expected to be the most difficult to resolve:

5. Osborn, "Theology in the Consultation," 64.
6. Dillenbeger, "Theological-Cultural Factors," 58–68.

the continuity of the ministry from the time of the apostles onward, with special attention to bishops as successors to the apostles. The Presbyterian, Methodist, and United Church of Christ traditions held distinct understandings of authorized ministry. Even with these theological distinctions, however, these ministries were, for the most part, able to function, when invited, in one another's churches. Not so, with the Episcopal Church because in that communion the ministry's historical and theological efficacy and validity were major factors. The Episcopal Church's ministry included bishops in apostolic succession, while the ministries of the other churches fell short, the Episcopal Church believed, because they stood outside of this succession.

To analyze this issue, the delegates used a paper by Episcopal theologian, Theodore O. Wedel that had been published a decade earlier.[7] Referring to Ephesians 4:4–6, Wedel proposed that the "Body-Spirit paradox" is "the crux of the doctrine of the Church as our ecumenical era at last must deal with it." He affirmed the Reformation insight that for Christians the essence of the New Covenant in Christ is a personal relationship with God the Father through Jesus Christ, in the Fellowship of the Holy Spirit. Since the resurrection, however, this personal relationship is "given exclusively to a visible society, and to individuals only as they became members of this society." To become a Christian "meant incorporation into a corporate visible body where Christ now [is] a continuing life and power."

Wedel noted that this visible Body of Christ, the church, has been divided into the many churches. These divided communities of faith have been responsible for guarding doctrine and providing authentic worship. In all of churches, maintaining a proper ministry generation after generation has been "the chief sacramental means and symbol of structural unity, in time and space." Therefore, Wedel concluded, "The problem of which [form of ministerial] succession can best unify the scattered flocks of Christ's Church is not on the periphery of ecumenical concern, but at its very heart."

In addition to engaging in theological discussion, delegates from the four churches began the process of converting theology into practical action by projecting a pattern for future work. They named their venture the Consultation on Church Union (COCU was the inevitable shorthand), projected annual plenary assemblies, with the participating churches rotating as hosts at or near theological seminaries of their denomination. They established a budget ($2,800 for the first year) and made arrangements to keep the press informed. At this meeting, they also appointed George L.

7. Wedel, "The Body-Spirit Paradox," 69–82.

Hunt, pastor of the Fanwood Presbyterian Church in Fanwood, New Jersey, to be part-time executive secretary of their consultation.

Recognizing that the United Church, Episcopal Church, and Methodist Church were engaged in bi-lateral union negotiations, the Consultation invited their partners—the Christian Church (Disciples of Christ), the Polish National Catholic Church, and the Evangelical United Brethren Church—to join the Consultation as full members. The Christian Church and the Evangelical United Brethren Church accepted. The Consultation also invited other churches in North America, the National and World Councils of Churches, world confessional bodies of which the COCU churches were members, and the executive officer of the Anglican Communion to become observer-participants in the Consultation's work.

They listed four topics for further study and clarification: (1) the historical basis for the Christian ministry that is found in the scriptures and the early church; (2) the origins, use, and standing of creeds and confessional statements; (3) the theology of liturgy; and (4) the relation of word and sacraments.[8] They also appointed committees on topics for future consideration: faith; liturgy; education; social and cultural problems; polity, order, and power structure. Each committee would make reports to the larger body for discussion, further exploration, and determining next steps.

The cherry trees were in full blossom during the days that these four churches conferred. As they left Washington during the nation's spring festival, some of the representatives of the participating churches may well have realized that they were embarking on a process that was much more promising—and also much more demanding—than any prior unity effort in the United States had been. The nature of the work ahead, and the portents both hope inspiring and fear-laden, soon came to light in responses published in months following.

"Enthusiastic and hopeful" are the words that Martin E. Marty, Lutheran historian and rising star on the American religious scene, used to describe the meeting. The delegates were wary in their comments to the press, he noted, because they recognized that they were meeting one another in a new mode. Working with one another in councils of churches, they operated "from guarded centers, from behind facades, from within protecting walls." In this new discussion, they were becoming acquainted "not as a present cousin but as a future brother in the confessional life of the church." Marty reported that some people were "opposed to merger talk of any sort because they fear it will assault current traditions, preconceptions, prejudices and relationships." Others were disappointed because there was no word

8. *Digest of the First Meeting*, 23.

of immediate success. Rather than expressing an understanding of "the dire situation of the church in a revolutionary world," Marty commented, this attitude represented "theological and moral laziness that simply would like to see a denominational picture simplified, a confusion rendered clear." For these people, the conversations in Washington were too slow.[9]

With amazing dispatch, Robert McAfee Brown and David H. Scott enlisted a group of scholars to write chapters for a book that would address the issues raised by this new movement to establish a united church. Shortly before the convening of the first full-fledged plenary assembly in Oberlin, Ohio (March 19-21, 1963), their book came from the press. Entitled *The Challenge to Reunion*, the volume consisted of twenty-one essays that presented the context for the COCU process and a widely ranging set of evaluations and opinions. In his introduction to the book, Brown, who was becoming one of the nation's prophetic Protestant voices, briefly described the range of ideas discussed in the essays. Although he did not state his own judgment concerning the proposal by his fellow Presbyterian, Eugene Carson Blake, Brown's extended discussion of four objections—bustle, bigness, bureaucracy, and bishops—gives the impression that he was one of the doubters. Reviewing the book, Kyle Haseldon confirmed its importance when he wrote that the authors had dealt with the factors that "clash in the Blake proposal and will clash in any other proposal for the mending of the church's division."[10]

The book's most important statement, however, is the challenge that Brown gave to leaders of the churches. For decades they had been talking about "the imperative to unity" with little to show for their efforts. "A responsible church leader has finally put the challenge to reunion in concrete terms." If the churches are unwilling to give this proposal full seriousness, they are "abdicating their ecumenical responsibility" and demonstrating once again "that Christians are more proficient at mouthing their convictions than in acting upon them."[11]

Blake had been asked to write a response to the essays, which was included as its last chapter and therefore available to the Oberlin delegates as part of this analytical and provocative book. After calling attention to the favorable and sustained response the sermon had elicited, and to the fact that official conversations had begun, he responded to questions that he was hearing.

9. Martin E. Marty, *Christian Century,* April 25, 1962, 514–15.

10. Haselden, "Review of *The Challenge to Reunion*," 441.

11. Brown and Scott, *The Challenge to Reunion,* 17.

"Is American church union really important on Christian grounds?" Blake answered that while beneficial practical results could come from union, its primary justification was Christian and theological.

"Would the proposed union create an organization "so mammoth and complex that the life and witness of the church would be burdened rather than enhanced?" Blake answered that "the new united church could create a more effective, responsible and democratic organization than any of us has so far achieved."

"Is not the difference between the evangelical and catholic understanding of the gospel, church and ministry so deep and essential that union of the kind proposed would water down the Christian faith and make unwarranted compromise of Christian principle?" The only hope of a united church, Blake responded, was that Christians on both sides of this divide would learn "to be concerned about the other man's conscience and conviction." To support his answer, Blake discussed evangelical and catholic views of salvation and grace, with the strong conclusion that in these matters "evangelicals need catholics and catholics need evangelicals if this historic distortion is to be overcome." By dealing with the issues of ministry as he had proposed in his sermon, Christians of both types would come to see the possibility that their "understanding of the mystery of Christ's redemption" would be enriched.[12]

Developing the Theological Foundation for a New Church

The Graduate School of Theology at Oberlin College near Cleveland was a fitting location for the first plenary assembly with representatives from all six churches present. Founded in 1833 by two Presbyterian ministers, Oberlin was the first American collegiate institution to admit women and African-Americans as full students. Charles Grandison Finney had been one of its early presidents, and he had done much of his work as the nation's leading evangelist from that location. The seminary's quadrangle and Fairchild Chapel, designed by Cass Gilbert, provided a splendid setting for the sessions. In addition to the delegates from the six member churches, observer-consultants from seventeen churches attended the assembly. Although Lutheran and Roman Catholic representatives were not listed, three Canadian churches were registered, as were Baptist, Moravian, Orthodox, other Methodist, and other Presbyterian or Reformed churches from the United States. Nearly 100 people, not counting media representatives, were present for the assembly.

12. Blake, "The Union Proposal Two Years Later," 394–98 (italics added).

Following the example of the previous COCU gathering, which had discussed issues related to ministry, delegates to the Oberlin assembly focused attention upon another foundational issue that often separated churches in the catholic and reformed traditions: the relative importance of Scripture and church tradition as authority and guide for the theology and life of the church. All of the churches held the Bible in respect, honored earlier generations of church leaders, especially theologians like Augustine and heroic figures like St. Francis, and accorded a certain honor to the early councils of the church, especially the Nicene Council of 325. They differed, however, in their understanding of the authority of post-biblical documents. In order to resolve differences with respect to ministry (especially the office of bishop), worship, the sacraments, and even the central tenets of the Christian faith, the churches had to reach agreement concerning the basis on which these matters would be settled. The Consultation's executive committee commissioned background papers and appointed study commissions to develop reports, drawing upon those papers, for discussion at the Oberlin meeting.

Methodist historian and noted Wesley scholar Albert C. Outler wrote one of these papers—"Scripture, Tradition, and the Guardians of Tradition"—in which he reflected upon the convergence that the Faith and Order Commission set forth at its Fourth World Conference held in Montreal later in the year (July 12–26, 1963).[13] Outler offered a series of "Comments in Search of Perspective" on the "dilemma" that he described as "the primacy of Scripture *and* the omnipresent of tradition" that has "plagued the Faith and Order Commission on Tradition and the Traditions throughout its decade of work." He also referred to an idea that "has come generally to be taken for granted in any and all ecumenical enterprises that there is such a thing as the *co-existence by right* of plural and varied traditions—hermeneutical, liturgical, doctrinal, political, etc.,—among the churches and even in a united church." He offered his own summary of the "*sola Scriptural*" tradition of the Reformation churches.

Outler then turned to "one aspect of the problem of tradition that was almost deliberately avoided in our study: the nature and function of the guardian(s) of tradition." Throughout Christian history, the churches have been interested in identifying the guardians or trustees of tradition, the people who were assigned the responsibility to preserve both The Tradition and the traditions. Always, it seemed, the authorized ministers were assigned this function and the result was that both in schism and in unity movements

13. Outler, "Scripture, Tradition and the Guardians of Tradition," 83–95. For the text of the Montreal report "Scripture, Tradition and Traditions," see Kinnamon and Cope, *The Ecumenical Movement*, 139–44.

"the reconstruction of the ministry has been the *conditio sine qua non*. More often than not, it has been the actual crux of the matter."

Outler concluded that if the representative ministries of the participating churches were to serve "as guardians of THE Christian Tradition," these churches would have to develop a "more validly authorized ministry" than any of them now has. In order to create an adequate ministry, they could not go back to "any existing ecclesiological tradition." Instead, the ministries in all of their churches, in a fresh and penitential manner, would have to offer themselves in new acts of commitment to the ministerial office in the Body of Christ. Only then could they adequately serve as the church's distinctive and historical witness to and proclaimers of The Christian Tradition in the church and the world.[14] It was clear that for Outler, none of the existing ministries, not even the Episcopal Church's historic episcopate, was adequate, in its current state of being, to serve in this new church.

The main point of the report to the plenary by its study commission on ministry was the relation of Scripture, Tradition, and the traditions in the life of the church.[15] Here, the language was clear and conclusive. "The churches represented in this Consultation affirm the Holy Scriptures to be canonical, that is, the norm of their total life, including worship and witness and teaching and mission." The report also speaks clearly about Tradition, by which "we understand the whole life of the Church, ever guided and nourished by the Holy Spirit, and expressed in its worship, witness, way of life, and its order." The report acknowledged that the churches also had traditions, but it affirmed that they all needed to be brought under the judgment of the Scriptures. As they discussed these matters, the Oberlin delegates concluded that they had reached agreement on the central issue. In their final report, they declared:

> We believe that the Consultation has reached an important consensus on the crucial question of authority in the Church. On the basis of this consensus we find ourselves now ready to grapple with the sharp issues that in our history have been the causes of division and the walls of separation between us."[16]

A second background paper may have helped the delegates reach their conclusion. Princeton sociologist Paul M. Harrison discussed the organizational systems in the participating churches.[17] Despite varied doctrines,

---

14. Outler, "Scripture, Tradition and the Guardians of Tradition," 95.

15. Report of the Study Commissions, *Digest of the Second Meeting*, 44–47.

16. Ibid., 50.

17. Some of the delegates would have known Harrison's 1959 book *Authority and Power in the Free Church Tradition* in which he analyzed the organizational systems of

terminologies, organizational patterns, and self-descriptions, Harrison proposed, the denominations functioned in demonstrably similar fashion. The driving force was goal achievement, the need to accomplish the various missions and services that each denomination, its congregations, clergy, and constituents needed. The result was a strong movement, even in congregationally governed churches, toward the concentration of power in the church's executive officers. One of Harrison's most interesting observations was lodged in a footnote: "Congregational and Presbyterian churchmen will assume some form of the historic episcopate. The hierarchy and its functions already exist at the informal level and only await official legitimation of existing powers."[18]

It was generally known that ideas and practices of worship varied widely among the churches represented at the Oberlin gathering of the Consultation on Church Union. They were agreed that the Eucharist is the definitive form of Christian worship, but except for the Disciples and a minority of Episcopal parishes, the principal act of worship on most Sundays was a service of the Word without the Sacrament. The Episcopal Church required that pastors and congregations use the approved the liturgies and prayers from the *Book of Common Prayer,* whereas Disciples depended primarily upon extemporaneous prayers developed by local elders. The other churches in the Consultation encouraged pastors to use their denominationally approved worship books, but allowed them varying degrees of freedom in actual practice.

To begin the process of resolving potential conflicts about worship, the Consultation's executive committee commissioned Massey H. Shepherd Jr., to write a paper on the church's liturgical tradition. Shepherd was an Episcopal historian and liturgical scholar who taught at the Church Divinity School of the Pacific in Berkeley, California. [19] Among his books was *Worship in Scripture and Tradition,* a collection of essays that he had edited on behalf of the Theological Commission on Worship (North American Section) of the World Council of Church's Commission on Faith and Order. In his COCU paper, Shepherd compared two ways of understanding worship. The *theocratic* approach emphasized worship for the glory of God. It easily used "symbol and ceremony and myth" and seemed comfortable with archaic patterns even though they might have lost "something of intelligibility and relevance." The *Christocentric* approach understood that each service of worship could be a new occasion for a "specific revelation of the Word."

---

the American Baptist Church.

18. Harrison, "Sociological Analysis of the Participating Communions," 106.

19. Shepherd, "Toward a Definition of the Church's Liturgy," 120–34.

This kind of worship was indifferent or hostile toward the senses other than hearing, and it tended toward emphasizing the instruction and nurture of the worshipers.

Shepherd acknowledged that in a united church there would be a mixture of worship patterns. Some churches would use forms that were fixed by church authority while others would follow the custom of allowing pastors and congregations to give form to worship. In some of the "essentials in Christian worship," however, the united church would demand "uniformity of expression" in order to maintain "the unity of Christian fellowship." Discussing the Words of Institution in the eucharistic prayer, Shepherd noted that "the question is whether local ministers and congregations may be allowed any form that is pleasing to themselves without regard to what is acceptable to the Church as a whole." He acknowledged that Anglicans preferred a form of worship that "bears the authority of the whole Church" and that governs the role of the clergy in worship no less than that of the laity . . . A liturgical Church prefers to take the risk of formalism in preference to the risk of banality . . . Liturgical worship is a means of protecting the laity, at the most solemn and sensitive moment of their confrontation with God, from all tyranny of clericalism. It is also a protection of the clergy from themselves."

Under the leadership of Elmer J. F. Arndt, a member of the United Church of Christ, a study commission developed a response to this paper. [20] It pointed out that "the vocabulary of worship . . . comes primarily from the Scriptures," while "the pattern of worship stems primarily from the traditions." Neither the "Living Tradition of the church" nor "cultural and sociological factors" should be finally determinative, however, because liturgy focuses the whole response of Christians upon God in Jesus Christ." The report stated that it would be desirable to have "three or four orders of service set forth as approved forms for a united church, with an agreed upon statement of the elements that are necessary for a whole and proper worship," and that "the reverent use in agreeable proportion of all the proposed forms should be asked of every congregation in a united church."

The "renewal of the Church depends in large measure upon the finding of a new liturgical life," which would have three components: "worship, witness, and mission" all focused as the church's response to the gospel gift. Delegates had no interest in coercing the churches into patterns of worship that were unfamiliar or alien to them, but instead sought to provide a framework that would stabilize practices, extend experience with unfamiliar ways

---

20. *Digest of the Second Meeting*, 47–49.

of worship, and lead toward developing new ways of worship in the united church.[21]

The Oberlin assembly adopted a budget of $4,800 to fund the Consultation during the 1963-64 year, and each church was asked to contribute $800 (the previous year's asking had been $700). A clear sign of serious intent was the action asking each church to request authority from its plenary body "to enter into the development of a plan of union when and if the Consultation decides that it is appropriate to begin such work."[22] By making this request, delegates indicated that the reason for the Consultation's existence was "challenged if we allow ourselves indefinitely to discuss unity in general." They knew that discussion soon had to be turned into action.

Before they could make this shift, however, the churches had more theological work to do. Since they could see consensus emerging on the relation of Scripture and Tradition, they decided to focus their next plenary assembly, in Princeton April 13–16, 1964, on three classic themes that had traditionally divided the churches from one another: Baptism, Eucharist, and ministry.

Finding a Common Mind in a New Era of Freedom

Delegates to the Princeton plenary assembly were greeted by COCU's chairman, James I. McCord, who was also the president of Princeton Theological Seminary, which was hosting the gathering. In his introductory statement, McCord acknowledged that there had been "some expression of disappointment in the progress of the ecumenical movement" since their previous meeting. One reason, he suspected, was that "those of us who had been hoping for a great deal of forward progress had our patience tested by the lateral progress, as the ecumenical movement reached out and engaged in depth branches of Christendom which had not been so engaged until 1963 and 1964." He noted that the six communions in the Consultation "are North American, and that we stand in a position in North America today in which the church may well be freer to move than she has been in generations." Referring to the cultural disestablishment of "the church as we know it," McCord told the delegates that "the church today has a chance to *become* the church, to be free, to be emancipated from her culture so that she can be that for which she is intended to be." That freedom "can be used to overcome our introversion; this freedom can be used to possess our catholicity, the fullness of our heritage and our faith; and this freedom can

21. Ibid.
22. Ibid., 31.

be used to overcome our fragmentation."[23] With this exhortation in mind, the delegates to COCU's Princeton gave their attention to the topics that had been assigned to this gathering, the historic sacraments of the churches and the continuing topic of the ministry.

Because five of the six churches ordinarily practiced infant baptism (usually by sprinkling or pouring) and one of the churches, the Christian Church (Disciples of Christ), exclusively practiced believers' baptism by immersion, the theology and form of baptism had to be considered. Anticipating a challenging discussion, the executive committee asked Ralph G. Wilburn, a Disciples' theologian and dean of Lexington Theological Seminary, to draft the background paper, which he entitled "The One Baptism and the Many Baptisms."[24] During the discussions of this issue, to the surprise of many, Disciples did not make believer's baptism an issue to be debated, but instead affirmed the consensus that emerged during the assembly.[25] George G. Beazley Jr, head of the Disciples delegation later explained that his church had recently engaged in unity conversations with the American Baptist Church. They realized that their views of the meaning of baptism were closer to those of the COCU churches than to those of the Baptist tradition.[26]

In its statement "One Baptism," the Princeton plenary assembly affirmed that baptism existed in the Church from the beginning and "as an act of Christ in his Church." They agreed that baptism formed the "visible basis" of their unity, united the baptized with Christ in his death and resurrection, and was the way that the baptized were born again and "incorporated into the body of Christ." They affirmed the classic theology that baptism was done by God rather than by those performing the act. The most important practical decision was that both infant and adult baptism would be "accepted as alternative forms in the united church," though neither would be required "if contrary to the sincere conscience of a member or minister." The baptismal rite itself would use water in the name of the Father, the Son, and the Holy Spirit. It would include a confession of sin and an affirmation of faith by the one being baptized or that person's sponsors. Baptism ordinarily would be administered by an ordained minister in the presence of a congregation. The report stated that baptism was essential and should be preceded or accompanied by careful instruction. It is to be administered

23. *Digest of the Third Meeting,* 2–3.
24. Wilburn, "The One Baptism," 72–107.
25. *Digest of the Third Meeting,* 25–28.
26. Beazley, "Editorial Introduction," *Mid-Stream* 3/4 (1964) vii.

once. "Neither infant baptism nor adult baptism should be imposed contrary to conscience."[27]

The background paper on "one table" was drafted by Franklin W. Young, a prominent New Testament scholar. He described his paper as a "blunt look at certain major problems" that confront people turning to the New Testament in order to interpret the meaning of the Lord's Supper.[28] With the guidance of its study commission on "one table," the Princeton plenary assembly adopted a comprehensive statement about the Eucharist in the life of the church. Early in the statement, it acknowledged that the question of who is authorized to preside at the One Table continues to be a divisive issue among the churches. Apart from that unresolved matter, however, they could testify to "a growing consensus of interpretation in all our churches." It describes four elements in this understanding, but the spirit of the agreement is expressed in the final element on the list. "The Holy Communion is the presence of Christ who has come, who comes to his people, and who will come in glory. It is the anticipation and foretaste of the heavenly banquet where the redeemed people of God will eat and drink with their crucified and risen Lord in His kingdom."[29]

Because issues related to ministry were so important, the Princeton assembly continued to discuss this topic. Paul A. Washburn of the Evangelical United Brethren Church led the assembly's discussion of ministry in the united church, linking the discussion to ideas adopted by the Fourth World Conference on Faith and Order that had met in Montreal in 1963.[30] The report stated that the theological foundation for ministry comes from Jesus who invites the church to relive the saving work, "which was accomplished through the saving work [of] his life, death, resurrection, and gathering of the Church." This ministry of prayer and loving service for both the Church and the world was given to "the entire people of God [who share] in Christ's priesthood, proclaiming the mighty acts of God in Christ Jesus, mediating Christ's atoning and reconciling work to the world."

"Within the community of his people," the report continued, "God calls forth an ordained ministry which he gives for the life, growth, and mission of the Church." The responsibilities of this ordained ministry include leading worship, guarding the tradition, preaching the Word, overseeing the Church's mission in the world, and providing pastoral care to Christians.

27. *Digest of the Third Meeting,* 25–28.

28. Young, "One Table," 119–42.

29. *Digest of the Third Meeting,* 32.

30. Ibid., 20–25.

The report recommends that the Consultation study union movements around the world that were addressing the problems and solutions with respect to ministry. "We believe," it continues, "that in a servant Church that is truly catholic, truly reformed, and truly evangelical, the ministerial orders should include the historic ministries of bishops, presbyters (elders) and deacons although we acknowledge that the particular functions of these ministries require further clarification." Equally important is this assertion: "We further believe that these ministries can be constituted for the united church without prejudice to the existing ministerial orders in the several churches." A list of ten questions requiring further study, however, made it clear that there was much work yet to do before the ecclesiological convictions and practices of the participating churches could be brought into the united church that the Consultation anticipated. Not least of these questions, at a time when the ordained ministry was almost completely male, was the place that women would have "within the ordained ministry of the united church."

As delegates to the Princeton meeting seemed to be coming close to agreement on issues related to ministry in a united church, William J. Wolf, professor of theology at the Episcopal Divinity School in Cambridge, Massachusetts, spoke a disquieting word to the assembly.[31] His church, he explained, was bound by the Chicago-Lambeth Quadrilateral, a document that outlined the factors that Anglicans around the world regarded as essential principles on which church union could take place. The Episcopal delegation would "discuss the ministry within the context of the historic episcopate," which Wolf explained by reading the delegates a three-page section from a statement by his church's Joint Commission on Approaches to Unity.[32]

Many of the delegates understood Wolf's statement to be an indication that the Episcopal Church was likely to take a hard line in the discussions about ministry and, perhaps, on other topics where its theology and practice differed from other churches in the Consultation. Later in the plenary's schedule, Robert F. Gibson Jr., bishop of the Episcopal diocese of Virginia who had just been elected president of the Consultation, spoke to the assembly. He would not have accepted this position if he had not believed that his church would continue as a serious participant in the Consultation's work.

Before the delegates could leave for home, they received a second sign of resistance. Charles Parlin, one of the Methodist Church's most prominent

31. Ibid., 9.
32. Wolf, *Documents on Church Unity,* 15–18.

lay leaders and secretary of COCU's executive committee, presented a statement that had been prepared for The Methodist Church's forthcoming General Conference.[33] The statement listed five problems that COCU had not yet resolved, and Parlin stated positions that he thought Methodists were likely to take. Referring to Anglican ideas about the connection of communion to the historic episcopate, he asserted that Methodists were unlikely to abandon open communion. They would not sacrifice their connectional system to the congregationalism of the United Church and the "Disciples Church." Methodists would not "abandon infant baptism and adopt total emersion [sic.] as the only valid rite." Even though the Consultation had earlier adopted a statement, with the Disciples voting in favor, "acknowledging the validity of other forms of baptism," Parlin said that the Methodist delegation would not revise their statement. Methodists resisted the COCU process, he added, because their communion was a world church and because it had taken stands on social issues such as alcohol and gambling that were not matched by the other churches.[34]

Characterizing Parlin's report as "pessimistic and partially inaccurate," Harold E. Fey commented in a *Christian Century* editorial that in light of this development the Evangelical United Brethren Church might have second thoughts about its union discussions with Methodists. Presbyterian leaders Eugene Carson Blake and James I. McCord, joined by the Disciples' George G. Beazley Jr., and David G. Colwell of the United Church of Christ, declared that the Consultation would continue forward and grow stronger. And this would take much less time than the 20 to 25 years that Methodist bishop Glenn R. Phillips had declared that it would require.[35]

When the Princeton plenary assembly closed, its members who had come to this Presbyterian stronghold anticipating further movement toward Christian unity, left town with two sober reminders that long-standing challenges to Christian unity remained. The creation of a new American church might be more difficult than they had anticipated.

33. Without mentioning the Methodists or the points of disagreement, the *New York Times* (April 18, 1964) depicted the underlying issue by the headline for its report: "Protestant Dissonance; Leaders Move for Unity at Princeton But the Congregations Stayed at Home."

34. Ibid.

35. Harold E. Fey, *Christian Century*, May 6, 1964, 599–600.

3

Second Thoughts on Church Union

Pressing on to become "God's instrument for peace and reconciliation
across boundaries of nation, race, and class . . ."

—EUGENE CARSON BLAKE

A MONTH AFTER THE Princeton plenary assembly, Eugene Carson Blake gave a speech in Kansas City in which he spoke to the signs of resistance that had surfaced. He described four motives for the churches to continue their work: to be obedient to Christ; to challenge the world with the gospel "with an effectiveness impossible in their separation"; to "strengthen the ethical witness of Christianity"; and to enrich each of the churches and remove from them some of the distortions caused by the divisions among them." At a time when the nation and world were facing new challenges "over civil rights, claims that churches were infiltrated by communists, the continuing struggle for racial justice [and] the politico-moral issue faced by the United States and the whole world—that of peace," our churches "look like a group of competing religious clubs, more often behaving like Greek-letter fraterni-ties in a college than like the bride or body of Christ, which we all claim the Church to be. Such a spectacle makes our preaching sound like biased propaganda and reduces the Lord's Supper to agnostic ritual for initiates."

A few months later, on January 24, 1965, Blake returned to the pulpit of Grace Cathedral where he had preached the sermon that had initiated the Consultation. In a sermon entitled "Second Thoughts on Church Union," he declared that American church union of the kind proposed four years earlier was "an obligation upon the members and leaders of our churches, challenging us all to a costly and risky seeking of the first step on our way toward reunion of the whole Church now." He cited two events in the years from 1961 through 1964 that were favorable to church union: the overwhelmingly positive response that the proposal had elicited and the positive impact upon church union of Vatican II. Events that were having a negative impact included the recovery of interest in world-wide connections of churches in confessional families and the vital involvement of American churches in the nation's racial crisis, which was leading to schism in churches, and lethargy in some quarters and overt opposition in others with respect to church union.

Blake warned that they should be against any church union "that is established at the expense of truth" or "motivated by, or aimed at, an outmoded triumphalism . . . Those who still want the church, or churches, to dominate American life misread the signs of the times. The churches and their leaders must learn how to serve the world rather than to go on trying, as in the past, to rule it." Finally, we must be against any church union that would "threaten the Ecumenical Movement or diminish the obligation to continue to cooperate with all Christian churches in their common witness to the Lordship of Jesus Christ." The sermon closed with a renewed exhortation: "Led, I pray by the Holy Spirit, I propose that we press on in North America to form, with all who will join with us, 'a united church, truly catholic, truly reformed, and truly evangelical,' lest in this revolutionary world we find ourselves so bound to our own past histories that we are unable to be God's instrument for peace and reconciliation across all boundaries of nation, race, or class."[1]

A Deeper Understanding of Ministry

The plenary assembly immediately after Princeton was scheduled for Lexington, Kentucky (April 5–8, 1965), with a pilgrimage to Cane Ridge, one of the most storied sites in American religious history and one that contrasted sharply with Princeton. The eastern city manifested the sophisticated, cultural aristocracy of American Christian life. There Jonathan Edwards, America's greatest native theologian and a representative figure of New England Puritanism, was buried. Princeton was also the place where John Witherspoon developed into one of the leaders of the new rationalism in American religious life and became a proponent of the political system that was emerging in eighteenth-century America. A Presbyterian scholar, he was the only clergyman to sign the Declaration of Independence. In later

1. Blake, *Church in the Next Decade*, 117–24.

years, Princeton became increasingly identified with the new economic system of the northern states and one more location in the rapidly increasing opposition to slavery and the southern culture of which slavery was an integral part.

In contrast, Lexington was the cultural center of the border state that suffered more bloodshed in relation to its population than any other state in the Civil War. While other southern cities, like Richmond and Atlanta, were more doctrinaire in their support of slavery and the way of life that it made possible, Lexington was very much within the orbit that revolved around the deeply ingrained plantation system. Although derived from Presbyterian lineage, the Christian Church (Disciples of Christ), whose seminary in Lexington would host COCU's fourth plenary assembly, represented distinctive traits of what United Methodist historian James F. White later called the frontier tradition of American Christianity.[2] With their emphasis upon patterns of faith and practice derived from the Bible, Disciples had developed a unique ecclesiology that combined believer's baptism, eucharistic worship every Sunday conducted by lay elders, extemporaneous prayer, congregational government, a non-creedal approach to theology, and an insistence that by affirming these qualities all of the churches could come together in a non-denominational form of unity.

The primary task for the Lexington meeting would be to develop as much agreement about ministry in the united church as already had emerged in discussions about faith, worship, and the sacraments. Was the sword that Eugene Carson Blake had unsheathed in his first San Francisco sermon sharp enough to sever the central issue the churches would face, the issue that Blake labeled "the Gordian knot of the ministry." Could the COCU churches create a united ministry by accepting the fact of the historic apostolic succession without insisting upon a particular theological interpretation of that ministry? Or did William Wolf's forceful introduction of the Lambeth Quadrilateral during the Princeton plenary assembly mean that it would be necessary for all participating churches to affirm one particular doctrine of ministry from the several that had been promulgated over the centuries?

If well-established historical precedent without specific theological justification was sufficient, then the Consultation could establish a reunited ministry with bishops in apostolic succession, practice varied forms of baptism, strengthen the eucharistic character of worship, use historic confessions of faith, and resolve other problems that had kept the churches apart for so many generations. If, however, accepting certain practices because

---

2. White, *Protestant Worship*, 171–73.

of their historical precedence was insufficient reason, if the churches had to agree on specific theological explanations and justifications, then the debates would continue indefinitely and the likelihood of creating a new church—especially a church that crossed the Catholic-Reformed divide—was greatly diminished.

The test case continued to be the ministry, and especially the controverted issue of apostolic succession. Following their established practice, COCU's executive committee commissioned research papers that would provide the information and insight that delegates to the Lexington meeting would need. George Beazley described this body of material as "the most significant collection of papers on the ministry which has ever been produced in America."[3] Among many themes discussed in the seven commissioned papers, three areas of concern were especially important.

The first task was to determine if a ministry ordained by bishops in apostolic succession was mandated by the New Testament or by explicit church teaching later in church history. Papers by Presbyterian Floyd Filson, Methodist John Deschner, and Ernest Best (St. Andrews University) led to the conclusion that there is no one model prescribed either in the New Testament or later in the church's history. Therefore, the inclusion of this pattern of ministry in the United Church would need to be on grounds other than biblical and historical doctrine. The episcopate should be included "in the orders of the united Church," Filson wrote, "not because it is prescribed in the Bible or found in unbroken line in history "but because it is an acceptable order which can symbolize the unity of the Church and serve for the working expression of unity without depriving the pastors or priests of the Church their freedom and dignity."[4]

Disciples historian Ronald E. Osborn presented a comprehensive survey of church traditions concerning the ministry from apostolic times until the present in the several traditions represented by the Consultation. He concluded that none of the churches in the Consultation taught that

---

3. In their published form these papers cover 210 pages in the *Digest* of the fourth assembly (Lexington, Kentucky, April 5–8, 1965). The authors and the titles of their papers are: "The Ordained Ministry in Uniting Churches," by William J. Wolf (Episcopal Church); "The Ministry in American History: A Reflection in the Light of Ecumenical Encounter," by Robert T. Handy (American Baptist Church); "The Relationship Between the Ministry of the Whole People of God and the Ordained Ministry," by A. T. Mollegen (Episcopal Church); Freedom Within Unity" by Floyd V. Filson (United Presbyterian Church); "Ministry or Ministries," by Ronald E. Osborn (Christian Church Disciples of Christ); "Ministry and Ministries," Ernest Best; "Church Order as Continuity in the Church," by John Deschner (The Methodist Church). Beazley's comment appears in *Mid-Stream* 4/3 (1965), i.

4. Filson, "Freedom Within Unity," 157.

ordination—which was the focal point of the debate—was a sacrament. Furthermore, in the official affirmations of the six churches "no one is required to believe 'as of the faith' that non-episcopal orders are defective, even though they may be regarded as irregular by being outside the continuity of the historic episcopate." Osborn's third and most important conclusion followed immediately: "Those who believe in the necessity of ordination by a bishop in the succession seem prepared to admit that ministries otherwise ordained may be 'real' ministries, that is ministries de facto, although some of them insist that these are not 'valid' ministries, are not ministries de jure." He then quoted Article XXIII of the Episcopal Church's *Articles of Religion* to support the principle that had been present from COCU's beginning, that historical practice is sufficient ground for the ministry of the new church to be organized around the office of bishops in the apostolic succession. Nothing concerning sacramental theory was at stake.[5]

Although two of the papers were written by Episcopal scholars, neither of them spoke directly to Osborn's paper and the conclusions he had drawn.[6] Episcopal scholars outside of the Consultation followed the COCU discussions and some of them conveyed varying degrees of discontent over COCU's plan to establish the episcopal office on a foundation that appeared to be organizational and procedural rather than theological and sacramental. A common sentiment among these writers was that the Episcopal Church should be more interested in uniting with the Roman Catholic Church than with the Protestant churches in COCU. They feared that the office of bishop as it was being described in the Consultation would be unacceptable to other catholic churches. They were adamant in their claims that a sacramentally defined doctrine of episcopacy was necessary in any COCU ecclesiology. It is not surprising that this reservation should arise since the Episcopal Church was actively involved in serious conversations with the Roman Catholic and Orthodox Churches, both in the United States and internationally. In both venues, the nature of the ministry and its place in the church's authoritative tradition was at the center of the debate.[7]

Some scholars who agreed that a ministry in apostolic succession had served as a means of maintaining the church's connection with the apostolic age and tradition also were agreed that this was not the only means of maintaining the church's apostolic character. After declaring that "the ultimate authority in the Apostolic Church is God acting through Christ by

5. Osborn, "Ministry or Ministries," 198.

6. Writers who were members of the Episcopal Church were William J. Wolf and A. T. Mollegen.

7. Episcopal discussions with Orthodox, Roman Catholic, and Lutheran Churches are described in Jones, *Joy in the Struggle*. See also Macquarrie et al., *Realistic Reflections*.

the Spirit in the Church," Episcopal scholar Albert T. Mollengen discussed five lesser authorities that "reside in the whole people, the United Church": a canonical scripture, a dogma ("an agreed upon norm for the doctrine, teaching, preaching, and theological content of worship"), a liturgical structure, Baptism and the Lord's Supper, and "an authorized ordained ministry." Following the death of Paul the apostle, Mollengen observed, the churches that he had shaped took the lead in formulating a rule of faith and an authorized ministry.[8]

Delegates to the Lexington plenary assembly faced a second challenge concerning ministry, which was to understand why there was such strong opposition to the proposal that the reunited church would include the ministry of bishops in apostolic succession. Most participants in the discussion understood historical and theological factors that separated the churches. Much of the resistance, however, seemed to be at a more personal, visceral level, and before progress could be made on resolving this issue, the underlying emotional distress needed to come to the surface. This is what Robert T. Handy, an American Baptist church historian on the faculty of Union Theological Seminary in New York, offered in a paper on the uniquely American experience of church life. He noted that during the nation's formative years many Americans (especially those in Congregational and Presbyterian churches) carried unhappy memories of conflict with Anglican bishops in Great Britain. Because they embodied Anglican theology and maintained Anglican patterns, Episcopalians felt that they were under attack and therefore had to strive mightily to defend their ecclesial forms.

In more recent times, Handy reported, another challenge had come to American ministers, especially those in the traditional Protestant churches who were facing theoretical and practical challenges concerning their ministerial identity. "All this is part of the reason," Handy proposed, "why the form and meaning of the ministry has become such an ecumenical sticking point; no church and no minister can risk having a precious link with Christ and the Christian tradition severed, more especially when everything else is shifting." This may mean, Handy proposed, "that one important way to proceed in church union consultation is to focus first on ministerial role and functions in the present stormy time, in the light of the revelation of God in Christ and the continuing presence of the Holy Spirit." Then, in approaching the formal definitions of ministerial forms and meanings, in an age that needs every authentic link to the Gospel it can have, is there not need for all to cherish and appreciate one another's ministry in past and present for whatever of Christ is in them?"

8. Mollengen, "The Relationship Between the Ministry," 138–40.

Handy concluded by suggesting that the churches needed "the courage to face the glories and achievements as well as the distortions and limitations in the history of the ministry of our own as well as of our brother's communion. May God choose to reveal his will to us as together we seek to minister and together ask the deeper meaning of one another's ministries."[9]

Handy's paper opened the door to a third issue on ministry. How would the existing ministries of the separated churches be united into one? How could the ministries of the participating churches, all but one of them not yet within the pattern of apostolic succession, be brought into a ministry with this character? Episcopal theologian William J. Wolf addressed this question in a paper that described how this unification had been treated in church unions around the world.[10] The most important of these unions was the Church of South India because it had included episcopal and non-episcopal churches and had been functioning effectively for nearly a generation.

Wolf outlined seven features that could be derived from the South India example. (1) A united church would maintain a ministry ordained by bishops of the historic episcopate. (2) No doctrine of episcopacy or specific claim concerning its historicity would be made mandatory. (3) The office of bishop would be constitutional. (4) A liturgical process for the unification of existing ministries would take place, and it would include the laying on of hands by bishops in the historic succession and by designated representatives of all participating traditions and churches. (5) The faithfulness and effectiveness of the ministries of the participating churches would be affirmed and honored. (6) Ministers coming into the ministry of the united church would not be required to minister in ways that were contrary to their faith and conscience. (7) It was understood that the process of unification would require more than a brief period of time. Wolf stopped short of advocating the South India pattern, but for some of the COCU delegates it offered a way forward that they could affirm.

The Resurgence of Hope

In order to facilitate discussion of issues related to ministry, two study commissions prepared reports to the people who assembled for the Lexington plenary assembly. One dealt with "The Ordained Ministry in a United Church" and the other with "Ordination in a Church Catholic, Evangelical and Reformed." After full discussion, debate, and revision of the drafts, the delegates adopted two reports, "which we have now recorded as a

9. Handy, "The Ministry in American History," 132.
10. Wolf, "The Ordained Ministry in Uniting Churches," 37–106.

consensus," and in which we have "broken fresh ground." They were beginning to imagine "a united church embracing the heart of all our varying
traditions and binding in visible unity companies of Christian people who
for generations have been led in separate ways by conscience and our separate readings of the gospel."[11]

Essential to this visible unity would be "a united ministry, capable of
bearing undoubted and unquestionable authority everywhere." There were
agreed that three conditions had to be met: (1) "a statement of the meaning
and structure of ministry" that would "sustain the test of universality"; (2)
the will to look forward for new understandings that had not been possible
in their separateness; and (3) "a corporate act in which and through which all
would offer our existing ministries to Almighty God, asking him to receive
our offering through Jesus Christ, to complete and perfect what is amiss or
incomplete in our ministries and to give us whatever of his authority and
grace we need to serve in the united ministry to which we are called."[12] Although the unresolved issues described in the two reports were formidable,
the discussions—in sharp contrast to those in Princeton—were marked by
a renewed sense of the possibility of achieving the goal of establishing a
church that was truly evangelical, truly catholic, and truly reformed.

The movement to create a new American church was still young. Only
four years and four months had elapsed since the sermon in San Francisco
had launched the enterprise and only three years since the organizing
conference at Mount St. Alban in the nation's capital had given it shape.
Through a process of serious theological engagement some of the nation's
most important theologians and church leaders had tested and confirmed
the central thesis of the proposal that Eugene Carson Blake had promulgated: that despite their many differences these four (now expanded to
six) American churches held similar views concerning the central ecclesial
factors around which their worship and work were organized. As they had
pushed deeper into the biblical, historical, and theological foundations of
church life, they had found basic ideas that all of them affirmed.

Furthermore, they had become increasingly aware of the fact that their
actual operations were similar despite significant differences in structures
and nomenclature. What might be considered an unexpressed corollary
was that despite their alignment with worldwide confessional families, these
churches were distinctly American and their primary mission field was the
rapidly changing people and systems of America. Surely, it seemed to many

11. "Minutes," *Digest of Fourth Meeting,* 19–29.
12. Ibid., 1–32.

of the delegates as they returned to their work places around the nation, they were ready to move forward with new eagerness and energy.

The time had come to translate their theological consensus into effective action. The first step, it seemed to the people gathered in Lexington, was to begin work on an outline plan of union. They stated the character of this next task with considerable care.

"We need not say that such a draft outline will be very far from a completed plan ready for submission to our constituent churches. Indeed, from one point of view, it will be no more than material for our next discussion. But it is far more important to note that this marks the first time we have felt able, and therefore compelled, to begin the delicate and equally commanding task of sketching, realistically and practically, the outline of the united church which we have imagined—perhaps all too easily—in time past."[13]

Delegates at the Lexington assembly received another report that pointed toward a new aspect of creating a new church. The executive committee announced that the "Continuing Commission on Liturgical Approach to Unity" had had one meeting, in Chicago on May 28, 1964. It was to study worship in "parallel with the activities of COCU in the hope that when and if union is achieved some of the basic agreement on worship will have been reached and will, during the process of study, have influenced the worship of all six churches. It was agreed that the nature of the ministry in a united church is not in the purview of this committee."[14]

Among the reasons for the new spirit was the plenary's Eucharist celebrated at one of the places of origin of the Christian Church (Disciples of Christ), the historic Cane Ridge Meeting House, twenty-five miles distant from Lexington. COCU delegates, guests, and friends left their hotels at 8:00 on the morning on April 7 and traveled in a caravan of buses through Kentucky's resplendent countryside, along roads bounded by sharply angled fieldstone fences, to the church and cemetery where in the summer of 1801 the Cane Ridge Meeting, one of the nation's most memorable religious events, had occurred—the outpouring of the Holy Spirit at a Presbyterian sponsored eucharistic festival. During the course of the revival, Presbyterians, Baptists, Methodists and other frontier Christians had listened to impassioned preaching in cleared land around the little church, received Holy Communion, and then were overwhelmed by dramatic moments of ecstatic behavior experienced by many of the vast assemblage.

On an April morning, one hundred sixty-four years later, the COCU assembly crowded into Cane Ridge's dimly lighted log church with its large

13. *Digest of Fifth Meeting,* 31.
14. Ibid., 15.

pulpit-centered platform and diminutive communion table. Congregational singing was supported by a restored reed organ. Using a liturgy that had been prepared by George Beazley who served as "host pastor" and with instructions by Paul Crow who taught history at the Lexington seminary, the congregants were able to "do this in remembrance of me" in circumstances that were distinctly American, egalitarian, and personal.

It was during the Eucharist at Cane Ridge, Eugene Carson Blake told an audience later in the year, that delegates could see illustrated the "mutual enrichment" that was one of the goals of the Consultation. It could be assumed by most people, he said, that "the Anglo-Catholics' and the Disciples' points of view on ministry and Sacrament would be at the extremes of the theological spectrum" since in Disciples' churches laypersons administer the sacrament. "They are not even in the argument whether we non-episcopally ordained ministers can administer a Sacrament valid in Anglo-Catholic tradition." At that service, however, many of the participants came to realize "for the first time that the chief reason for the Disciples' tradition and practice was because, like the Anglo-Catholics, they believed that the frequent and regular celebration of the Sacrament was essential to Christian worship."

Addressing people who were dissatisfied with the current state of the church but had little interest in church union, Blake declared that "to produce a united church, evangelical, catholic, and reformed, was not essentially an organizational matter." Denominations have no basis in the Bible, and "denominationalism, as such, distorts our understanding of the gospel, cripples the effectiveness of our witness, and encourages 'culture religion' in the place of Christianity."

At this point, Blake made another statement that was to become an increasingly important theme in the Consultation on Church Union. The purpose of the proposed union was not to "produce an upper-middle-class Protestant Church," but instead a church "more fully inclusive, racially, economically, socially, and ethnically than any of the present denominations." Referring to the Plan of Union that was already in the process of becoming, Blake said that they would be praying for "a miracle not unlike that which we have seen in our time wrought by God through his charismatic servant, Pope John XXIII."[15]

The "miracle" to which Blake referred included dramatic developments in worship across much of the Christian world. On December 4, 1963, three years to the day since Blake's precedent-setting sermon at Grace Cathedral, Pope Paul VI, promulgated the first of the Second Vatican Council's major

15. Blake, *Church in the Next Decade*, 125–31.

documents, the *Constitution on the Sacred Liturgy.* Among its decisions was that the Roman Catholic Church would use the vernacular languages when celebrating the Mass and other liturgies wherever Catholics gathered to worship God. That same year bishops from English-speaking countries who were in Rome for the Council established the International Commission on English in the Liturgy (ICEL) in order to prepare the new materials for English speaking countries. One reason why this decision impacted the COCU churches was that many of their liturgical leaders were encouraging the continued use of archaic forms of English in public prayer, despite the fact that Evangelical churches were increasingly adopting contemporary versions of English. The fact that the nation's Catholics would soon join Evangelicals in addressing God as You instead of Thou tipped the balance for many musicians, professors, and pastors.[16]

The newly elected chairman of the Consultation on Church Union, Episcopal bishop Robert F. Gibson Jr., left the Lexington meeting with much the same feeling that Blake had expressed in his post-assembly address. He too believed that by focusing attention on worshiping together, especially at the eucharistic table, COCU's leaders could move their process forward while they continued to struggle over issues of ministry and church order. Gibson recognized that the existing COCU group dealing with worship—the Continuing Commission on Liturgical Approach to Unity—could not do its work until its full complement of members had been appointed. He encouraged his colleagues on the executive committee to name the remaining members of the commission and clarify its assignments. With a new name, the Commission on Worship, this small group (initially one person from each participating church) would develop its own docket of work, meet at times of its own choosing, and focus attention primarily upon developing provisional liturgies for study and trial use. In order to keep the commission focused, Paul Crow, the part-time general secretary who worked with COCU committees and working groups other than the executive committee, would serve as its moderator. While members of the commission on worship were encouraged to attend the plenary assemblies, they would report their work directly to the executive committee, which also would authorize publications.[17]

The *Digest* of COCU's fifth plenary assembly (Dallas, May 2–5, 1966) lists the members of the commission on worship, five of whom attended

16. I made the decision in the spring of 1967 and used a research leave during the next school year to learn how to pray in contemporary English. When I returned to my duties as professor of worship a year later, I was ready to help my colleagues and students as they learned a new vocabulary of public prayer.

17. Paul A. Crow Jr., pers. comm.

the assembly as observers: W. Barnett Blakemore (CCDC) dean of Disciples Divinity House at the University of Chicago and director of worship at the university's Rockefeller Chapel; Paul H. Eller (EUB), a church historian and president of Evangelical Theological Seminary in Naperville, Illinois; Joseph D. Quillian Jr., (MC), formerly professor of homiletics and worship and now dean of Perkins School of Theology and co-author of a book on worship; David W. Romig (UPCUSA), pastor of the Sea and Land Church in New York City, who was gaining prominence in his church's program to develop a new worship book and hymnal; and R. Howard Payne (UCC), pastor of St. Thomas Reformed Church of Reading, Pennsylvania, who gave special attention to the liturgical tradition that the Evangelical and Reformed Church had brought to the newly formed United Church of Christ.

The one member of the Commission not at the Dallas assembly was Massey H. Shepherd Jr., professor of Liturgics at Church Divinity School of the Pacific, who was known to people in the Consultation because of the background paper, "Toward a Definition of the Church's Liturgy," that he had prepared in 1963 for COCU's second plenary assembly in Oberlin. Ohio. Early in the worship commission's work, at Gibson's urging, its members decided to draft a liturgy for the Lord's Supper, and Shepherd was chosen to do the drafting.

With these decisions, the Consultation became an active participant in the liturgical movement that was moving with increasing force among Protestant churches. As might be expected, the Episcopal Church was a leader in this renewal. Its Standing Liturgical Commission was preparing a revision of the revised *Book of Common Prayer* and as part of that process was publishing a series of booklets entitled *Prayer Book Studies* in order to involve the church fully in the process. In 1964 the Episcopal commission started work on a new eucharistic liturgy (which was approved for trial use by its General Assembly in 1967).

In the 1950s, conversations developed among Presbyterian churches in the United States, the Reformed Church in America, and the United Church of Christ concerning the possibility of developing a book of worship that all could use. Although these conversations were unsuccessful, the United Presbyterian Church decided to revise *The Westminster Directory of Worship* that for three hundred years had shaped worship in Presbyterian Churches. Working with the newly formed Joint Committee on Worship, Robert McAfee Brown drafted the new *Directory of Worship* that was approved by the church's General Assembly in 1960 and the next year by all but seven of its 213 presbyteries. In his book, *Presbyterian Worship in the Twentieth Century,* Arlo D. Duba notes the "amazing similarity" between this "theologically revolutionary Directory of Worship 1961" and the

Vatican Council's *Constitution on the Sacred Liturgy*.[18] Soon thereafter, the Presbyterian Joint Commission on Worship began preliminary work to develop a new lectionary and a new liturgy for celebrating the Sunday service of Word and Sacrament.

Similar activities were taking place among Lutherans in the United States and Canada. In 1965, four national synods formed the Inter-Lutheran Commission on Worship (ILCW) in order to develop a common hymnal and book of worship. Following the Episcopal Church's example, the ILCW began publishing a series of trial-use booklets, *Contemporary Worship,* to be used as the basis of conversations with pastors, musicians, and theologians. Also in 1965, the Methodist Church adopted a new book entitled *The Book of Worship for Church and Home.*

In order to enrich its discussions and drafting of new worship materials, the Consultation's commission on worship decided to invite representatives of other churches to send representatives to its working sessions. Among those who responded to the invitation, representatives of the Lutheran ILCW and the Catholic Church's U.S. Bishops' Committee on the Liturgy were especially constructive in their participation. During the next few years, this regular gathering of liturgical leaders of churches at the center of American life served as a source of life for the Consultation and as a forum for liturgical leaders of American churches to share the ideas and resources pointed toward liturgical renewal. Some of the COCU representatives hoped that the commission on worship would be able to develop an ecumenical worship book that could be used by all of the participating churches as they moved closer to one another.

Despite the hope that the renewal of worship would lead toward the closer communion of the churches, the challenging issues of ministry and church order had to be resolved in order for a new American church to arise.

---

18. Duba, *Presbyterian Worship,* 21.

4

Principles of Church Union

A more inclusive expression of the oneness of the Church of Christ than
any of the participating churches can suppose itself alone to be . . .

—PREAMBLE TO *PRINCIPLES OF CHURCH UNION*

BEFORE LEAVING LEXINGTON, THE church delegates approved a drafting
committee, with Eugene Carson Blake as chair, "to begin work on an outline
plan of union." The part-time COCU executives, George L. Hunt and Paul
A. Crow Jr., developed the initial draft, but following the first meeting the
committee asked one of its members, Episcopal bishop Stephen F. Bayne Jr.
to do the drafting. After nearly a year's work, the committee sent its document to COCU's executive committee, which suggested minor clarifica-
tions and released it to the Consultation. A month before delegates were
to gather in Dallas, Texas, for their fifth plenary assembly (May 2–5, 1966),
the "Outline for a Possible Plan of Church Union" was made available for
their review. The drafting committee hoped that this outline, modified in
light of suggestions from the churches, would become "the basis on which
to formulate a Plan of Union."

The plenary assembly revised the document, gave it a new title, *Principles of Church Union,* and sent it to the churches for study. The book included three appendices: "An Open Letter to the Churches," A Paper on
"The Structure of the Church," and A Paper on "Stages and Steps Toward
a United Church." COCU's chairman, George G. Beazley Jr., wrote that the
Consultation was "moving into a new phase as the churches begin to recognize the seriousness and dedication with which the goal is being pursued."

Referring to a new challenge that had arisen during the meeting, Beazley noted the irony that "having found acceptable solutions to the thorny problems of faith and order during the Dallas meeting, the Consultation on Church Union should have skidded near to the precipice of disaster over a matter of organizational structure." The Consultation, he hoped, could resolve this issue as it had done with others in the past, "by moving to some higher ground from which to survey the full meaning of this gift of God."[1]

Quickly, the executive committee published *Principles* so that it could be distributed broadly. Designed in the same small format that had been used for earlier COCU publications, this ninety-six-page book went through four printings during the next few months. Following actions taken at the 1967 meeting, the Consultation published a revised and expanded edition. Although the "Principles" and "An Open Letter to the Churches" remained unchanged, the new edition included "Guidelines for the Structure of the Church" and "Stages and Steps" which replaced papers on these subjects in the 1966 first edition. Other new materials were "A Study Guide," drafted by Janet Harbison, a suggested reading list, and an evaluation form.

Midway through the second edition, the editors printed "A Resolution on Developing a Plan of Union," which the Consultation had adopted on May 3, 1967. The resolution states that the Consultation "resolves to take certain immediate steps appropriate to the development of a plan of union." This plan would "include in detail" the procedures for uniting the memberships and ministries of the participating churches and "the structure and functions of the Provisional Council, to be organized at least on a national and regional basis."[2] The Consultation's confident mood was expressed in the foreword to the revised edition in which COCU's chairman, UCC pastor David G. Colwell wrote this confident sentence: "It is increasingly clear that the Consultation on Church Union will find the way to a united church, catholic, evangelical, and reformed."[3]

In March 1967, McCormick Theological Seminary's journal *McCormick Quarterly* published a series of essays interpreting the Consultation and the *Principles*. Since the authors of these interpretations were among COCU's most prominent leaders, their statements could be interpreted as unofficial but significant commentaries on *Principles of Church Union*.

The second edition of *Principles* begins with "An Open Letter to the Churches" that declares the theological foundation for everything in the

1. Beazley, "Editorial Introduction," *Mid-Stream* 5/3 (1966) i–v.

2. *Principles of Church Union*, 74–75. Unless otherwise noted, references are to the 1967 revised edition.

3. Ibid., 5.

main document: "We are one . . . because the "self-giving God, who comes to us in his Son Jesus Christ . . . has called into being a single family in the Son and the Spirit. He has sealed with us all a single covenant, grounded in the same ultimate demand and promise." The world around us "is unimpressed by our claim to love one another, when it sees how we are fractured and divided by our lesser loyalties." To people around us, our churches often appear not "as servants of the servant Christ but as affluent, self-perpetuating enterprises competing with one another." The new church would not overcome all that has divided the churches and it would "still be far from the wholeness of the Body of Christ." It therefore would keep itself open to all others who "seek a wider unity of catholic and evangelical traditions, alike reformed by every true obedience to God."[4]

Acknowledging the long history of their disunity, the "Open Letter" notes that "one century's divisions may be pointless in another century." These divisions may be "simply the excuses we use for retaining separatenesses which have little or nothing to do with the gospel in our day." Calling attention to "the deep impulse toward unity" in American life, the document states that "even those forces which seem quite secular in origin may [be] but an intimation of God's will which we are bound to hear and obey, if the Church is to retain integrity and faithfulness in its mission."[5]

This new church would remember, if God be willing, "every lesson he has taught his Church in history" and would incorporate every one of these lessons into the new church's way of life "so that it will continue to guide and nourish." Summing up, the "Open Letter" states that the Consultation had been guided by two principles: "first, that we be true to every essential link with the apostolic gospel and community; second, that we guard every opportunity of action that will assist us better to bear responsibility for the future."[6]

The "Preamble," which the revised edition entitles "Road to Union," contains one of COCU's most memorable lines. The new church would be "a more inclusive expression of the oneness of the Church of Christ than any of the participating churches can suppose itself alone to be . . . and a truer expression of the fullness of the Church of Christ than any of the constituting churches can suppose itself to be."[7] Of course, more work would have to be done. After *Principles* had been given "careful consideration," the delegates would need to provide "wise amendment" and make "judicious

4. Ibid., 10–11.
5. Ibid., 14.
6. Ibid., 15.
7. Ibid., 21.

decisions within the areas covered by subsequent chapters." Six criteria—"commanding objectives" is the phrase they used—would guide the process: (1) obedience to mission, (2) mutual enrichment, (3) existing relationships, (4) maximum protection to existing diversities and liberties, (5) maximum openness for continuing renewal and reformation, and (6) being a uniting as well as a united church.

To counter the fear that unity would require the churches to give up some aspect of the gospel, Christian teaching, or church practice that was important to them, the "Preamble" lists six "agents of continuity" that are "precious in each of our churches separately" because they link the churches of their time with the authentic church of earlier times: (1) the authority of Scripture, (2) faithfulness to the Tradition, (3) the witness of the historic statements of Christian faith, (4) the central sacramental gifts, (5) a ministry with authority as close to the universal and undoubted as any authority in a still-divided church can be, and (6) the unfailing, steadfast community of worshipping Christians in their congregations through the ages.

The main body of the green book consists of four chapters, which state in concise and graceful language the substance of the COCU proposal as it had developed to this point. Here the theological understandings which representatives of the participating churches had clarified and confirmed, were set forth in words they hoped would be understood and affirmed by people across the land in every manifestation of their churches' life and work.

Chapter One, The Faith of the Church. Since the churches, ministers, and members held a wide range of views concerning the doctrines and practices of the Christian faith, the central issue for a church union movement was to determine what everyone would be required to acknowledge or confess in order to participate in the life and worship of the new church. For some, the expected answer would be that the ancient creeds would have to be affirmed and recited, while others would resist any requirement that creeds would have to be used. Chapter One of *Principles* states that the united church would acknowledge the Christian faith in five ways: (1) by affirming the Scriptures as the norm of the church's life; (2) by recognizing "the historic Christian Tradition" (defined as "the whole life of the Church ever guided and nourished by the Holy Spirit); (3) by honoring and using the Apostles' Creed and the Nicene Creed; (4) by developing new formulations of faith; and (5) by using the various confessions that the churches had developed in their separate histories.[8]

8. Ibid., 27–35.

The united church would confess its faith both in worship and in mission, both of which were to be understood as translating the faith into forms of suffering love for the world. The Consultation would hold both Scripture and classic formulations of the Christian faith in high honor, with a slight leaning toward the priority of Scripture. In his essay in the *McCormick Quarterly,* George Beazley explained that while the two historic creeds would be honored and their use encouraged, *Principles* stopped short of requiring that they be used in worship in the congregations of the new church.[9]

Chapter Two, The Worship of the Church. Everyone knew that there was a wide range in the ways that the COCU churches conducted worship on Sunday mornings. The Episcopal Church required priests and parish churches to conduct worship according to the forms in its officially approved *Book of Common Prayer.* Presbyterian, Evangelical United Brethren, and Methodist Churches recommended denominationally approved books of worship but allowed pastors and congregations to design their services and select their own words for prayer. The Christian Church (Disciples of Christ) and the United Church of Christ gave pastors and congregations even greater freedom to do what they believed best in their worship on Sundays.

Aware of these differences, *Principles* declares that worship "is a response of thanksgiving to God's holy love revealed in Jesus Christ," and an offering of the "response of praise for which universe and humanity are created." All congregations would be encouraged to participate in planned use of forms of worship already in use in the uniting churches "so that unity-in-diversity may be characteristic of the united church from the start." There would be steady movement "toward the creation of new forms of worship expressive of the enriched new tradition of the united church itself," and "diverse traditions of ceremony, appointment, vesture, music, and the like. Public worship would include reading from the Scriptures, preaching, prayer, congregational participation, and the ordering of time through the Christian year. The early period of time in the united church's life would be a time of "mutual exploration and discovery of one another's traditions."[10]

In the *McCormick Quarterly,* Stephen F. Bayne Jr., the Episcopal bishop who had been principal drafter of *Principles,* called attention to three "deeper concerns" concerning worship. First on his list was "the part that liturgy plays in both the expression of cultural patterns and the determination of these patterns." Although "the prevailing winds in the Consultation,

9. Beazley, "Faith of the Church," 200.
10. *Principles of Church Union,* 38–39.

no doubt, are American," the implications of this fact had not yet been discussed. Bayne's second concern, "the social relevance of liturgy," was tied to the Consultation's emphasis upon reading scripture, including the Old Testament, in worship, and on the "regular preaching of the Gospel within all liturgy." Implied in these factors were "the responsible freedom of the individual Christian" and the need for liturgy to challenge "the superficial Anglophilia of many of the participants." Bayne's third concern was the tension between liturgy's "relevance to our immediate situation" and its "conserving function" as it reminds us "that we are not simply creatures and victims of our times, but part of the age-long pilgrimage of humanity."[11]

Chapter Three, The Sacraments of the Church. The chapter on worship was followed by a chapter dealing with the sacraments of Baptism and Lord's Supper, which were essential to worship in the COCU churches. Here *Principles* affirms that the church always has to frame its doctrine and practice in light of the past and at the same time remain fully open to the leading of the Holy Spirit in every time and place. Although the churches differed in their ideas about when Baptism should occur and what should happen thereafter to bring about Baptism's full meaning, they agreed that the "confessing believer [is] incorporated into Christ by death, burial and resurrection with him." In Baptism, people renounce sin and are grafted into the church. As "divine symbol, ordinance, sacrament, and mystery," Baptism "forms the visible base of our unity in Jesus Christ." This new life must be "confirmed in the baptizand and continued in full, glad commitment to Christian discipleship."

Infant baptism and believer's baptism would be accepted as "alternative practices in the united church," but neither would be "imposed contrary to conscience." The basic elements of the rite itself would be immersion, pouring, or sprinkling in the name of the Father, Son, and Holy Spirit, a confession of sin and repentance, affirmation of faith, and promise to live a faithful life. An act for confirming these vows would be part of the plan, and this would be especially important for those whose baptisms had occurred before they were able to speak for themselves.[12]

Principles defines the Eucharist as "an effective sign," an action of the Church, which becomes the means whereby "God in Christ acts and Christ is present with his people." When celebrated in the united church, the Eucharist would include "Christ's words of institution" and the two elements he ordained, the visible acts of taking the bread and cup, and a blessing or prayer of thanksgiving for "the gifts of God in creation and redemption," the

11. Bayne, "Worship of the Church," 206.
12. *Principles of Church Union*, 44–47.

breaking of the bread, partaking of the loaf and cup by the congregation, and "a prayer invoking the Holy Spirit." The service would be conducted by an ordained bishop or presbyter, with the assistance of unordained men and women. Baptized Christians eligible to receive in their own churches would be eligible to receive in the united church.[13]

Commenting on this chapter in the *McCormick Quarterly,* David G. Colwell, pastor of First Congregational United Church of Christ in Washington, D.C., and chair of COCU's executive committee, noted that the Consultation had come to consensus "more readily than had been anticipated." The reason, Colwell proposed, was that eucharistic practice would be affirmed and continued but no theological explanation would be required of the churches. There had been "no attempt to lay down a sacramental theology as such." Instead, *Principles* stated a "consensus as to the essential and central place of the sacraments in the life of the Church." Colwell noted that the Consultation had not felt it necessary to set down "exclusive liturgical forms," but had stated "the essential elements which would preserve the Holy Communion from caprice and ignorance."[14]

Chapter Four, The Ministry of the Church. The chapter dealing with the ministry proposed for the united church is the longest in *Principles of Church Union.* Even with the significant body of work already done by COCU's historians and theologians, this topic was far from settled. *Principles* could declare, however, that the foundation for all ministry in the church— including the new church they sought to establish—is the ministry of Christ who extends his "royal priesthood," to all who come into the church through Baptism. A second declaration was that within this general ministry there have always been "representative ministries," called by God, set apart by the Church, and "ordained for distinctive functions in the Church."[15]

What may be the "breakthrough" in *Principles* is the way the document discusses continuity—how the church in any time and place is connected to the one church presented in Scripture and Tradition: a ministry in which bishops and those whom they ordained continued the line begun by the apostles themselves. While acknowledging the continuing importance of apostolic succession, however, *Principles of Church Union* states a significantly broader basis of continuity. The church "is bound to the Christian past "through Scripture and Tradition, through liturgy and creeds, through the life and witness of the people of God, and through their ordained

13. Ibid., 47–50.
14. Colwell, "Sacraments in a United Church," 214.
15. *Principles of Church Union,* 51–53.

ministries." All of "these modes as well as all manner of ministerial ordination must be grounded in the historic deed of God in Christ."[16]

While affirming this theological foundation, the COCU churches
faced the challenge of uniting previously separated ministries into one new
order of ministry fully recognized for theologically valid service in this new
church. *Principles* states two factors on which most people would probably
agree: the process would need "a statement of meaning" that would command allegiance within the new body and meet the test of universality; and
"a united, mutual will to turn our faces resolutely to what lies ahead" while
anticipating new understandings that would come in the context of unity.
A third factor, however, would undoubtedly push the churches and their
ordained ministries into new patterns of relationship and commitment:
"a corporate act in which and through which all would offer our existing
ministries to Almighty God, asking him to receive our offerings through
Jesus Christ, to complete and make perfect what is amiss or incomplete in
our ministries and to give us whatever of his authority and grace we need to
serve in the united ministry to which we are called."[17]

The challenge, as COCU would come to realize, would be to design the
liturgical act that would embody this idea. In future services of ordination,
"representatives of all offices of ministry in the Church, not excepting the
general ministry of those not ordained, should be included." Under normal
conditions, "office and authority in the Church are conveyed through the
action of those officers who have been duly chosen to convey it." As though
the drafting committee had already forgotten its claim of multiple modes of
continuity, *Principles* declares that the historic episcopate "commends itself
as personifying the continuity of churchly authority." This orderly transmission of authority and function "helps guard the continuity of the Church's
faith expressed in word and sacrament."[18]

Structure of the Church. More than half of the chapter on ministry
discusses matters that at every point of COCU's activities henceforth would
become increasingly important and problematic: the translation of theological consensus into the practicalities of church life and practice. In the chapter on ministry, *Principles* begins the process of describing what bishops,
presbyters, and deacons would actually do. It makes a distinction between
ministerial labors that would require special training and the full-time work
of those in that office and other labors that were not "professional" in this
sense. It acknowledges that more study would need to be given to the roles
of the deacon in the united church.

16. Ibid., 52.
17. Ibid., 47.
18. Ibid., 54.

Knowing that the churches needed a more complete understanding of the structure, the Consultation had included a "paper" in the 1966 version of *Principles* that outlined how this new church would be organized. The draft contains four sections, "dealing respectively with *local* (i.e., neighborhood, parish, community, and also functional and specialized) units, *district* (i.e., diocese, presbytery, county or state) units, *regional* (i.e., provinces, synods, or areas embracing several states) units, and *national* units."[19] It then provides twenty-two numbered paragraphs describing an organizational system for the new church. A group assigned to study this paper at the 1966 assembly, however, concluded its report by stating that structures in the new church must be tested by three criteria: "the preaching of the good news of Christ, the fellowship of life in Christ, and the carrying forward of the ministry of Christ in service to his people in the world. Each of these demands a balance of freedom and authority, of leadership and discipline, of democratic process and executive action." Its final words were that at this stage in the Consultation's life "we find it easier to agree on such general goals than to identify the best means to achieve them, and would regard any final decisions at present as premature."[20]

Acknowledging this impasse regarding structure, the COCU leadership prepared a new paper for the 1967 assembly in Cambridge, Massachusetts, with the title "Guidelines for the Structure of the Church." All efforts to describe an organizational structure for the new church were dropped and, instead, the new document presented a broad set of principles that would shape a structure that would have to be developed later. In order to "be faithful to its missionary task," the rewritten draft proposed, the church's structures would need to "be adapted to the changing world in which and to which it ministers and therefore its structures for mission must be open to change." The structures of the new church "should reflect its continuity with the past" and provide "for creative freedom, for unfettered response to the Spirit of God and for faithful obedience in mission."[21]

The body of the rewritten document consists of ten "guidelines," each one accompanied by two or three paragraphs of interpretation. "As a united church develops its structures," the introduction concludes, "it will give the guidelines concrete application. The guidelines are not structures; they are criteria of structures."[22] The church's structures should be "functionally determined" and there should be provisions so that they could be established, changed, or eliminated "as needs arise or conditions of life require."

19. *Principles of Church Union* (1966 edition), 58.

20. Ibid., 77.

21. Ibid., 64.

22. Ibid., 65.

There should be many forms of ministry by persons both ordained and unordained. Policy decisions should be made by "representatives, ordained and unordained" and "democratically selected by their constituents." Structures should "provide for inclusiveness with respect to all kinds of people, especially racial and ethnic groups." They should provide for ministry to the church's members and to the world, to persons in their individual lives and in the larger systems in which they function. The Guidelines state that structures needed to provide "for the exercise of freedom and order under Christ" and for the maintaining relations with other churches and ecclesial organizations in the United States and the world. The final guideline emphasized the importance of providing "for the mutual support of the various parts of the church by one another in the fellowship of witness and service."[23]

This paper on guidelines for the structure of the church enabled the Consultation to step back momentarily from the potential impasse over the radical reorganizing of its systems that union would require. It helped them, at least momentarily, focus attention on what they wanted their new church to accomplish. The hard work of devising a structure, however, could only be postponed and to that task the Consultation would soon have to return.

While many people in the academic world supported the Consultation's objectives, the publishing of *Principles* served as the incentive for some scholars to register their dissent. Episcopal theologian John Macquarrie invited a group of professors to provide their assessment of COCU's *Principles,* which he published in a 64-page book with the title *Realistic Reflections on Church Union.* In addition to himself, Reginald H. Fuller and Paul L. Lehman were members of the faculty of Union Theological Seminary in New York. Five contributors were Anglican, one was Roman Catholic, and Lehman was Presbyterian. Macquarrie summarized the contributors' conclusions that COCU should be slowed down and that it was inappropriate at that time to move toward organic union. They had three reasons. 1) Despite its positive features, *Principles of Church Union* did not provide an adequate foundation for building a church that would be truly catholic and reformed. 2) Even if the principles could be improved, the union of these churches would be a setback to genuine Christian unity. 3) The very idea of organic union was old-fashioned.

Fuller wrote that *Principles* treated the Lambeth Quadrilateral positively but inadequately and was deficient concerning matters that were important to catholic Christians, including the sacerdotal character of the ministry, especially of bishops, and the sacramental nature of Baptism and

23. Ibid., 65–73.

Eucharist. As they worked for unity, Episcopalians always looked three ways—toward Rome, Eastern Orthodoxy, and Protestantism—and used the four points of the Lambeth Quadrilateral as criteria. Fuller believed that the Anglican interest in unity possibilities with the Orthodox and Catholics would be significantly compromised by participation in COCU.

Macquarrie and his associates were unwilling to accept the COCU proposal for solving some long-time disagreements, which was that the uniting churches would accept certain structures and systems as necessary for the life of the united church (the office of bishop, for example) but would not insist on any one theological explanation for that structure or system. Two writers mentioned that if Lutherans had also been participants in the process, doctrine would not so easily have been underplayed. Because of their confessional character, Lutherans would have insisted that *Principles* deal more fully with ecclesiological issues.

Some of the contributors expressed their disagreement with the intention that the new church be *evangelical*. One writer saw this emphasis as a veiled way to insisting that the Word would be dominant in the new church. Another feared that the evangelical emphasis provided a way to preserve the two major "aberrations" in Protestant theology, liberalism and pietism.

The harshest rejection was offered by Paul L. Lehmann, a Presbyterian professor of systematic theology at Union Seminary. *Historically*, the experience of the church had been that the emphasis upon structural union leads to the church's disobedience. *Procedurally*, this proposal was a top down approach to unity and failed to involve the grass roots members of the church. *Ethically*, the proposed union failed because it focused attention upon the church's own life when it ought to be focusing their attention upon the world that was "riven by war and injustice and driven by powers" that were threatening humankind. "What would it profit, if through COCU the Church gained her life and lost her soul?"

These scholars represented a three-fold point of view concerning unity movements that has been held by many people then and now: 1) Christian unity is to be highly valued, but it can only be affirmed when it leaves the ideas and practices of one's own tradition exactly as they currently exist. 2) Even when viewed in the most charitable way possible, efforts like COCU are trying to create a new church that is built on unacceptable principles that would contribute little of value to the church's own life or to the life of the world. 3) The leaders of COCU and similar ventures probably mean well, but they are wrong and if they have their way the possibilities for more genuine unity would be obstructed. With ideas like these in the air, leaders of the COCU churches still had much work to do.

5

Uniting Christians Separated by Race

New Members, New Challenges, New Hopes for the Future ...

THE POSITIVE SPIRIT OF the 1966 Dallas plenary assembly—COCU's fifth meeting—was encouraged by the reception of more churches into full membership in the Consultation. The African Methodist Episcopal Church (AME) became the seventh church to join the Consultation. This action gave reason to hope that the new American church would reunite Christians who for more than a century had been divided from one another because of differences of race, ethnicity, and culture. This church would finally be able to speak to the larger society knowing that its own life was consistent with its prophetic message. The action of the AME Church encouraged the COCU churches to anticipate that the other predominantly African American Methodist churches would follow their example. In 1967, the African Methodist Episcopal Zion Church (AMEZ) continued the momentum by becoming COCU's ninth participating church, and in 1968 the Christian Methodist Episcopal Church (CME) became the tenth church.

COCU was not the only way that the three African American Methodist churches were showing their interest in ecumenism. They had joined the Federal Council of Churches, which in 1950 was restructured and renamed the National Council of Churches. During the mid 1950s, these three churches had also joined the Greenwich Plan, an alliance of Protestant churches that had unsuccessfully tried to unite nine denominations. Except for the Episcopal Church, all of the COCU churches had participated, although briefly and nominally, in that venture that had carried a name easily confused with COCU's—The *Conference* on Church Union.[1]

In the 1960s, the three black churches had lodged episcopal offices in the Methodist Building in Washington, D.C., which at that time also housed several regional and national offices of The Methodist Church and offices of the National Council of Churches, the United Presbyterian Church, the Church of the Brethren, and the United Church of Christ.[2] In January 1964, eighty-six representatives of the AME, AMEZ, and CME churches met at Wesley Theological Seminary in Washington D.C., "to re-open discussion on organic union among their respective bodies." Two conveners of the conference, John Satterwhite (AMEZ) and Charles S. Spivey Jr., (AME) soon were to become prominent voices in COCU debates. Representatives met again in 1965, 1968, and 1969, but after the 1969 meeting, Raymond R. Sommerville Jr., reports, "the thrust for union among the three denominations appeared to dissipate, although the CME and AMEZ churches continued to pursue merger." Sommerville offers two reasons for this diminished interest: COCU's "competing vision of . . . a more expansive form of merger, one that proposed to unite multiple Protestant traditions into a single, racially integrated church," and "the rise of black consciousness and militancy among African-American clergy in the 1960s."[3]

The Presbyterian Church in the United States (PCUS) became the Consultation's eighth participating church. It was often referred to as the southern Presbyterian Church, to distinguish it from the northern church, the United Presbyterian Church in the United States of America (UP-CUSA). As had happened with their Methodist and Baptist counterparts, the nation's Presbyterian Church had broken into northern and southern branches during the years prior to the Civil War. Although the northern and southern Methodist Episcopal churches, along with the Methodist Protestant Church, had reunited in 1939, the two Presbyterian churches had continued their existence as separated denominations. Serious conversations toward reunion were in process, however, when the PCUS became a participating member of the Consultation.

The resolution with which the PCUS requested membership in the Consultation included a paragraph based upon the "New Delhi Statement," an important summary of what unity entails that had been issued in the report of the World Council of Church's third assembly in New Delhi in 1961. It listed, perhaps more clearly than COCU's earlier documents had done,

1. Morrison, "The Ecumenical Trend," 9–13.
2. Sommerville, *An Ex-Colored Church,* 196.
3. Ibid., 199–200.

the characteristics that would mark the new church. This church would (1) hold the one apostolic faith, (2) preach the one Gospel, (3) break the one bread, (4) join in common prayer, and (5) have a corporate life reaching out in witness and service to all. It would be "united with the whole Christian fellowship in all places and ages in such wise that ministry and members are accepted by all, and all can speak and together as occasion requires for the tasks to which God calls His people."[4]

During this period, Lutheran, Baptist, and Brethren Churches chose not to become full members.[5] The result was that all of COCU's participating churches had strong connections with the Reformed Tradition, the branch of the Protestant Reformation in which John Calvin, Ulrich Zwingli, Thomas Cranmer, and John Knox were the preeminent founding theologians, and which John and Charles Wesley had later modified in important ways.

COCU's earliest, and perhaps most creative, years coincided with some of the most contentious and transformative years in American history. A short list of major events of the 1960s indicates the extent and power of this decade. In 1960, two busloads of "Freedom Riders" began their journey from Washington, D.C. The violence they encountered in places like Birmingham, Alabama, gave President John F. Kennedy little choice but to order federal marshals and the National Guard to protect them until they reached their destination at Jackson, Mississippi, where they were arrested by a pre-arranged agreement. In 1963, a proposed conference by the Southern Christian Leadership Conference led to confrontation in which Martin Luther King Jr., along with others, was imprisoned and where he drafted his "Letter from a Birmingham Jail." By June, President Kennedy had decided that a new approach to civil rights was necessary and he addressed

---

4. *Digest of the Fifth Meeting*, 19. This sentence is a "whereas" clause in the resolution: "*Whereas*, the official representatives of these Churches have now bound themselves into seeking a unity in which all who are baptized into Jesus Christ and confess Him as Lord and Saviour may be brought by the Holy Spirit into one fully committed fellowship, holding the one apostolic faith, preaching the one Gospel, breaking the one bread, joining in common prayer, and having a corporate life reaching out in witness and service to all, united with the whole Christian fellowship in all places and ages in such wise that ministry and members are accepted by all, and all can speak and together as occasion requires for the tasks to which God calls His people."

5. For reports on these decisions not to join the Consultation, see Handy, "For the Record"; *Christianity Today*, December 3, 1965, and February 18, 1966; "Church Unity: Current Attitudes in the Church of the Brethren," *Brethren Life and Thought* 11/1 (1966) 4–51; "The Consultation on Church Union: Two Open Letters," and "Before COCU'ing: Stop and Look Both Ways," 12/4 (1967) 44–64; and "Brethren Response to the Consultation on Church Union," *Brethren Life and Thought* 14/4 (1969) 227–47; "COCU Too Vague About Creeds," *The Lutheran*, March 5, 1969, 29, 84.

the nation to describe this new understanding, with the Golden Rule as a guiding principle. On August 28, 1963, 250,000 people gathered in front of the Lincoln Memorial where Martin Luther King Jr. delivered his "I Have a Dream" speech. Later that year—November 22, 1963—President Kennedy was assassinated in Dallas. In 1964, the U. S. Congress passed the Civil Rights Act and the next year followed with the Voting Rights Act.

In August 1965, six days of rioting in the Watts district of Los Angeles led to thirty-four deaths and forty million dollars of damage, requiring 14,000 National Guard troops to restore order. In five days of rioting in Detroit, July 1967, forty-three people died, 7,000 were arrested, and more than forty million dollars of property damage was incurred. Order was restored by police, the Michigan National Guard, and US Army troops. Watts and Detroit dramatized the fact that racism was a far deeper problem than most people had recognized and made it clear that racist systems were deeply ingrained across the nation rather than being a southern problem only.

Although the digests of COCU's annual meetings convey little sense of the tumult that was taking place all around them, these events were inescapably present, contributing to the sense of urgency that the nation would have to change and sustaining their hope that a new church could be a leader to this new era. What many people in the Consultation did not yet understand, however, was how much their existing churches and the new American church would have to change.

The one exception may have been The Methodist Church, which during these same years was struggling to overcome its own systemic racism and segregation. In his book *Methodists and the Crucible of Race, 1930–1975,* Peter C. Murray writes that in colonial America "early Methodists, both African American and white, worshipped together, preached together, prayed together, and contended with one another over the breadth and length of God's liberating message." During the latter eighteenth century and early nineteenth century, "African American membership hovered around 20 percent of the Methodist Church . . . To a degree unfathomable a century later, African Americans were integral members of a predominantly white Protestant church in America, both as worshipers and leaders."[6]

In the early 1800s the Methodist Church experienced schism "over ministerial rights, although segregation and paternalism were integrally involved." The first fracture occurred in Philadelphia, culminating in the formation of the African Methodist Episcopal Church in 1816. A similar set of circumstances in New York City led to the formation of the African Methodist Episcopal Zion Church in 1821. In 1830, the predominately

6. Murray, *Methodists,* 9–10.

white Methodist Protestant Church came into being in order to provide "a more egalitarian, democratic structure." In 1844, the Methodist Episcopal Church broke into two regional churches when the southern jurisdictions withdrew from those in the North, with conflicting attitudes toward slavery as the primary reason, and the next year formed the Methodist Episcopal Church, South. In 1870, most African Americans who had remained in the southern church were encouraged to join the newly formed Colored Methodist Episcopal Church (which in 1954 changed its name to Christian Methodist Episcopal Church). The result was that during the later decades of the nineteenth and early decades of the twentieth centuries, there were six largely parallel Methodist churches, three predominately white and three predominately African American.

In 1939, the three white churches culminated nearly a half-century of serious conversation by joining together in a new denomination with the all-inclusive name *The Methodist Church*. The southern church had tried to preclude African American members from membership, but had failed. Instead, the new church created a church within a church, the Central Jurisdiction, which extended across two-thirds of the continent and acted in parallel with the geographically organized jurisdictions of white Methodism. African American congregations, annual conferences, and clergy, including bishops, were assigned to this entity. At its formation, The Methodist Church was the largest Protestant denomination in the country and the largest Methodist church in the world.

This new church, Murray writes, "had the most segregated church structure in the country, and it hardened Jim Crow lines within the church." Murray also observes that this new church was "a vivid reminder of how segregated worship was in the United States." African American members, however, "had more autonomy over their affairs and more leaders in the upper echelon of the institutional church than in any other predominately white church."[7] Almost from the beginning, many people in the Methodist Church were unsatisfied with this compromise and by the 1950s segregation in some of the church institutions began to be discontinued in parallel with changes elsewhere in American public life.

The predominately white southern Presbyterian Church also had African American members, but that membership had been proportionately smaller than in its Methodist counterpart. Even so, in 1898, the PCUS created the Afro-American Presbyterian Church, which it continued to support financially for two decades. In 1916, the southern church "took these African American churches back into their church as a separate synod,

7. Ibid., 43.

the Snedecor Memorial Synod," which resembled the Methodist Church's Central Jurisdiction. African American and white Presbyterians "were officially members of the same church, but they came together only at the General Assembly."[8] Murray also summarizes the history of the Episcopal Church during this same period. Although it did not break into northern and southern denominations, this church also experienced serious conflict over race and related sectional issues. As a way to segregate black members of their church, some Episcopalians tried unsuccessfully to establish what was called "a missionary district" in the south.[9]

The Christian Church (Disciples of Christ) responded to America's racism in a less obvious manner. Largely because of its congregational polity and scanty denominational structure during the crucial years surrounding the Civil War, the Disciples had managed to stay connected. Attitudes toward slavery, however, had divided the movement. One reason that Disciples in Indiana established their own church college, initially named North Western Christian University and later changed to Butler University, was so that young people would not have to go to Alexander Campbell's Bethany College in Virgina (later, West Virginia) and be influenced by issues related to slavery. Sectional issues festered, however, with the result that in the beginning years of the twentieth century a significant portion of the Disciples movement in the middle south and south withdrew, forming a new religious body, the Churches of Christ.

Following the close of the Civil War, African American Disciples of Christ developed schools across the South. They were committed to a broad education—of head, heart, and hands—so that their people could enter fully into the post-slavery American society. Gradually, the sponsors of these schools established relationships with the mission boards of their church, which were based in the North and operated by a predominately white membership. Although the schools benefited from financial support, their African American constituents lost control. The mission boards emphasized the industrial model of education and suppressed those aspects of study that would have helped African Americans advance in autonomy and self-determination. As Lawrence A. Q. Burnley has shown in his book *The Cost of Unity,* northern leaders of the mission boards during this period accommodated their practices in order to maintain the support of their white southern constituency.[10]

8. Ibid., 51.

9. Ibid., 49–51.

10. Burnley, *Cost of Unity,* 7, 202ff.

In 1966 and 1967, however, when the three African American Methodist churches joined the Consultation on Church Union, much of this long, painful history was overlooked, at least in public discussion. Instead, there was a rising sense of excitement that COCU's multi-church framework provided the context for all of the churches to discontinue their segregated existence. The one COCU church that understood the complexity and comprehensiveness of the changes in church life would be required was The Methodist Church because during these same tumultuous years it was in the throes of dismantling its own structural racism while at the same time engaging in union negotiations with the Evangelical United Brethren Church.

One of the organizing presuppositions of the Methodist-EUB merger was that the new church—the United Methodist Church—would not contain a racially segregated structure. These deliberations, however, had revealed how difficult it would be to free the church from inherited structures. White racism was firmly fixed, leading to virtually full segregation at every level of the church's life, and these attitudes and practices were resistant to change. Furthermore, African American Methodists, who had experienced dignity and self-determination within the systems of their churches, were reluctant to jeopardize these important factors in any new system that integrated them into a structure in which the dominant white constituency would be in charge. Despite these challenges, The Methodist Church developed a persistent process to negotiate changes and require conformity at every level and in every geographical region of this large, complicated church. The merger was consummated in 1966, and the final meeting of the Central Jurisdiction, which marked the formal and public transformation of The Methodist Church, was August 17–19, 1967.

One of the most important factors in this lengthy process, which can clearly be seen in Murray's account, is that Christian conviction and voluntary action need one more factor in order to bring about systemic change. That additional factor is a structural connection that requires constituent parts to move forward even though conviction or courage are insufficient in their own power to accomplish the change. At this point in the Consultation's attempt to create a comprehensive new church, these three factors could only have been partially realized. The new American church that COCU envisioned, however, would have provided the strong, inter-connected organization that would enable the churches to translate carefully reached, theologically coherent decisions into specific and effective action.

It is fortunate for the churches participating in the Consultation on Church Union that the new churches entered when they did. Despite the rapid growth of tension over issues of power and race in American life, established institutions such as the COCU churches continued to maintain civil relationships and open lines of communication. People could come together to discuss matters of mutual interest and coordinate plans for limited patterns of social ministry in the nation. As the turmoil of the next decade broke open, it would have been increasingly difficult for the Consultation to become, as it did, an active agent in America's struggle to overcome its long history of racism.

6

Poised on the Edge of Success

> The law of man is secondary. We move today
> under command of the law of God.
>
> —OLIVER SHROEDER JR., AND THE PANEL OF LAWYERS

THE EXPANDING OF THE denominational base from the six churches to ten brought new people into the leadership core—people with distinctive bodies of experience and insight, new energies, and new skills at the very time when the infusion of new energy and creativity would be increasingly important. Momentum was building and it looked as though a new American church really would come into being within the decade of the 1970s. Much work, however, remained to be done in order to achieve this goal that a few years earlier would have seemed impossible.

An important part of that work was to continue the Consultation's efforts to communicate the vision of a new American church to the people who would finally make the decisions and live in the new ecumenical era—the executive staffs of their national agencies and regional organizations, the thousands of pastors all over the country, and the millions of members in congregations everywhere. From the beginning, the Consultation had published reports of the plenary assemblies. These *Digests of the Proceedings* included minutes of the meeting, financial reports, lists of participants, and the papers and documents prepared for its use by delegates.[1] The Princeton

1. The Disciples' Council on Christian Unity had greatly assisted COCU by publishing each digest, with supporting papers, in a subsequent issue of its quarterly journal *Mid-Stream*. The plates were then made available to COCU for publishing its own

64

office distributed 1,934 copies of the first volume, which included materials for the Washington and Oberlin assemblies, 1,108 copies after the Princeton meeting, and 785 following Lexington.

To communicate to a broader audience, the Consultation's leadership published a 96-page "miniature book" in 1966 with the title *COCU: The Reports of the Four Meetings*. Two years later, the treasurer reported that the book was still in print and that 99,966 copies had been sold.[2] A more comprehensive account of the movement was a book edited by COCU's part-time executives, George L. Hunt and Paul A. Crow Jr.: *Where We Are in Church Union*.[3] Although printed in a small format, this 128-page volume contained essays by the two editors and six other scholars, a study guide, and an index. It sold for fifty cents a copy, or twelve for five dollars, so that the book could be widely distributed among the churches. The denominations bought 34,615 copies "for distribution to their ministers," and by the 1965 plenary assembly the number sold had increased to 45,534, resulting in some royalties to the Consultation.[4]

During 1965, editors of five magazines published by participating churches commissioned a series of articles, which "tried to deal in laymen's language" with several of the key issues involved in the Consultation's work: That We All May Be One, Authority in A United Church, Baptism, The Lord's Supper And Worship, and Ministry in A United Church. Some of these articles were also published in a Lutheran magazine and in a publication of the United Church of Canada. The most widely published and used document, however, was the "Prayer for the Consultation on Church Union," which was written for each plenary assembly and published not only in denominational papers, but also in some non-church newspapers.

During this same period of time, there was a concerted effort to develop an annual COCU Sunday for celebration in the participating communions. These observances were developed locally and included features such as pulpit exchanges, services of common worship, and "other acts of fellowship." In 1966, local study groups took place in many parts of the country. It was recommended that as many of the COCU churches as possible should

---

official Digest.

2. The "miniature books" were published by Forward Movement Publications, an official, non-profit agency of the Episcopal Church.

3. Hunt and Crow, *Where We Stand in Church Unity*. This was one of a series of similar books published by Association press, a publishing entity of the National Board of Young Men's Christian Associations. These books, written by well-known theologians, dealt with a broad range of topics thought to be important to members of American churches.

4. *Digest of the Fifth Meeting*, 24.

be represented in each of these groups. Although local groups could develop their own plans, a reading list was prepared for their use, and groups were asked to send reports to the COCU staff. Although it is nearly impossible to determine how many localities set up programs and how many people participated, these processes represented a determined effort to take the union movement from the academic halls, administrative offices, and convention centers to the congregations and mission locations across the nation where the people of the churches could experience the unity movement.

The two editions of *Principles of Church Union* continued this aggressive program of communicating COCU's decisions and official documents. The churches used their own methods to distribute the small, inexpensive books to their constituencies, and these publications could easily make their way into the hands of the executives and pastors of other churches, and to professors in seminaries and members of the news media.

The most important responsibility facing COCU's leadership following the 1966 Dallas assembly was to expand the *Principles of Church Union* into a plan of union on which the churches could unite and form a new American church that would be fully catholic, fully evangelical, and fully reformed. This work would occupy the full attention of four plenary assemblies from 1967 through 1970.[5] Approximately 200 participants came to each of these conferences, including representatives of participating churches, members of COCU commissions, observer-participants from non-COCU churches, representatives of ecclesial organizations such as the World Council of Churches, and media representatives.

COCU's executive committee and executive staff responded to the theological issues by commissioning scholars to analyze them so that the representatives of the churches would have a theoretical foundation for the practical decisions that they had to make. The pragmatic side of the Consultation's work was entrusted to a lengthening list of commissions, committees, and work groups that were expected to examine issues under consideration, gather factual data already available, and propose solutions. The most important task assigned to commissions established during this period was to draft the documents that would enable the new church to come into being. One of the remarkable aspects of COCU's history is that pastors, professors, and church executives were willing to devote the time and energy that this process demanded.

5. Cambridge (March 1–4, 1967), Dayton (March 25–28, 1968), Atlanta (March 17–20, 1969), and St. Louis (March 9–13, 1970).

The Consultation Goes Full Time

The volume of work was increasing significantly despite the fact that CO-CU's staff consisted of two part-time executives who essentially volunteered their time while continuing in full-time jobs, and a part-time salaried secretary. George L. Hunt, the general secretary, was pastor of the Fanwood Presbyterian Church, in a community about an hour's drive north of Princeton, New Jersey. Doris Pettibone, the secretary, worked in an office in the Fanwood church. Paul A. Crow Jr., the associate general secretary, taught church history at Lexington Theological Seminary in Kentucky.[6] By 1967, it had become clear that COCU's budget had to be increased so that a full-time executive staff could be appointed. The executive committee presented a resolution to the plenary assembly in 1968 recommending this expansion. It was passed unanimously, which authorized the executive committee to employ two full-time executives and clerical staff and to rent appropriate space for their work. COCU's disbursements for the 1967–68 year were $11,106.42; the budget approved for the first year with full-time leadership was $75,000. This would come from the $2,000 assessment each participating church was expected to contribute, plus voluntary gifts that were to be contributed by the churches primarily on the basis of membership.[7]

In consultations with other Consultation leaders, Eugene Carson Blake and William Gibson concluded that their associate general secretary, Paul Crow, brought the academic credentials, experience with COCU, and administrative skills that they needed. At the Hartford Seminary Foundation, he had written his STM thesis on the Church of South India, perhaps the most significant union of churches on the mission field, and his PhD dissertation on "The Concept of Unity in Diversity in the Faith and Order Movement." When they came to Crow with the request that he leave his assured position on a theological faculty for an insecure position with the Consultation, Blake and Gibson persuaded him that the unity movement

---

6. Hunt was appointed to this position at the Washington organizing meeting (April 9–10, 1962) with an annual stipend of $1,000. Crow was appointed to his COCU position prior to the Princeton assembly (April 13–16, 1964), with an annual stipend of $500. The budget approved at Princeton provided $900 for secretarial support (*Digest of the Third Meeting*, 12–13).

7. The relative strength of the churches can be seen in the budget adopted for 1969 when nine churches were participating members of the Consultation. In addition to the $18,000 received from the churches in equal assessments, "special contributions" were proposed: AME, $500; AMEZ, $1,500; CME, $500; D of C, $5,000; EC, $10,000; PCUS, $4,500; UCC, $7,000; UM, $21,000; UPUSA, $10,000 (*Digest of the Eighth Meeting*, 50).

was a cause to which he could devote himself in the confidence that it offered remarkable opportunities for service in the future.[8]

During the summer before Crow assumed his new position, the executive committee labored over other decisions. The first was the location for
the office, whether it should continue in Princeton or be moved to space in
New York City, perhaps in the National Council's building at 475 Riverside
Drive. A metropolitan location would relate COCU to the contemporary
world and demonstrate its commitment to dealing with the urban crisis,
whereas the Princeton location, which some perceived to be an aristocratic,
easy going, and cultured university town, would demonstrate that the Consultation had little interest in the problems with which the world and the
church were wrestling. In Princeton's favor were its library, suitability for the
families of the staff, and a strong leaning within the executive committee to
continue in the community where the offices already were established.

The executive committee also struggled to name the members of the
committee that would begin work on a plan of union, and after settling
upon those names chose, again with some difficulty, William A. Benfield
Jr., a pastor of the Presbyterian Church U.S., to be its chair. The third issue
under discussion during the summer was choosing a person to serve as associate general secretary. The executive committee members were agreed
that the person would have to be African American, but they were divided
concerning the leadership qualities that the person should possess. Some
urged that the foremost factor had to be close identification with the "black
revolution," while others urged that the nominee be someone well adapted to
performing the executive and administrative responsibilities of the COCU
office. In his letter to Paul Crow summarizing the summer's work, George
Beasley remarked that "the Consultation was confronting every problem
that was present on the American scene."[9]

Crow began his full-time work in October 1968. Since Princeton had
been chosen as the location for the COCU office, he settled on office space
and appointed Doris Pettibone to continue as secretary, but with expanded
hours and work. At the Atlanta plenary in 1969, W. Clyde Williams became
the associate general secretary, thus completing the staff. Williams was a
minister of the Christian Methodist Episcopal Church and a member of the
staff of the Interdenominational Theological Center in Atlanta.[10]

8. Paul A. Crow Jr., pers. comm.

9. George G. Beasley Jr., to Paul A. Crow Jr., May 31, 1968.

10. Unless otherwise noted, quotations from materials related to the Atlanta meeting are drawn from *Digest of the Eighth Meeting, Proceedings*.

Serving with Crow and Williams as chair of the Consultation was James K. Mathews, bishop in The Methodist Church's Northeastern Jurisdiction. Mathews had graduated from Lincoln Memorial University in Harrogate, Tennessee, the Biblical Seminary in New York, and Columbia University where he earned the PhD degree. He had served as missionary in India, where he married a daughter of missionary E. Stanley Jones. As the Methodist bishop in Boston, he was taking an active role in the Civil Rights Movement and he was instrumental in the closing of his church's segregated Central Jurisdiction. Mathews was finishing work on a book, *A Church Truly Catholic,*[11] which consisted primarily of the Gray Lectures that he had delivered at Duke University in 1967. Published in 1969, it dealt directly with one of COCU's major themes.

With a full complement of churches, committed and experienced officers, a strong executive staff, and a widely acclaimed set of principles, the Consultation on Church Union seemed poised on the edge of success.

Facing Organizational Challenges

It may have come as a surprising realization to many participants in the Consultation on Church Union that resolving the theological issues, which for centuries had seemed intractable, would be the easy part and that resolving organizational challenges would be more difficult. Although the details differed, the participating churches were roughly parallel organizations—denominations, to use a much-avoided word—extending across the nation. For all of them, the parish church or congregation was the place where individuals held membership, met for worship, study, and mission, and contributed the money that supported the entire system from congregation through highest-ranking national body. Nearly all congregations occupied buildings that they had built at some point in the past and continued to maintain as their own, although in some of the denominations the title and final control were vested in some other non-congregational unit of the church.

All of the COCU churches maintained ecclesial organizations at regional levels, in many cases coterminous with metropolitan regions or state boundaries. Each had a national organization, with executive offices, some form of general assembly, and an overlapping set of program agencies,

---

11. Two of Mathews' later books also bear directly upon topics that would be important to church union processes: *Set Apart to Serve: The Meaning and Role of Episcopacy in the Wesleyan Tradition* (1985), and *A Global Odyssey: The Autobiography of James K. Matthews* (2000).

boards, and ministries. Each of the participating churches maintained special relations with one or more publishing companies, colleges, and seminaries. The complexity of bringing all of this together was staggering. Statistics reported in 1972 indicated that the membership of COCU churches totaled 23,961,000, which was 47 percent of all Protestant membership in the nation (including the Latter Day Saints and Jehovah's Witnesses). The COCU churches reported 85,212 congregations and 40,687 pastors with charges.[12] The United Methodist Church reported 10,672,000 members and the three African American Methodist Churches reported 2,573,000 members, making the Methodist component 55 percent of the COCU constituency.

Steps toward simplifying and consolidating this overlapping system had been reported at the 1966 (Dallas) plenary assembly. "Professional Christian educators from the staffs of our denominations" have been meeting "to consider how they may interpret the Consultation through their publications and what they can do together." Even more promising was the fact that representatives of youth ministry staffs were meeting to consider how they could "combine the resources of their several youth ministries for the purpose of creating a totally new response to the youth of this generation through a common ministry that will be ecumenical [sic.], catholic, and reformed."[13]

At this stage in COCU's life, however, determining the local form of the new church was a topic of greater importance. There was, of course, the organizational task of connecting congregations in communities all over the country. Needed would be new patterns for relating pastors and members with one another, procedures for uniting or merging congregations, and a systematic educational process that would help Christians in all of these places learn how to be members of the new united church.

The greater challenge, however, came from one of the ideas that had become a new orthodoxy among prophetic voices in the church, that the congregation itself was the problem. In these local enclaves of like-minded people, the accusation declared, the prejudices and problems of life in America fester and from these congregations the infections spread into the rest of the society. The conclusion to this line of thought was that in order for the united church to become an agent for renewal a new way for the church to be local had to be devised. As they prepared for the 1967 plenary assembly (Cambridge, Massachusetts, May 1–4), COCU leaders asked two established scholars to write papers analyzing the issues and proposing solutions that they would be facing. Surely they knew that these writers would push the Consultation toward a new future.

12. *Statistical Abstract of the United States 1972*, 44–45.
13. *Digest of the fifth Meeting*, 23.

John Dillenberger, former dean of the Presbyterian Seminary in San Anselmo, California, and the founding president of the Graduate Theological Union in Berkeley, provided a historical template for his analysis. In the past, churches developed constructive responses to the challenges they faced, but as time and circumstances moved on, these responses no longer were adequate, and new patterns had to be developed. The Consultation had followed this pattern in its handling of the relation of Scripture and Tradition and in its discussion of the sacraments, Dillenberger wrote, and the discussion of the relation of episcopacy to Christian freedom seemed to be a tentative affirmation that this aspect of COCU was also moving along satisfactorily.

To this point, however, COCU had failed to provide a suitable pattern for the local presence of the united church. The system of coherence for churches had long been geographical: "denominational interests could fit into parish structures . . . in which geography and function coincide." Because "the structures and forces with which the Church must deal in any area involve many levels, centers of influence and work which do not follow geographic patterns," its functioning groups in the future would need to be based on "factors other than geography." This strategy, he proposed, "may in due time result in the substitution of the cathedral style for the community celebration as a whole, elimination of many church plants, with their place taken by house and smaller groups on the one side, and multiple office centers or task force types on the other." Old organizational patterns would not equip the churches to be ready for the new world. The church needed to create "a provisional possibility" pointing toward the future.

They needed to hurry, Dillenberger insisted. "While the Consultation has made progress, judged in terms of itself, it is further behind than when it started, judged by what is happening around it; its time-table is devastatingly long and in my judgment only an escalation of our activities and deliberations will save us."[14]

Similar ideas were proposed by Colin W. Williams, a Wesley scholar and staff member of the National Council of Churches responsible for Christian Life and Work. He based his paper upon a report by the World Council of Churches, "The Missionary Structure of the Congregation," and upon the work of other scholars, such as Gibson Winter of the University of Chicago.[15] The thousand-year-old pattern of residential congregations, largely rural in their defining characteristics, could not be the organizing base for the new forms of ministry that the rapidly changing world required.

14. Dillenberger, "Theological Givens as Theological Orientations," 42–52.

15. Gibson Winter's most influential publication was his book *The Suburban Captivity of the Churches: An Analysis of Protestant Responsibility in the Expanding Metropolis.*

Instead of ordinary residential churches, four types of structures would be needed: 1) Family-like structures (house churches); 2) Permanent availability structures (cathedral or community service established by the church); 3) Permanent community structures (Taizé Community and Evangelical Academies); and 4) Task forces (Civil Rights organizations). Williams theorized that decision-making would best be done at the regional level. Yet, he acknowledged that "there is still a sense in which the local residence community must be the basic unit for the Church." Here the Church meets the family and "the largest amount of personal time" is available "for gathering and training in basic Christian discipleship."[16]

With these papers very much in mind, the executive committee appointed a committee consisting of six denominational executives, chaired by William P. Thompson, a Wichita, Kansas, lawyer who had succeeded Eugene Carson Blake as Stated Clerk of the United Presbyterian Church. This high-level committee soon recognized that cooperation and union at the local level needed encouragement and guidance, and that a larger, more diverse committee would be necessary to do the work. Thompson, who continued as chair, was the one person to serve on both the earlier and later versions of the committee. Its seventeen-page report to the Atlanta plenary assembly (1969) was one of the most comprehensive and practical documents that any COCU committee or commission had produced.[17] The committee positioned its work carefully; it offered guidelines and suggestions for local church action during the "consulting stage" prior to the larger church union that would develop from the Consultation's work. One result of being in the pre-union stage was that the guidelines gave a considerable amount of attention to preserving relations of congregations and other local bodies with the denominational systems within which they operated.

The report's focus, however, was one of the principles that had guided COCU from the beginning: that church union should bring about greater effectiveness in serving God's mission in the world. The "creation of a united church will require great changes in structure and spirit at all levels of the churches as they now exist," the report declares, and these changes will be worthwhile only if they give new power "to the mission of the people of God, which is to proclaim and hear the Word, and participate in the Sacraments and in the healing of the world's wounds."

The report organized its models in two categories. *Interchurch cooperation at the local level* described ten patterns by which congregations and other local ministries (chaplaincies, neighborhood centers, and university ministries were given as examples) could join together. While

16. Williams, "The Structure of the Church," 68.

17. "Guidelines for Local Interchurch Action," *Digest of the Eighth Meeting,* 120–36.

denominational structures and loyalties were "technically unchanged . . . the resulting action program" would have "a united base for operation and a united identity to the public." *Local church union* would ordinarily require changes in "denominational structures or loyalties," involving both "the official statuses of congregations" and "the public identity of the resulting action program." The report offered four models for local church union. It also provided a bibliography of nine books, published from 1965 through 1969, that provided impetus to and guidance for local cooperation and union. The Consultation, of course, did not have jurisdiction over local efforts that this report discussed. All that it could do was "transmit" the report to the participating churches in the hope that they would in turn refer it to their respective constituencies.

The Unification of Ministries

At this point in COCU's work, a further complication developed with respect to the ministry. Even if they were to reach agreements on theological issues such as ordination in apostolic succession and the importance of having bishops in the united church, they still had to settle organizational issues. How many bishops would there be in the new church? Would all of the bishops in the uniting churches continue as bishops in the new church? What about churches that did not have officers with that title? Would their closest counterparts be assigned the title bishop? Would there be ceremonies that regularized existing ministries? Who would be in these ceremonies? Would bishops hold their positions for specified terms or for life? Would bishops belong to local congregations? To what degree and in what ways would they have to share power and responsibility with others in their communities of faith?

An even more challenging task facing this new church was to unite their ordained ministries, thus bridging centuries of separation. Clear signs of the importance of this topic was that a commission was appointed to work on it and Presbyterian theologian James I. McCord, one of the most prominent and influential leaders of the consultation, was appointed to chair the commission. With oversight provided by the commission, UCC theologian Roger Hazelton and Disciples historian Ronald E. Osborn prepared background statements. Both men analyzed the variations that existed among the churches with respect to the ministerial offices of deacon and presbyter. They also offered proposals that they believed could resolve differences of understanding and practice concerning ministers of word and sacrament in the uniting churches and lead to the renewal of the churches and their ministries.[18]

A third paper, however, developed a line of thought that significantly complicated the process of unifying the ministries. It was drafted by Methodist historian Albert C. Outler whose 1957 book *The Christian Tradition and the Unity We Seek* had analyzed issues of unity in a substantive way that was only partially compatible with the ideas being developed in the Consultation on Church Union. In his paper on the unification of ministries, Outler explored a topic in which theology was overwhelmed by emotionally charged issues of faithfulness to the gospel, honor, status, and relationship. In COCU's previous work, only the paper by American Baptist historian Robert T. Handy four years earlier had dealt with these issues in such a direct manner.[19]

Outler made four points that would necessarily generate significant discussion among delegates to the Consultation. First, a considerable degree of catholicity already existed in the ministries of the separated churches. The baptisms they performed in their churches were accepted in all of the participating churches. Furthermore, all of the ministries in their separation from one another represented Christ to their people. Second, the central factor of the challenge they faced was to extend the limited catholicity that already existed. Third, the work now being done by these separated ministries was already made holy by the Holy Spirit who was at work within them. Fourth, the churches couldn't go back and undo history. The only direction that they could go was forward.

Outler acknowledged that "it is agreeable" to accept the historic episcopate as one of the church's principle modes of continuity and regularity" but then stated unequivocally that "the notion that episcopal ordination is an absolute prerequisite for ministerial *validity* is a manifest *non sequitur*—on grounds historical, ecclesiological, and pneumatological." He objected strongly to any "easy and uncritical acceptance of a Service of Reconciliation (however well-intended) in which the ecclesiological issue of 're-ordination' is obscured by high-principled but ambiguous rhetoric." His constructive proposal was that COCU follow the example of the Church of South India. The reunited church could achieve the historic episcopate "by means of a *per saltum* acceptance *by all,* of those existing ministries already in COCU, and already recognized by all, as *valid.* This could and should be followed by some sort of reinstitution of the process of *regularization* of the ministry

18. Hazelton, "The Diaconate in a United Church" and Osborn, "The Meaning of Presbyter in the United Church" are published in *Mid-Stream* 8/1 (1969) 74–106.

19. Handy, "The Ministry in American History."

of the united church in its consequent polity and practice." The Episcopal Church could in this way "supply to the united church and its ministry its distinctive treasure of the historic episcopate . . . but not to the existing ministries of the churches that would form the union." A mutual service of ordination or re-ordination would be ruled out.[20]

Bringing Things Together in a Plan of Union

By the time of COCU's seventh meeting, the plenary assembly at Dayton, Ohio (March 25-28, 1968), it was clear that the time for theological discussion was disappearing and that the way to resolve these issues was to create the documents that would define the new church and be the basis for binding decisions by the churches participating in the Consultation on Church Union. The responsibility for doing this work was entrusted to the Plan of Union Commission, which consisted of ten members, each one appointed by his or her church.[21] Nine more persons met regularly with the commission, five described as special appointees, two as consultants, and two as the secretariat. All participants in these discussions were men except for two of the special appointees. Five of the nineteen were African-American.

William A. Benfield Jr., pastor of a large and influential congregation in the Presbyterian Church U. S., chaired the commission. In his personal style, Benfield was a commanding presence, and he brought considerable skill to the process of discussion and deciding. It became clear to the people who worked with him that he had developed a deep commitment to the vision of Christian unity and to the impact that this new church could have on American life. Three other members of the commission, representing widely disparate interests, also exercised much influence on the commission's work. Episcopal theologian William J. Wolf had gained the trust of major segments of his church and was determined that the *Plan of Union* had to be written in such a way that the Anglo-Catholic wing of his church would stay with the process. William P. Thompson, a lawyer, conservative ruling elder of the United Presbyterian Church USA, and Eugene Carson Blake's successor as Stated Clerk, was firmly committed to the vision of unity. Having the ear of conservative members of his church, he pressed the commission to produce a document that would maintain their support.

20. Outler, "The Mingling of Ministries," 106–18.

21. Although The Methodist Church and the Evangelical United Brethren Church had united, becoming the United Methodist Church, each of the former bodies maintained membership on the commission, thus giving the United Methodist Church two positions in the list of commission members.

George G. Beazley Jr., president of the Disciples' Council on Christian Union, was aware of points in COCU's documents that challenged long-held practices in his church, among them the acceptance of infant baptism, the definition of "elder," the office of bishop, and acceptance of the historic creeds as statements to be used in the united church. With full commitment to the purposes of the Consultation, these leaders were determined to shape the document in ways that they believed could command the consent of the constituencies that they represented.[22]

Although they knew that their document would leave many issues unresolved and that drafting a constitution would be a later stage, the commissioners were convinced that the plan they developed had to flesh out COCU's vision in sufficient detail that churches would know what they were committing to. It also had to provide enough detail that the new church could become a functioning entity, with both a spiritual-theological heart and an organizational body.

At the Atlanta plenary assembly (March 17–20, 1969), Benfield presented the commission's interim report "with evangelical zeal for church union."[23] It consisted of "a preliminary outline of a plan of union," which even in outline form was twenty-one pages long. Under ten headings, the report laid out the details of the plan, dealing with the faith of the church, its worship and sacraments, membership, ministry, and organization. At appropriate places in the outline, the commission highlighted topics or questions that needed further work. One topic was "The Name of the United Church." Three of the questions dealt with membership, including would "membership of church members be in the congregation, parish, or district," and should there be statements on standards of belief and behavior? Two questions asked about the location of membership of presbyters and deacons and two more focused on roughly parallel questions related to bishops. Eight of the highlighted portions raised questions or offered proposals concerning "the organization and government of the church."

The theological focus of most COCU documents had given little attention to practical matters such as who would hold title to church properties, what proportions of clergy and laity, men and women, younger and older members, and racial and ethnic constituencies would be maintained in the church's governing structure. By identifying these topics, the commission helped to establish the docket for completing COCU's work.

Since this was an interim report, the assembly was invited to comment on its features but delegates did not have to take action. In presenting

22. Paul A. Crow Jr., pers. comm.
23. *Digest of the Eighth Meeting*, 7.

the document, the executive committee announced its confidence that the commission would have a plan of union ready for consideration at the 1970 plenary assembly in St. Louis. As the Consultation moved steadily toward its climax stage, one of its most imaginative and prophetic statements was presented to a plenary assembly, drafted not by theologians or pastors but by a panel of lawyers that the executive committee had convened to consider "the concerns and anxieties of certain participants in the Consultation regarding the legal implications of our current Consultation work." The four-person panel presented "three facts of legal evidence to support our unanimous opinion in much the same manner as clergymen cite biblical scripture to support religious opinion."

The first fact was that in America every great issue "eventually ends up as a legal problem." Since the problems with which COCU was dealing, such as issues of race and poverty, were "great," they would *end up* as legal problems, but COCU now was only in the beginning stage. Second, much can be learned from current explorations into space and advances in medicine such as heart transplants. Only after doing these great things is it possible to form the laws that impose order on society and establish justice. The time was not right for COCU to move to that stage. "More talking, more doing, more experimenting are in order. Law can and must wait more definitive accomplishments by our Consultation." The third fact was that "dynamic change in law and legal institutions" was taking place in America, illustrated by new criminal justice procedures that were developing and the unfolding implications of the "one man, one vote legal principle."

Then came the panel's recommendation: "On such evidence we four lawyer panelists unanimously urge our Consultation to advance without struggling with the legal implications of our work. At this time and in this position, the law of man is secondary. We move today under command of the law of God—to consult, to act, to do in our ecumenical pilgrimage toward a meaningful church union experience in America."[24]

Perhaps buoyed by these words, the Plan of Union Commission continued its work, completing its draft in December 1969. Paul Crow arranged to have the document printed by February 15, 1970, so that it could be in the hands of delegates before they gathered at COCU's ninth plenary assembly less than a month later. The committee work invested in preparing the draft had been intense, requiring a full three months of time. Although several members of the committee had been involved in composing the document, William J. Wolf had carried major drafting responsibilities, especially for

24. *Digest of the Seventh Meeting,* 6–7. The four panelists were Robert Frieberg, William P. Thompson, James Tunnell, and Oliver Schroeder Jr., chair.

the sections dealing with faith and order. As was true with other COCU drafting processes, the committee itself often overruled the drafter so that the final document represented the committee's judgment. In a letter to fellow Episcopal delegates to the Consultation, Wolf indicated his hope that the Plan would be an instrument for renewal similar to the way that Vatican II was serving the Roman Catholic Church. He strongly endorsed the draft, especially its catholic features, and spoke positively of the value of multilateral approaches toward union with the Roman Catholic Church.

In order for COCU's Plan to be a constructive instrument for use in developing relations with the Catholic Church, however, the catholic features that the committee had included needed to be preserved. As he prepared for the plenary assembly, it was clear that Wolf was determined to work in that direction. At the same time, he urged the other commissioners of his church to "have fun" at the St. Louis meeting, a positive word of good advice for all who would be attending this gathering.[25]

25. William J. Wolf, Letter to Dear Fellow Delegate to C.O.C.U., February 3, 1970.

7

At Last a Plan of Union

> Whatever the decision may be, the lives of all of us will be changed
> by it and the shape of the church in this country will have been
> drastically altered.
>
> —JAMES K. MATHEWS

LOCATED AT THE JUNCTION of the Missouri and Mississippi Rivers, the jumping off place for America's westward expansion, St. Louis was a city rich in symbols and therefore an auspicious location for COCU's climactic plenary assembly, March 9–13, 1970. Architecture alone would have been enough to point delegates toward a new American future: Minoru Yamasaki's four-domed terminal at Lambert Field (built in 1956) through which many of the delegates would come to the city, Busch Memorial Stadium (built in 1966), with its 96-arch "Crown of Arches" designed by Edward Durrell Stone, and Eero Saarinen's Gateway Arch that had been opened to the public on June 10, 1967. Vice President Hubert H. Humphrey's speech at its dedication on May 25, 1968, easily could have been applied to the Consultation on Church Union. The arch is "a soaring curve in the sky that links the rich heritage of yesterday with the richer future of tomorrow" and brings a "new purpose" and a "new sense of urgency to wipe out every slum . . . Whatever is shoddy, whatever is ugly, whatever is waste, whatever is false, will be measured and condemned" in comparison to the Gateway Arch.[1]

---

1. http://www.interestingamerica.com/2011-04-09_Gateway_Arch_Architecture_by_R_Grigonis_41.html.

Although the downtown St. Louis that most delegates would see was valiantly seeking renewal, the rapid deterioration of American cities was on display just across the Mississippi River in East St. Louis, a community that had reached its cultural zenith in 1958 when it had been named an All American City. Its musicians had been a creative force in blues, rock and roll, and jazz. The deindustrialization of America, restructuring of railroads, and construction of freeways through vibrant neighborhoods, however, had decimated East St. Louis as a place. Polarization between rich and poor and black and white intensified. With the changes came gangs, rioting, and other modes of violence. COCU's commitment to the renewal of the church's mission received graphic validation by the presence of depressed communities so close to the urban center where its deliberations would be taking place.

Delegates from the participating churches came to St. Louis to debate and revise *A Plan of Union for the Church of Christ Uniting,* a ninety-page, closely spaced document that described in full detail COCU's proposal for a new American church. The time for debating ecclesiastical and sacramental theology had morphed into the time for structuring the organizational life of a 24 million-member church that would be fully catholic, fully evangelical, and fully reformed. In less than a decade, the vision proclaimed by Eugene Carson Blake at San Francisco's Grace Cathedral had been embodied in a plan that the delegates could debate, revise, and commend to their churches for serious study and revision.

For many of the delegates, a dramatic portrayal of the vision of the proposed new church took place on Christmas Day only a few weeks before the assembly. The National Broadcasting Company featured an hour-long televised broadcast entitled "A Christmas Service of Word and Sacrament." As George Dugan reported the next day in the *New York Times,* this special liturgy at the Episcopal Church's National Cathedral in Washington, D.C., was designed to "point the way toward a united Protestant church." The service "combined the solemn responsive readings common to Methodism and Presbyterianism with the colorful processionals of high-church Anglicanism." Participants "partook of the wine from a common chalice, a practice favored by many Episcopalians. Intercommunion, or sharing the elements, is regarded as a first priority in any church union."

Intercommunion was more fully expressed in another feature that the reporter had also noted in his article, when "a Methodist bishop, an Episcopal dean and representatives of seven other churches received Holy Communion" together, transcending custom, theology, and church discipline as they gathered around this one table. Dugan also noted that "a highlight of the liturgy was the recital by the congregation and the participants of a revised version of the Lord's Prayer."[2]

In an earlier review of the COCU order of worship that was used in the televised service, *New York Times* reporter Edward B. Fiske had noted that the problem faced by the churches was "to produce a liturgy that was continuous with each of the traditions involved yet avoided becoming simply a common denominator without artistry or religious integrity." Quoting Paul Crow, Fiske said that the solution had been to go past the post-Reformation period to "the liturgical traditions of the early Christian church." The liturgy represented current theological understandings in two ways: its mood was celebrative rather than penitent, and it assumed that the regular Sunday service in congregations should include Holy Communion in addition to Bible reading and preaching. Another distinctive element of the liturgy was that it included a strong interest in social issues.[3] This liturgy, although it was not included in the *Plan of Union,* illustrated one of the ways that worship in a new church might be conducted.

Following Christ to the Cross

The climactic character of the St. Louis plenary assembly was presaged by the selection of Lesslie Newbigin to deliver the Bible lectures and preach at the plenary Eucharist. More than any other person of his generation, this missionary theologian and church leader embodied the vision that COCU was seeking to develop in the United States. In 1936, at twenty-nine years of age, Newbigin had gone to India as a Church of Scotland missionary. He had become proficient in the Tamil language and read extensively in the literature that expressed the culture and religion of India. This grounding in the culture of the people with whom he worked shaped Newbigin's theology of mission and became a central feature in his lectureships and the six books he had already published.

In his writings, Newbigin focused attention on the ecclesiological implications of the breaking up of Christendom—the synthesis between the Gospel and European culture, which had become the folk religion for this part of the world and had been taken to other continents by the missionary

2. George Dugan, "Protestant Communion Stresses Unity," *New York Times*, December 26, 1969. The translation of the Lord's Prayer had been developed by another ecumenical body, the International Consultation on English Texts.

3. Edward B. Fiske, "When Protestants Get Together," *The New York Times*, February 9, 1969. Because the Methodist-Evangelical United Brethren merger had been consummated, there now were nine churches participating in the Consultation.

movement.[4] He was interested in a theme that had motivated and led Eugene Carson Blake to work so vigorously for Christian unity: the importance of proclaiming God's revelation in Jesus Christ by which a new humanity was coming into being."

More important to delegates of the St. Louis plenary assembly, however, was the fact that Newbigin, a missionary in the Presbyterian tradition, had become one of the first bishops of the Church of South India, that had come into being in 1947, eleven years after Newbigin had come to India and twenty-nine years after the union discussions had begun.[5] This new church brought together for the first time churches from the Anglican, Reformed, Congregationalist, and Methodist traditions, and it had done so while remaining faithful to the Anglican Lambeth Quadrilateral, which included bishops in apostolic succession as a necessary mark of a united church. The Church of South India was the one place where a ministry such as COCU envisioned had been established, and more than any other church leader Lesslie Newbigin embodied the unification of ministries that American churches were hoping to achieve. The South Indian method for developing a ministry in apostolic succession had three features: an act by which bishops for the new church were ordained and confirmed so that all would be within the succession; the agreement that henceforth all ordinations would include at least one of these bishops in the act of laying on of hands; and the authorizing of all ordained ministers of the uniting churches to function as ministers in the new church.

In his COCU lectures, Newbigin's thesis was that the church—both leaders and people—must follow Christ to the cross. Paradoxically, church leaders were commissioned to do all that they could to bring the church to the highest level possible in every aspect of its life and then be willing to give it all away in order to follow Christ. "There is one history of man and nature . . . and the cross and resurrection of Jesus are its center, the hinge on which it turns. The events of the past few months," he continued, "have made us suddenly aware of this basic reality." Although he did not list any of these events, he might have been thinking of the Apollo program that had landed people on the moon for the first time, the Woodstock Festival, the inauguration of Richard Nixon as U. S. president, the My Lai Massacre in Vietnam, violence in other parts of the world, and the events that were inexorably leading to closing down the Vietnam Conflict.

Newbigin spoke plainly to his hearers: "The whole emphasis of the New Testament eschatology is not upon our escaping out of this world into

4. Shenk, "Lesslie Newbigin's Contribution," 3–6.

5. 1947 was the year that India regained independence.

another one, but on Christ's coming into this world to manifest and consummate God's rule over all things." Referring to 1 Corinthians 15, he said that "neither we nor our works qualify for eternity. For us as we now are, immortality would be a disaster. Nor do we pray that eternity should be given to the draft plan of union which will issue from this meeting. But it is this perishable, this flawed and stained and twisted thing which is sown, that God can raise up imperishable—fit to find a place in the Holy City."[6]

The Basic Elements of the Plan

The dominant focus of attention in COCU was, of course, the much-anticipated document entitled *A Plan of Union for the Church of Christ Uniting*. William A. Benfield Jr., the Presbyterian pastor (PCUS) who chaired the drafting committee, reported that the fifteen-person body had met twelve times, with most meetings lasting from five to seven days. In addition, there had been countless hours devoted to study and writing. He called attention to four features in the plan. It is faithful to earlier documents that the Consultation had developed. It calls for the united church "to be characterized by inclusiveness in every phase of its life and work. It "strongly relates the ministry of the laity to the renewal of the church." It presents "a new concept,"—the parish plan—for the local presence of the united church."[7]

In his analysis of the document, *New York Times* reporter Edward B. Fiske highlighted two features. First, "the proposed denomination would be run by bishops whose powers would be checked by an elaborate system of lay-dominated councils and part-time moderators." At least on paper, the new church's structure would be "more decentralized . . . than that of any of the member churches and would require the systematic involvement of youth, women and minority groups at the local, district, regional and national levels." The second distinctive feature was that the new church would be organized around mission, which Fiske described as "a new euphemism for serving the world in its social as well as political needs." He highlighted *A Plan's* intention to abandon "the concept of a geographical parish," with the expectation that this action would make possible "all sorts of new relationships, such as inner city and suburban congregations working and worshiping together." Fiske stated that the Church of Christ Uniting, with 24.8 million members would constitute approximately one-third of America's

6. Newbigin's lectures and sermons appear in *Digest of the Ninth Meeting*, 193–231. Quotations above appear on 193, 214–15, 225.

7. Benfield, *Digest of the Ninth Meeting*, 73–80.

70.2 million Protestants. In a pie chart, he noted that there were 23 million Baptists, 5.8 million Lutherans, and 16.6 million "others."[8]

These brief summaries, however, fail to express the comprehensive character of the document, which intermingled succinct statements of what this new church would do with extended expositions of the theological and historical rationale that justified these actions. For people acquainted with COCU's previous theological work the expository sections would have seemed familiar and perhaps extraneous to a document intended to present the basis for union. The Plan of Union Commission, however, recognized that despite the Consultation's many efforts to communicate its work to the constituencies of the churches, most readers of A Plan would be unfamiliar with the theological consensus that had emerged. The commission hoped that by surrounding the specific provisions on which the churches would unite with a full theological and historical rationale they would help their constituencies understand and affirm these provisions.[9]

The first six chapters of A Plan present matters that had been thoroughly discussed in earlier meetings of the Consultation. They deal with central ecclesial and sacramental ideas and practices on which delegates from the uniting churches had discovered common ground more quickly than most of them had expected. This level of agreement had, in a way, confirmed one of Eugene Carson Blake's initial premises: that the churches he named already were in substantial agreement on many aspects of church life and practice. Chapters seven through ten and the first appendix propose a way forward on organizational issues and the process of uniting. While some of these factors had been agreed upon in earlier plenary assemblies, there were others that delegates were seeing for the first time.

The Church of Christ Uniting. The first chapter—"To Begin Anew"— compresses the entire purpose of the Consultation on Church Union on one page, and the rest of the document provides the detail of what this church would be like and how the union would be achieved.

We

The African Methodist Episcopal Church,

The African Methodist Episcopal Zion Church,

The Christian Church (Disciples of Christ),

The Christian Methodist Episcopal Church,

The Episcopal Church,

8. Edward B. Fiske, "Protestant Urge to Merge: It's Not That Easy," *The New York Times*, March 15, 1970.

9. Paul A. Crow Jr., pers. comm.

The Presbyterian Church in the U.S.,
The United Church of Christ,
The United Methodist Church,
The United Presbyterian Church in the U.S.A.

———————————————————

———————————————————

a company of the people of God celebrating the one God,
Father, Son, and Holy Spirit,
moving toward his coming Kingdom
and seeking in faithfulness to
unite under the Gospel for Christ's mission and service in the world,
open ourselves individually and corporately
to renewal from the Holy Spirit,
struggle against racism, poverty, environmental blight,
war, and other problems of the family of man,
minister to the deep yearning of the human spirit for fullness of life,
provide for the common use of the resources and gifts
of many traditions
in a church
catholic, evangelical, and reformed,
do covenant together in this
Plan of Union
for
The Church of Christ Uniting
(C.C.U.)

One of the most important lines on this one-page depiction of the proposed church states the name for the new ecclesial body: *The Church of Christ Uniting.* The use of the present participle *Uniting* implied that this new church hoped to enlist other communions to come into the venture, an intention that was stated more fully later in *A Plan.* Special attention will be given to other churches in the United States and to churches in Canada and the West Indies.

Primary Objectives. Eight "primary objectives" were to guide the Church of Christ Uniting: celebration of God's grace in all its actions, faithfulness to the gospel, inclusiveness of all members, mutual enrichment, honoring ecumenical relations, protection of diversities and liberties, uniting as well as united. This union, though costly, is made necessary by the Gospel, which again is "releasing its revolutionary impulses into our history." The new church will embody all that has been important in the separate traditions but in ways that are dramatically new. "Visible unity should take away from us nothing essential; we will lose only our separateness" (II.18).[10] The Church of Christ Uniting makes no claim of being the whole church, " but instead seeks to be a representative of the whole people of God in this place and to "participate with Christians in this nation and other nations in the upbuilding of the whole body, in faithfulness to the Gospel, and in the fulfillment of our Lord's total mission" (III.28).

Membership. A *Plan* states that in the Church of Christ Uniting "all members, including lay persons, presbyters, bishops, and deacons shall be members in the parish where they worship, study, and serve and to which they give their financial support" (IV.4). The initial members of the Church of Christ Uniting will include "all who are members in good standing of the uniting churches at the time of union," and the "unification of memberships will be symbolized and effected at the time of union by appropriate acts of worship in the service of inauguration" (IV.17). New members will be received by baptism and confirmation. "Full members of other churches that baptize in the name of the Father, Son, and Holy Spirit and require a confession of faith in Jesus Christ as Lord and Savior" will also "be received as full members of the united church by transfer" (IV.12)

The Living Faith. In keeping with agreements already reached, "the Holy Scriptures of the Old and New Testaments [will be] the supreme norm of the church's life, worship, witness, teaching and mission" (V.4). Referring to the Apostles' and Nicene Creeds as "witnesses of Tradition to the mighty acts of God recorded in Scripture," A *Plan* states that the united church will "use these creeds as acts of praise and allegiance . . . for the guidance of the members of the church. (V.9, 10)." Contemporary confessions will be welcomed in the united church and it will also confess its faith through its liturgies and its actions in the world.

Worship, Baptism, and the Lord's Supper. Forms of worship and service books already in use will be continued in the united church, and parishes will be encouraged to familiarize themselves with patterns of worship conducted in other participating churches. New liturgies are to be encouraged and in the united church "there will be room for wide variety and manner of ceremony, furnishings, vestments, music, and the like" (VI.9). A *Plan*

---

10. Quotations from the Plan of Union use Roman numerals for chapter and Arabic numerals for paragraph numbers.

affirms the importance of reading, hearing, and proclaiming the Scriptures, and encourages the use of the common Christian year and new lectionaries.

A Plan states that "both infant baptism and the baptism of consenting believers shall be maintained as alternative practices within the united church," but neither shall "be imposed contrary to conscience" (VI.18, 19). The baptismal rite shall include the use of water, "in the name of the Father, the Son, and the Holy Spirit," confession of sin, affirmation of faith, "promise of continued life in the church and a life of obedience to Christ." The rite will include "a solemn act of confirming baptismal vows" (VI.20, 21).

The celebration of Holy Communion shall "include the use of Christ's words of institution and of the two elements ordained by him . . . the visible acts of taking of the bread and the cup, the giving thanks or 'blessing' over them for the gifts of God in creation and redemption, the breaking of the bread, and the partaking of the elements by the congregation in communion. There shall also be prayer invoking the Holy Spirit" (VI.29). A bishop or presbyter shall preside over the rite, and Christians not members of the united church who were eligible to receive Holy Communion in their own churches "may communicate in the united church" (VI.31).

Ministers in the Church of Christ Uniting. The chapter on ministry states that all Christians, including members who are not ordained, are members of the "ministry of the whole people of God." "The main sphere of Christian lay activity is society at large," but lay persons also "share responsibility with the ordained ministry for preaching the Word, teaching the gospel, leading in worship, assisting in the administration of the sacraments, providing pastoral care and discipline, and leading in mission" (VII.25). Most of *A Plan's* discussion of ministry, however, refers to the ordained leaders of the church who are described as a "particular ministry representative of God who calls and of the church which ordains" (VII.28). Persons already "recognized as ordained ministers in any of the uniting churches at the time of unification" will be recognized as ordained ministers by the uniting church." Accommodating Presbyterian and Disciples polities, lay elders who "had been ordained to celebrate the Lord's Supper" or to serve as ruling elders could become presbyters in the uniting church or choose to become deacons or lay persons. Following unification, the uniting church will ordain persons to the ministry in services of prayer with the laying on of hands, with a bishop presiding using the ordinal (liturgy of ordination) published in *A Plan.* All offices of the ministry and representatives of the laity would participate in the laying on of hands.

A Plan uses the word *presbyter* for the office of ministry ordinarily referred to as *priest, pastor,* or *minister.* The eight functions assigned to presbyters are those that already were performed by ordained clergy in all of the COCU churches. Provisions for the office of bishop are described with great care. Especially important is this sentence: "In accepting and maintaining the historic episcopate, the Church of Christ Uniting neither implies, excludes, nor requires any theory or doctrine of the episcopate which goes beyond what is stated in this plan." It develops the intention that the ministry of bishops will be corporate (functioning within the life of the church), personal, and collegial. "No bishop can be completely autonomous in function." Seven functions are assigned to bishops, again the functions that already were exercised by bishops, conference ministers, and other ecclesiastical executives in the participating churches (VII.57-79). Because the office of deacon was not well developed either in the current practice of the uniting churches or in COCU's earlier documents, A Plan's treatment of this office is brief.

Organizing the Church for Mission. In its description of the structure that is being proposed for the new church, A Plan suggests that its polity includes elements "previously identified as congregational, presbyterian, connectional, or episcopal." There will be four levels: local parish, district, region, and nation. Some of the most critical practical issues for the uniting church to solve are in this chapter: where laity and ordained ministers will hold membership, how the various levels of the church will be administratively connected, how ministers will be "settled" in their places of leadership and how they can be removed from these positions, the authority and power of bishops, and the nature and function of church courts.

The most distinctive element in this chapter, however, is the proposal that in the united church "the local governmental unit shall be the parish." The new entity will embrace the functions previously exercised by residentially based congregations but in a broader geographical and missional pattern than was conducted by congregations. Although subject to the authority of the region, each parish "will be responsible for its own life and work." One or more congregations will be incorporated within each parish, along with task forces and mission groups of various kinds. Pastoral leadership and governance, as well as fiscal responsibility will be assigned to the parish. Although the traditional activities of congregations will be included in the activities of a parish, the focus, as described in A Plan, is more on developing organized mission in the communities where parishes are located. This focus and the organizational process makes the church at the local level more a social service agency than a worshiping body of Christian people.

Steps in the Process. Sooner or later, the churches going into the union had to face the challenging organizational process of merging their largely parallel systems into one new church. At an earlier plenary assembly, a small task force suggested that the way to do it would be to create a governing council at the national level, which would replace the comparable council or assembly of each participating church. Other parts of the church systems— their councils, agencies, conferences, program bodies, etc.—would continue in place for an unspecified period of time during which they gradually would be consolidated into the systems of the united church. In its broad outline, this gradual process is the one recommended in *A Plan*.

The uniting process would begin when two or more of the churches vote to unite with one another and concludes when a constitution for the Church of Christ Uniting has been adopted and made operative. The initial step will be to create a Provisional General Council, consisting of ten members from each of the uniting churches. This body will oversee the process of creating the Transitional National Assembly, which will have twenty-five members elected by each uniting church and would be "the highest governing body of the new church during the formative and transitional period." At the service of inauguration the Provisional General Council will be terminated and the Transitional National Assembly will begin its work. Step by step, outlined in *A Plan*, the rest of the united church's organization will come into being and the comparable parts of the uniting churches will disappear.

The Service of Inauguration. The most challenging aspect in the entire process would be the actions that bring the new church into being. It all can begin when two or more churches vote to unite and in a designated manner bring their previous corporate identities to a close. *A Plan* describes the liturgy—the act of worship—in which these actions will take place. There will be one central service of inauguration and closely parallel services in several locations around the country, perhaps taking place simultaneously. The inaugural service will "announce before God and man the decisions of the people of God in the uniting churches to be his people henceforth in a united church committed to serving him by serving men." These acts of unification will "bring the members and ordained ministers of the uniting churches together in mutual acceptance of one another" with the hope that this new united membership and ministry will be acceptable from that time forward to the churches with which the uniting churches had been in communion prior to the union.

The liturgy consists of several actions and might be conducted in two sessions with an intermission—perhaps a lunch break—between them. Early in the liturgy, a representative of each uniting church would read the official declaration of their church and place a scroll with that text on the Holy Table where the Eucharist would later be celebrated. These representatives would then exchange the peace of Christ with one another and the peace would be taken to the congregation who would continue extending this greeting until all had participated. In this simple manner, the members of the previously separated churches would be united with one another as members with completely equal status in the Church of Christ Uniting.

Three elements of the liturgy are to unite the ordained ministers of the uniting churches into one new ministry. Its members could thereafter, in principle, perform ministerial acts in any of the parishes and congregations of the Church of Christ Uniting. The liturgy's intent is to extend the classic sign of a ministry in apostolic succession to ministers who had not previously received this sign, but to do this in such a way that the action avoids any indication that any of these previous ministries lacked theological validity or religious efficacy. Following the sharing of the peace of Christ, a representative from each church will present a deacon, a presbyter, and a bishop from his or her church. A representative then places on the table the list of names of ministers who have signed the declaration indicating that they are ready to receive from God anew "such grace, gifts, and authority as he may deign to bestow" upon them to do the work of ministry in the united church.

After confessing the limitations of their ministries, they acknowledge in prayer their recognition of one another's ministries and pray that God will unite them as one ministry in the united church. Then all of the representative ministers in this central act go around the circle in silence, laying their hands upon the heads of all of the others until all have received this sign. Successive groups of ordained ministers come to the Holy Table and continue this action, until all ordained ministers have been accepted and welcomed into the Church of Christ Uniting. All would sing or say the hymn "Come, Holy Ghost, Our Souls Inspire," which was widely used in services of ordination. The Lord's Supper would be celebrated, with a minister from each of the churches sharing in the breaking of the loaf.

Deliberations and Actions

Despite the length and complexity of *A Plan of Union*, the delegates to the St. Louis plenary assembly became a deliberative body with the power to amend the document. The minutes of the St. Louis assembly show that members of the Consultation took an active role in determining the parliamentary process and in revising the language of the draft that the Plan of Union Commission had prepared. Small editorial revisions passed easily and subtle changes in emphasis were approved, especially in the chapter on the ministry. Some portions of the text, especially in Chapter II, were condensed, thus shifting the balance of the exposition away from theological explanation to a focus on the features that would characterize the new church.

The issue with longest record of debate and action in the minutes concerned the racial background of the presiding bishop. The uniting church intended to demonstrate its commitment to racial justice in its internal life as well as in its public ministry. Agreed procedures, therefore, had to guarantee full access to church office for people of color. An amendment that the church's first presiding bishop would have to be black was not successful, but in its place, the delegates revised *A Plan* so that it required that the one nomination presented by the nominating committee would be of a different race from that of the incumbent (unless the incumbent was the nominee). An additional amendment allowed nominations from the floor, but with the same stipulation concerning race. The minutes do not report the number of registered voters, but if full delegations had been present the number would have been 90. The number of votes cast was recorded twice: 37 to 32 and 48 to 27.

Late in the morning on Friday, March 13, 1970, the plenary assembly approved the Resolution on the Transmittal of the Plan of Union to the Churches." The executive committee of the Consultation had prepared the draft, and on their behalf Paul Crow, COCU's general secretary, presented it to the assembly. By standing vote, *A Plan of Union* was approved for transmittal to the churches. Following this action, the delegates "rose and sang the Doxology." The language of the resolution clearly stated the purpose of the document: "The Consultation on Church Union on March 13, 1970, commends this draft of the Plan of Union to the member churches and to all Christians for study and response, seeking their assistance in the further development and completion of this Plan of Union."

Responses were to be submitted no later than January 15, 1972, thus allowing the churches nearly two years to review the document. It was hoped that during this period the study, evaluation, and response to this document would be done through processes that included participation by all nine churches of the Consultation. During the 1970–1972 biennium, the Consultation was not seeking official votes from the churches. Instead, it was asking for "assistance in completing this Plan which is pointed toward the union and the vital renewal for mission of Christ's church."[11] In the "rather personal word" with which he concluded a paper prepared for the assembly, Roger Hazelton made a statement that expressed the mood of many delegates in the Consultation. "Any venture toward church union such as ours must reckon not only with the built-in inertia that inhibits

11. *Digest of the Ninth Meeting,* 30.

needed change, but also with the understandable impatience that falls easy prey to novelty and programmed manipulation of attitudes and opinions. Now, as we enter the planning and negotiating stages, this tendency toward polarization must be overcome. Both within the Consultation as a whole and within the delegations that compose it, we shall have to move forward soberly, advisedly, and in the fear of God, but *move.*"[12]

Even more indicative was the statement with which James K. Mathews, United Methodist bishop and COCU president for the assembly, had opened their meeting: "Whatever the decision may be, the lives of all of us in this country will have been drastically altered."[13]

---

12. Ibid., 85.

13. Mathews, "Introductory Statement of the Chairman," *Digest of the Ninth Meeting,* 45.

PART TWO

Negotiating the Terms of Agreement
(1971–1988)

8

Responding to the Nation's Deepening Distress

Still the best hope for a renewed, revitalized,
and reconciled Christian community . . .

—PAUL A. CROW JR.

"A CONCRETE MERGER PROPOSAL" is the way that Edward B. Fiske described *A Plan of Union* in the *New York Times* as the delegates headed home from the St. Louis plenary assembly (March 9–13, 1970). Within a decade, this plan would create "the largest Protestant denomination in the world," which despite its size—25 million members—"would actually be more decentralized in practice than any of the present denominations." Along with other news media around the country, the *Times* outlined major features of the plan and noted points of debate during the deliberations.[1]

"Quiet Victory in St. Louis" is the title that Alan Geyer gave his report in the *Christian Century* a few days later. Acknowledging that there was "no lack of criticism of the proposed draft," he cited its length, the "severe disproportion between the lavishness of rhetoric and the leanness of constitutional clarity," the Consultation's unwillingness to deal with power and political forms until doctrinal matters of ecclesiology were addressed, "theological fixations of a decade ago," and discontent with the name proposed for the new church. Geyer spoke favorably about the parish plan, which he described as the "clustering of congregations and task groups and

1. Edward B. Fiske, "9 Churches Vote Plan for Merger," *New York Times*, March 14, 1970. See comments about press coverage by Beazley Jr., *News on Christian Unity*.

the sharing of ministries through a common mission to the local community." He affirmed COCU's "unfeigned determination to establish the new church on the firmest possible foundation of racial justice and inclusive participation."[2]

The *Century's* evangelical counterpart, *Christianity Today*, published two accounts by Russell Chandler, entitled "The Nose on COCU's Face" and "Selling COCU to 24 Million." Although he reported that the unique parish plan and the stand against racism were considered "to be outstanding features of the plan," Chandler's disdain for *A Plan of Union* and the Consultation itself permeates both reports. [3] His magazine asked the participating churches about the procedures they would follow in order to join the new church and published earliest dates for approval ranging from 1973 to 1976.[4]

As their publishing schedules permitted, news magazines of the participating churches provided news reports and editorial positions concerning *A Plan of Union*. The *United Church Herald* listed six issues that were likely to prompt discussion: the parish of congregations; the task force; increased role of the laity; the "settlement" of clergy; the ministry of bishops; and forms of worship and confessions of faith. The *Herald* also published a three-page spread in which a representative from each of the nine churches described "Our Contribution to The Church of Christ Uniting."[5] UCC executive Theodore H. Erickson noted that the parish plan was not new. A similar approach had been proposed as early as the 1920s by H. Paul Douglass, based on his surveys of churches all across America. Despite his

2. Alan Geyer, "Quiet Victory in St. Louis," *Christian Century*, March 25, 1970.

3. Russell Chandler, "The Nose on COCU's Face," *Christianity Today*, March 27, 1970; and April 10, 1970. An example is when he quotes "COCU officials" as saying that the new church would have 2,000 bishops, which was 1,800 more than were then in the five COCU churches with bishops.

4. *Christianity Today*, April 10, 1970. The editors assumed, incorrectly, that action could take place on the basis of the *Plan of Union* adopted by the St. Louis assembly and provided this time-table: AME, AMEZ, CME—Approval by quadrennial General Conference, followed by approval by majority of annual conferences; earliest date for a final decision, late 1973 or early 1974; UMC—Action by General Conference followed by study and voting by annual conferences; earliest date, 1976; CCDC—Process would be set up in 1971; earliest date, not before 1973; EC—Approval by two consecutive general assemblies; earliest date according to current schedule, 1976. UCC—Approval by General Synod, followed by approval by conferences and then by congregations; earliest date, maybe in mid 1975; UPCUSA, PCUS—Referred by General Assembly for study and then for transmittal to congregations with final ratification by General Assembly; earliest date, 1975.

5. "Nine denominations receive Plan of Union," *United Church Herald*, March 1970, 47–49.

lack of enthusiasm for *A Plan*, Erickson believed that his church should remain in the Consultation, and he insisted that the COCU plan had to be studied seriously. If it is rejected, he concluded, then "it must be done for the right reasons—that it is an inadequate response to religious and social need today—rather than for the wrong reasons—that we don't trust each other, or ourselves, enough to engage in a venture of faith."[6]

Speaking to members of the United Presbyterian Church, Lois Stair and William Thompson, Stated Clerk of the General Assembly (both of whom had served on the drafting committee) supported the parish idea and encouraged other Presbyterians to respond positively to *A Plan of Union*. The "understanding of the church that pervades this entire plan," Thompson said, "is that the mission of the church is to the world and within the world. Mission, he continued, is what happens when the church members, and this includes the ordained members as well as the unordained, go out into the society in which the church is set and there act as reconcilers."[7]

Two pastors on the Disciples' delegation held contrasting views of the parish plan. Speaking to delegates at the recently inaugurated Disciples-Roman Catholic Bilateral Conversation, Cleveland pastor Albert M. Pennybacker described the parish plan as basically "a reshaping of church life" that would make possible new relationships "that more genuinely parallel the relationships in which life itself is being lived out" as churches deal with issues of race, homogeneity, fixation on property, and current patterns for the deployment of clergy.[8] Indianapolis pastor Paul A. Stauffer wrote that the parish plan was "an arbitrary and artificial structure" that would lead to "the lessening of the participation of the individual member at the decision making level—the parish" and generate a "bureaucracy which may displace even more the participation of the whole people of God in the decision making process."[9]

Writing to Episcopalians, Edward T. Dell, Jr., stated that *A Plan of Union* was like a tailor's "basted version of a new suit." It doesn't look very good, but "it's strong enough to try on for a first fitting." The COCU leaders hope that people in the pews "will take a good look at the new garment, take tucks, shorten, change the style or the buttons, or send it back with instructions for a major re-make." Dell reported that the "type of ministry reunification service COCU proposes to use has already been declared valid by the

6. Erickson, "Mission or Unity," 1–6.

7. Lois Stair and William Thompson, *Presbyterian Life*, November 1, 1970.

8. Pennybacker, "The Possibilities in the Parish," 97–104.

9. Stauffer, "The Parish Concept in a Plan of Union," 116–21. Another Disciples report was given by Paul A. Crow Jr., "Education for Church Union," 82–100.

Lambeth Conference of Anglican bishops in 1968," and that the Episcopal Church's thirty-two member Joint Commission on Ecumenical Relations, which had met in St. Louis immediately after the COCU assembly, was expected to ask the next General Convention to "commend the draft plan for a two-year churchwide study." This new suit for unity "may not turn out to be an overnight fashion smash. But it is the single most ambitious and serious ecumenical undertaking in Christendom today."[10]

Presbyterian activist Stephen C. Rose supported the *Plan of Union* because its commitment to renewal was clear. "COCU was based on a principle of compensatory justice (read 'reparation' shorn of rhetoric)," included "the imperative that each parish be racially and economically inclusive," and legitimated "the death of denominations." Rose acknowledged that some denominations (he named the Methodist Church) might be split by the *Plan* and that the united church might emerge from the process of uniting "with half the members now involved nominally in the old structure, but hopefully with a more alive membership possessing more dedication to the principles Jesus laid out to his disciples."[11] Citing the unwillingness of "the powers-that-be" at the St. Louis plenary assembly to discuss issues of power and money, Rose noted that black churchmen and white renewalists "will refuse to support the creation of a fundamentally white structure merging many of the worst features of present white structures. Thus these renewalists may soon be pushed into forming a new church—possibly along COCU lines but divorced from the COCU establishment."[12]

Empowering the Black Churches

Rose's comments bluntly stated a major challenge facing not only the COCU churches but also the nation as a whole. The Consultation's first decade coincided with a period of dynamic change in the basic structure of American society, beginning with the momentous decision *Brown vs. Board of Education* handed down by the U. S. Supreme Court on May 17, 1954, and followed eighteen months later by Rosa Parks' refusal to move to the back of the bus on December 1, 1955. Leaders of black churches, especially Martin Luther King, Jr., became increasingly active in the movement, giving voice, theological depth, and moral shape to the demand for justice by black Americans. Convinced by the theological and ethical message of King and many others, a growing number of white Christians knew that they had

10. Edward T. Dell Jr., "COCU: A New Suit for Unity," *The Episcopalian*, May, 1970.

11. Stephen C. Rose, "Renewal Lives!" *Renewal*, March 1970.

12. Rose, "The Coming Confrontation," 1209–11.

to repent of their past behavior, sinful as it was, and develop new ways for churches to maintain their inner lives and position themselves with respect to the public issues that were threatening to break America apart.

This challenge to the white churches came into sharp and painful focus at the Riverside Church in New York City on Sunday, May 4, 1969, only a few months before the St. Louis COCU meeting. More than any church in the nation, this congregation that had been endowed by John D. Rockefeller, with Harry Emerson Fosdick as its long-time pastor, represented the intellectual, spiritual, and cultural high-water mark of American Protestantism. This was the place that James Forman, a leader of SNCC (the Student Non-violent Coordinating Committee) chose as the site to unveil a new document entitled "The Black Manifesto," which demanded that the white churches contribute 500 million dollars to black organizations and programs that were named in the Manifesto. Forman and others working with him approached other congregations and church organizations with similar demands. In nearly every case, the Manifesto itself was rejected, but some church bodies responded with financial contributions and they accelerated processes to provide equal opportunity to people of color and women in their own systems.[13]

The Black Power Movement and the Black Manifesto created a difficult time of decision for leaders of the black churches in the Consultation on Church Union. "The rise of black consciousness and militancy among African-American clergy in the 1960s," as CME historian Raymond R. Sommerville Jr., reports, led them to distance themselves "from the integrationist goals of Martin Luther King Jr. and the Civil Rights mainstream that now dominated the denominational hierarchies . . . [I]ncreasingly critical of the paternalism and racism in the ecumenical churches . . . this younger generation of clergy was more likely to form broad-based coalitions with other African-American clergy/activists, including those in predominantly white denominations and church agencies, than to promote organic union among their respective denominations."

In order to respond to this challenge, the CME Church appointed a committee that drafted a statement in 1967.[14] "While the committee substantively agreed with the manifesto's analysis of racism in the United States," Sommerville writes, "it disagreed with the manifesto's theological assumptions, ideological commitments, and programmatic solutions." The committee "regarded race relations as a 'moral issue' that needed to

13. http://www.nybooks.com/articles/archives/1969/jul/10/black-manifesto/?pagination=false.

14. Sommerville, *An Ex-Colored Church,* 202–3.

be confronted by the totality of black and white institutions, not just by white religious bodies." It rejected the "presumption" that any one person or group—whether white or black—could "speak for all African Americans." Faithful to King's "nonviolent philosophy and strategy," the committee "renounced the manifesto's threat of violence." It rejected "the manifesto's explicit Marxist analysis of racism and critique of capitalism in the United States, affirming that 'all human economic systems are evil and that no system should be held up as that desirable by the black people of America.'" The committee objected to "the arbitrary amount of reparation money the manifesto demanded from white religious institutions." As its last point, the CME committee "rejected the manifesto's critique of African-American Christianity for its uncritical acceptance of Euro-American Christianity."

Sommerville's review of this report is based on an "undated mimeographed copy" in the papers of Henry C. Bunton. Although it is difficult to know how widely distributed it might have been, the ideas it contained represented a point of view that would likely have given rise to spirited debate and probable affirmation among many of the COCU church leaders, black and white.

Although progress was slower than many people would have desired, COCU delegates would have been aware of the changes, cautious and plodding though they had been, that had taken place in the Consultation since the black churches had joined the movement. As black Christians came into the Consultation, delegations of the white churches gradually had begun to change so that more women and people of color were becoming active participants and leaders. Although one of the major goals in drafting *A Plan of Union* had been to address this long-standing cleavage in the soul of the American church, it soon became clear that *A Plan of Union* had not gone far enough, and a conference was held at Gammon Theological Seminary in Atlanta, December 9-10, 1970, to figure out what to do. Black theologian Cornish Rogers reported that the COCU staff met with "black churchmen representing both denominational caucuses and black denominations . . . in order to grapple in an open way with the problems confronting blacks in COCU." Black denominations have shown "benign neglect" of COCU, fearing that regardless of how the relationship started, white church leaders would soon find ways of re-establishing "their plantation-style church again."

One leader had said that the three black denominations had been participating in COCU mainly as a courtesy gesture and to keep track of what was going on. They were unhappy with the way that some black churches were whitening their worship and the way that their black styles of worship were "amusedly dismissed by many whites as irrelevant." The result of this conference, Rogers reported, was that "substantial changes recommended for COCU's direction will be brought to the executive committee within a few months . . . The year 1971 shapes up as a pivotal one for the audacious COCU plan."[15]

Later in the year, Presbyterian scholar Preston Williams tightened the pressure in his address to the COCU plenary assembly that met in Denver September 27–30, 1971. Before coming to the faculty of Harvard Divinity School as the Houghton Research Professor of Theology and Contemporary Change, he had served as the Martin Luther King Jr., professor at Boston University's School of Theology.[16] COCU "was revolutionary in conception and consequence," Williams acknowledged, but then asserted that "the central question is whether it is sufficiently revolutionary and whether it seeks the proper type of revolution for our time and the days ahead." His answer was swift and abrupt: "COCU is not sufficiently revolutionary; COCU is not revolutionary about the issues that matter." In order to "persuade blacks, women, and youth who are cultural revolutionaries to join," COCU would have to provide further demonstration of its "appreciation of Christianity as a movement, its willingness to accept dissent and deviance, and its intention to include in the new uniting church particulars found outside the main stream of religious life."

Williams then deepened his critique, pointing out that since he was neither a woman nor a youth, he would speak from his own experience as "a black churchman." The women's and youth revolutions were basically white, and thus already on the inside of the congregation, denomination, and ecumenical movement. "If they are not present all one needs to do is tell wife, son, and daughter to join in the work of the Lord." The blacks, however, are on the outside. Most whites do not know any blacks, and if they do know some, the whites conclude that the blacks are "not domesticated and suitable for tasks in the ecumeni [sic.]." What is needed is "the empowerment of the black church," and to do this COCU needed to provide sufficient funds to black churches and black people for them to do well the mission in black neighborhoods. When "strong black churches comparable statistically and programmatically with the best white churches" have emerged, these churches could then minister effectively in their neighborhoods and "be better equipped for the ministry of racial reconciliation." Black churchmen would then have a base in the staff and hierarchy of the uniting church.

15. Rogers, "Blacks and COCU," 1554.

16. Biographical information: www.hds.harvard.edu/people/faculty/preston-n-williams.

COCU should also encourage "black churchmen to come together in a united black religious community prior to their merger into COCU. Black churchmen in white denominations and the black denominations together should decide about the nature of the church, boundaries of parishes, and the character of mission. They need to be represented in all aspects of church leadership. Williams concluded his address by declaring that "No return to the old is possible. If COCU does not succeed, a new COCU shall arise from the ashes."[17]

The Church's Need for a New Stance of Confidence

A second major address, which came later in the Denver assembly, took delegates by surprise because it seemed out of harmony with the prevailing theme as it was expressed by Williams and other speakers. Delegates and observers gathered in the hotel's ballroom for an address by Peter L. Berger, professor of sociology at Rutgers University and one of the most celebrated voices in the call for transformation of American church life. He began his lecture by referring to his book *The Noise of Solemn Assemblies* that had been published ten years previously. When he had published that book, the American church was "a secure, well-established and generally self-satisfied 'culture Protestantism'" and needed to be reminded that "Christianity always stands over and beyond any particular culture, and that this transcendence involves judgment as well as grace." Now, however, Protestant churches have hit an iceberg, the Roman Catholic Church that had "seemed to be sitting pretty on their Rock of Peter, are now looking for plausible lifeboats with the rest of us," and panic is even creeping up on Southern Baptists and Missouri Synod Lutherans. In these troublous times, the churches have been spending much time listening to the culture around them and have tended to give a positive evaluation to what they are hearing. Even more problematic was the tendency to join forces with these forces that were increasingly prominent. It was an easy transition from "ministering to the Canaanites" to "worshipping with them at the shrines of the ba'alim."

Berger suggested that he and other sociologists might have been mistaken in projecting the current social trends into the future. Instead of the continuation of "progressive secularization," there were signs that a deepening sense of demoralization was settling in and that there was "a widespread and apparently deepening hunger for religious answers among people of many different sorts." He couldn't anticipate what this religious renewal might be like. He was convinced that in American society, however,

17. Williams, "COCU and the Cultural Revolution," 131–43.

"a strong renaissance of religion" would be Christian and that it would not come from the churches that had made such strong efforts to be "relevant to modern man . . . Ages of faith are not marked by 'dialogue,' but by *proclamation*." And what would be proclaimed? Essentially the "old story of God's dealings with man, the story that spans the Exodus and Easter morning." While the accents would change, the story would remain the same.

Berger affirmed that "every enduring human enterprise must exist in institutional structures, and the enterprise of Christian community is no exception. What is more, anyone concerned for the institutional structures of the American church must *ipso facto* concern itself with the existing denominations and their relations to each other . . . I would even express the rather unfashionable opinion that there have been occasions when bureaucratic organizations may be vehicles of grace." But these institutions will be useful only if they are sustained by "a new conviction and a new authority in the Christian community." Changes will have to take place as the church responds to the travail in American society. "It seems to me, though, that these tasks will only be meaningful to the extent that the Christian community regains its 'nerve,' and succeeds in achieving a new stance of confidence in itself and its message." Were they living in one of the church's "historic moments?" Maybe. They would have to wait in hope.[18]

When Berger finished his address, the assembly seemed unable to respond, and no one spoke up with comments or questions. In an effort to break the eerie silence, chairman George Beazley, who was sitting at the podium with the leather bound English and Greek New Testaments that he always carried with him, summarized the message he had heard. With three hundred people, representing the significant leaders of American Christianity listening in, Beazley and Berger then conducted a candid conversation concerning the role of the church in the America that was emerging.

One reason for the silence following Berger's address was that leaders of the ecumenical Protestant churches and other institutions at the center of American life were increasingly unnerved and disabled by the changes that were taking place around them, changes that they scarcely comprehended and certainly could not control. The assassinations of Martin Luther King Jr., (April 4, 1968) and Robert F. Kennedy (June 5, 1968) were signs of the nation's deepening distress, which burst out in seemingly uncontrollable fashion in the events surrounding the Democratic National Convention in Chicago, in August of that same year. The Vietnam war continued to divide the nation, even though President Johnson had responded to the Tet Offensive in early 1968 by deciding no longer to escalate the war and President

18. Berger, "A Call for Authority," 113–29.

Richard M. Nixon, who had defeated Hubert Humphrey in the presidential election, had begun withdrawing U.S. troops early in 1969. Anti-war feelings, especially among young Americans, remained strong, and it had led to campus unrest throughout the decade in various places around the country. The Free Speech movement at the University of California, Berkeley, in 1964 had been unsettling to people in that state, and because of that reaction throughout California Ronald Reagan was elected governor four years later. Other schools, notably Columbia University in 1968 and the University of Chicago in 1969, experienced their own student actions that challenged the ruling powers in American life.

Other movements that may have seemed less fearful but were profound in their implications for changing American life were also taking place. Betty Friedan's 1963 book, *The Feminine Mystique,* challenged long-held assumptions about the place of women in American society, and the National Organization of Women, which she helped to found in 1966, gave institutional form to a movement to change the way that the nation lived its life. The Stonewall riot in New York City on June 28, 1969, made it clear that a new movement to secure gay rights was emerging. The deep chasm between the churches and popular culture was portrayed at the Woodstock Festival, August 15–17, 1969, when some 400,000 people gathered in an unprecedented campout in the mud, featuring music, sex, and drugs in a new and potentially volatile mix.

Paralleling these societal changes were two developments among the nation's churches. By the end of the 1960s, it was clear to everyone that the post-war return to religion had run its course in the ecumenical Protestant churches. From 1955 to 1960, membership of the United Presbyterian Church had grown by 20.5%, but from 1960 to 1965 the rate of growth had dropped to 3.2% and from 1965 to 1970 it lost 6.4% of its members. For those same periods of time, the Episcopal Church experienced growth rates of 13.5% and 7.2%, followed by a decline of 2.7%. Other ecumenical Protestant churches reported membership changes with similar patterns. During these same years, evangelical Protestant churches increased rapidly, the most prominent example being the Southern Baptist Convention which showed steady growth rates: 14.8% in 1955–1960, 10.7% in 1960–1965 and 8.0% in 1965–1970. During these same three periods, the Roman Catholic Church reported growth rates of 19.3%, 10.5%, and 4.0%.[19] As Dean R. Hoge and David A. Roozen were to write later, this "reversal caught many

19. Hoge and Roozen, *Understanding Church Growth and Decline,* 146. This book consists of studies by sixteen historians and social scientists who were describing and interpreting the dramatic changes taking place in American Christianity during this period midway through the twentieth century.

denominational leaders by surprise." The two questions that pressed upon them were "why did the declines occur, and why were they most acute in the more theologically 'liberal' denominations?"[20] Early in the 1970s, social scientists, theologians, and church officials would begin publishing studies and explanations, but in 1971, when Berger addressed the Denver assembly, bewilderment, uncertainty, and defensiveness prevailed.

Already in full swing, however, was a theological movement that increasingly alarmed many of the leaders of the nation's liberal churches. Often referred to as "the death of God theology," this movement challenged central ideas in the Christian faith. Among its best-known proponents were Gabriel Vahanian, Paul Van Buren, William Hamilton, and Thomas J. J. Altizer. The impact of the books these men were writing was clearly symbolized by the April 8, 1966, edition of *Time*. For the first time in its publishing history, the magazine did not feature an image on its cover. Instead, superimposed in deep red on an all black background was the three-word question "Is God Dead?" For ordinary churchgoers, the most influential of the books during this period was a surprise best seller, *Honest to God* by John A. T. Robinson, a former New Testament scholar who had become the Anglican Bishop of Woolwich in South London. His thesis was that he, along with an ever-growing number of people, was no longer able to believe in Christianity in its traditional form.

As the Consultation on Church Union hesitated in its forward movement, a new organization came into the picture that focused the energies of the evangelical Protestant churches that seemed unaffected by these societal changes: the Church Growth Movement established at Fuller Theological Seminary in 1965. Its founder was Donald McGavran, a third-generation missionary to India sponsored by the Christian Church (Disciples of Christ). During his years of missionary service, McGavran had developed a theory that people became Christians as part of peoples' movements. When he returned to this country and began developing an American version of this process, he found little acceptance of his ideas by his own mission board or by leaders of other ecumenical Protestant churches. McGavran found a home in the rapidly growing non-denominational seminary that had been founded in in 1947 by radio evangelist Charles E. Fuller and Harold John Ockenga, pastor of Boston's Park Street Church. Central to the church growth model was the principle of the homogenous unit: "Churches that realistically evaluate themselves culturally and that gear their ministry toward meeting the needs of people most like themselves are in a position to grow. On the other hand, churches which decide to try to meet the needs

20. Ibid., 17.

of a variety of people usually find that they have growth problems."[21] This principle was understood by many people to run directly counter to the Consultation's determined effort to unite people of differing cultures and religious traditions in local congregations.

The minutes of the Denver meeting record an extended and vigorous debate among delegates concerning how the Consultation and its churches should respond to the challenges that they were encountering. They drafted "A Word to the Churches" that asked their member churches to "act in two crucial and interrelated areas." First on the list was one that stated the aspect of their work that was increasingly energizing their activities. They asked their member churches "to initiate, participate in, and continue to promote programs leading to the achievement of racial justice and compensatory treatment for minorities in the churches and in the nation, the sharing of resources among the constituent churches, and cooperative action in mission."[22] Not until later meetings would the Consultation discover and implement the deeper implications of the ideas and issues with which they were contending. While this recommendation asked the churches to give ever more attention to new patterns of mission, the second recommendation sought to refocus attention on goals that had directed the Consultation's work during its first generation.

Reclaiming the Sacramental Center

At this critical moment of uncertainty in COCU's life, something had to happen to renew its vision and rekindle its flagging energies. Perhaps more than anyone else, the person who recognized this need was the Consultation's general secretary, Paul A. Crow Jr. His conversations around the *ecumene* and his reading of the literature that *A Plan of Union* already was generating convinced him that a major reason why COCU was losing momentum was the misplaced focus of *A Plan of Union* on organizational issues, the externals of Christian unity, rather than on the sacramental core of COCU's vision. On the afternoon of the assembly's last full day, Crow spoke to the delegates hoping to lead them back to the center.[23] Using the title "Commitment for a Pilgrim People," he noted that the decade-old Consultation was "reaching for balance and equilibrium, attempting to be flexible to the future, alert to the life and death issues of our world, increasingly conscious of our uniqueness in the one ecumenical movement." The united church

21. Wagner, "Church Growth Research," 27– 28.
22. *Digest of the Tenth Meeting*, 36.
23. Crow, "Commitment for a Pilgrim People," 165–76.

will "not be the result of some future decision enshrined in legislative acts. Rather, it will arise from new experiences in community, new relationships among persons, congregations, and institutions." These experiences would enable the churches to move beyond the "failure of nerve" and "pessimism" which Crow perceived to be the special challenges they faced.

Convinced that the churches of the Consultation on Church Union needed "to move boldly toward a common sacramental life," Crow proposed that in the near future they begin "an interim eucharistic fellowship on some regular basis." This would not be "an episode in shotgun ecumenism" but instead would be "a sign of the integrity of the church and a testimony to Christian truth." Referring to the long history of controversy over intercommunion, he acknowledged that some churches believed that intercommunion ought to take place only as a "sign of full reconciliation into a corporate union." He countered this position by saying that it was common knowledge that joint celebrations "without official approval" were taking place across a wide spectrum of the churches. These "underground celebrations" were prompted, in part, by joint statements in the ecumenical world on the centrality of the Eucharist to the life of the church. "Perhaps in these developments," Crow suggested, "God is at work as reconciler overcoming our disunity and proclaiming judgment on our hesitancy."

Interim eucharistic fellowship would be practiced "on the basis of the sacramental consensus" already expressed in *A Plan of Union,* and the churches would use the experimental liturgy that the Consultation had already produced. Almost as an aside, Crow added that these interim celebrations would encourage the eight churches that already could practice intercommunion with full ecclesial freedom to move forward and actually practice what was already permitted. These occasions when members of the separated churches came together at the Lord's table would bring "a new perspective . . . on those disunities of racism and social alienation which tear the body of Christ asunder . . . This is not to suggest that the Eucharist will become a magic cureall [sic.], but it does suggest that no model of reconciliation has full validity until it brings us face to face to break the one loaf and share the one cup. We need to confront each other at the Table in order that we might see Christ in each other. Instead of being peripheral to our attempts to overcome the hostilities and suspicions which exist in our society and in these conversations, the Lord's Supper jointly celebrated would become that place where these disunities are most realistically transcended."

After discussing organizational matters concerning the Consultation, Crow made one more proposal. In the face of "the mood of pessimism which prevails in so many corners of the *ecclesia Americana,*" the Consultation could express its sense of confidence that God was leading them in this venture by renewing the invitation that other churches become sojourners with them. "The Consultation still remains the best hope for a renewed, revitalized, and reconciled Christian community."

In the discussion following the address, the proposal for interim eucharistic fellowship received positive responses, including a strong statement by Roman Catholic observer participant John Hotchkin. "We watch with deep and keen interest. We would be impoverished if this process were suspended or stalled."[24] During the waning moments of the final business session, however, an underlying difficulty with Crow's proposal for interim eucharistic fellowship came to the surface in an amendment to the "Word to the Churches," which Episcopalian Peter Day offered on behalf of Bishop Arthur Vogel. The amendment seemed to require that before churches could participate in these eucharistic occasions they would have to have approved the chapters in *A Plan of Union* that dealt with sacraments and ministry. Presbyterian William P. Thompson responded by saying that his church would not approve those chapters "before *A Plan of Union* is adopted as a whole." Bishop Robert F. Gibson Jr., head of the Episcopal Church's delegation and one of COCU's most constant supporters, commented that some members of his church would not participate in these eucharistic gatherings and he was confident that there were people in other churches who for different reasons (such as the use of wine in the Eucharist) would not take part. He did not support the Day-Vogel amendment, however, and it was not adopted.

Careful drafting interspersed with hours of plenary debate produced three documents that the assembly sent to the churches. Two expressed the Consultation's administrative brain by offering ten proposals for action by the churches and four directives to the Consultation's executive committee.[25] More important, however, was "A Word to the Churches" in which the Consultation's *sacramental heart* was revealed to the churches. In earlier assemblies, the document noted, the Holy Spirit had spoken to the churches "primarily through one another as we shared the faith we have received through our separate traditions." At Denver, the voice of that same Spirit "has come to us particularly in the anguish of the oppressed as we listened to the cry of Chicanos, American blacks, and a black South African, with the hurt of Attica, Vietnam, and East Pakistan heavy upon our hearts." We must continue the process of working for racial justice and compensatory treatment for minorities in the church and nation.

24. *Digest of the Tenth Meeting*, 19.

25. "Recommendations to the Churches" and "Recommendations to the Executive Committee," *Digest of the Tenth Meeting*, 39–41.

The delegates told their churches that the Denver assembly was calling them back to first things, "the story of God's liberating work," and they declared with "new conviction the gospel imperative to organic union."[26] They recommended that the churches demonstrate this renewed commitment by moving toward a growing practice of interim eucharistic fellowship. The Lord's Supper, they declared, is "both cause and sign of unity."

This positive message, however, masked a growing sense of pessimism that was spreading among many of the people who had committed themselves to COCU's vision. There was no escaping the fact that the bold proposal which Eugene Carson Blake had proclaimed twelve years earlier had lost its imaginative power. It didn't take long for this sense of gloom to coalesce in an action that dramatized COCU's distress. At its 1972 General Assembly, the United Presbyterian Church U.S.A. voted to withdraw from the Consultation on Church Union. This action had been promoted by *The Presbyterian Layman,* a monthly newspaper established in 1968, which from its inception conducted "a sustained attack on COCU." The magazine claimed that the office of ruling elder would be discontinued, bishops would become more prominent, and the laymen would be disenfranchised in local congregations."[27]

The fact that this was Blake's own church invested this decision with especially strong symbolic value. The leadership of people like James I. McCord and significant contributions to COCU's annual budget would disappear. People couldn't help but wonder which church might be next? The Episcopal Church, with its deep commitment to the catholic patterns and beliefs? One or more of the Methodist Churches because of its commitments to the Methodist connectional system? The United Church of Christ because of its impatience with hierarchical governing systems? The black churches because the unity movement seemed irrelevant to their concerns for justice and a more satisfactory distribution of power inside the church and in society at large?

Or could the churches in the Consultation on Church Union find a new way to overcome division and express the unity that they believed to be Christ's intention? The next plenary assembly, in Memphis, Tennessee, would be the time when they would make their decision.

---

26. "A Word to the Churches," *Digest of the Tenth Meeting,* 35–37.

27. Coalter et al., *The Diversity of Discipleship,* 191.

9

Shifting the Focus from Plan to Process

Consensus on Theology But Still Searching for Agreement on Organization
and Structure ...

MEMPHIS, A PROUD AND complex city of the Old South, provided a sym-
bolically charged location for the 1973 plenary assembly during which the
Consultation on Church Union would decide its future direction. With an
estimated population of 667,000 within city limits—38.9% black—it was the
third largest city in the South. At one time an important slave market and
center of the cotton trade, Memphis continued to be the world's largest spot
cotton, hardwood lumber, and mule market. This was the city where the
machine politics of E. H. "Boss" Crump long had dominated life. At this assembly, some of the white delegates had their first experiences with duplicate
restrooms in public buildings, architectural reminders of the rigid segregation that had existed until outlawed by the Civil Rights Act only nine years
earlier. Some delegates to the meeting discovered that prominent Memphis
nightspots continued to be uncomfortable places for black patrons.

Very much on the minds of COCU delegates was the fact that Memphis was the city where Martin Luther King Jr., was assassinated on April
4, 1968, after delivering a sermon in which he had supported demands by
black sanitation workers for improved working conditions, higher wages,
and recognition of their union. Because Memphis was planning a march
from City Hall to the Lorraine Motel where he had been shot, to com-
memorate the fifth anniversary of his death, the COCU docket of meetings
was arranged to allow delegates to join in the commemorative events of the
day. What better way could they honor the slain leader and his non-violent

principles and at the same time confront the continuing tension over matters of race and justice in American life!

Paying Attention to What the Churches Had Said

The document that would shape the discussion and business dockets of this COCU meeting was the thirty-page report of the implications team, "The Significance of the Responses to a Plan of Union for the Church of Christ Uniting." Chaired by Rachel Henderlite, this thirteen-person commission examined and analyzed the significant body of material that had been generated since *A Plan of Union* had been sent to the churches for study and comment. After summarizing the responses, the commission presented its recommendations for the Consultation to consider.

Henderlite was herself an embodiment of one transformation that COCU was undergoing. Born in Henderson, North Carolina, she grew up in a world in which the role of women in academic and religious leadership was narrowly circumscribed. She studied ethics under H. Richard Niebuhr at Yale, receiving her PhD degree in 1947, and then taught at the Presbyterian School of Christian Education, a graduate school primarily for women. In 1965, at the age of 60, Henderlite was the first women ordained to the Christian ministry by her church, the Presbyterian Church, U. S., and the following year she became the first woman to hold a full-time position on the faculty of Austin Presbyterian Seminary.[1] When her church became a participating member of the Consultation, Henderlite was appointed one of its ten delegates. No one in her church had been aware of a tacit agreement among the COCU churches not to include ordained women in their delegations in deference to the churches that did not admit women to the ministry.[2]

The implications team outlined the seriousness with which *A Plan of Union* had been studied by the churches and union groups in North America and around the world. Half a million copies of *A Plan* and 180,000 copies of a study guide had been sold. COCU's Princeton office had received reports from 1,300 study groups from which more than 8,500 different expressions of opinion were gleaned. The United Presbyterian, United Methodist, and Christian Church (Disciples of Christ) had sponsored approximately 1,400 "contract response groups," each of which prepared a written report. "In all, several hundred thousand local church members have studied the Plan

1. Sherilyn Brandenstein, "Henderlite, Rachel," Handbook of Texas Online (http://www.tshaonline.org/handbook/online/articles/fhelx).

2. Henderlite, "Musings on Christian Education," 5–13.

and made some sort of response to the COCU office." Even though there had been few responses from the three African-American churches, all of them had indicated their readiness to continue in the Consultation.[3] The other churches had "in one way or another reconfirmed their commitment to the Consultation, although not without raising significant questions to be further pursued."

In addition to these responses, approximately 300 articles had been published in church periodicals and journals and a book of essays on COCU—*Church Union at Midpoint*—also had been published and widely distributed. The American Bishops' Committee for Ecumenical and Inter-religious Affairs had published a collection of essays—*COCU: A Catholic Perspective*—of which 30,000 had been distributed. It can safely be concluded that COCU's 1970 *A Plan of Union* was more widely disseminated and studied than any other document of that era that dealt with critical issues concerning faith, ministry, worship, and mission of the church.

With the assistance of the Huguenot Memorial Church, a Presbyterian congregation in New York, and using nascent computer technology, the Implications Team collated the findings and identified twenty-seven topics and ten issues for consideration. What the team heard was "general acceptance of six and a half chapters of *A Plan of Union*, which deal primarily with theology and worship, and general dissatisfaction with the chapters dealing with structure." The team concluded that the churches had "achieved a general consensus on which future work can build" but that the Consultation would have to find "a more flexible structure before it is ready for union."[4]

The most important section of the document was a seven-page summary of the mind of the American churches on the ten issues that the implications team had identified. Perhaps more than any other single document, this summary expresses the character of American Protestantism in the

3. William C. Larkin, minister of the CME Church and associate general secretary of the Consultation, discussed these actions under the title "COCU and the Black Methodist Churches," *The Christian*, September 24, 1972. The General Conference of the AME Church voted at its meeting June 21–30, 1972, to continue in the Consultation. In its General Conference May 3–13, the AME Zion Church voted to remain in COCU and acted to establish ecumenical commissions at every level of church life. The General Board of the CME Church voted at a meeting on May 3–4, 1972, to remain in the Consultation and, with the two other churches, "help determine what a church united ought to be." He discussed difficulties the black churches would face, including reducing the power of the bishops in making appointments.

4. "The Significance of the Responses to A Plan of Union," *Digest of the Eleventh Meeting*, 169.

tumultuous decade during which COCU had labored to create a new form of the church for the center of American life.[5]

Christian Unity and the Necessity for Actual Union of Churches. Despite general agreement with the idea that "unity is an essential mark of the church" and that "steps toward unity are an imperative of the gospel," the responses revealed hidden reservations that demonstrated that "there is obvious unreadiness for the structural union of the participating churches."

The Locus of Christian Identity. A major element in *A Plan of Union* was the parish as the local manifestation of the Church of Christ Uniting. Although sometimes praised in the responses, this feature "received a disproportionate body of criticism as the locus of membership and decision-making." One reason was that it subordinated the congregation to the more complex parish, thus giving rise to "the fears of thousands of people that their personal needs and capabilities will be by-passed." While the parish plan "provided for a variety of impersonal needs," it "failed to make sufficient provision for personal values: a person's identification with the church, his/her at-homeness in a supporting group, the need for pastoral care, the opportunity for decision making and consensus." These responses showed little sense of denominational loyalty, but instead demonstrated that for most people "their sense of personal identification with the church is with the congregation" rather than the denomination. The implications team concluded that the failure of the parish plan to take these factors into consideration was a sign that more work needed to be done.

Deployment of Leadership (Professional Leadership and the Role of Bishops). Responses indicated that most people affirmed two theological ideas in the Plan: that "the ministry of the church is Christ's ministry," and that this ministry has been delegated "to the whole people of God." Criticisms and questions also were freely expressed, leading the implications team to conclude that the people were asking for clarification concerning terms used to describe ordained ministers and concerning their responsibilities in the united church. The list of examples that the team reported, however, could with perhaps greater accuracy be described as rejection of the ministerial system that *A Plan* proposed for the new church.

Search for Inclusiveness. At the heart of COCU's hope for the new church was the determination to open the church to full participation at every level to people of all ethnic groups and to provide full representation for women and youth. Yet, as the implications team worded it, "probably no feature of this ecumenical venture is more promising and more fraught with suspicion and misunderstanding." The black churches "were unable to

5. *Digest of the Eleventh Meeting,* 169–76.

respond as the other churches did to *A Plan of Union*," and "responses from predominantly white churches are not encouraging." Responses indicated that "there was no theological ground for the economic inequality" in the church's life and affirmed that more study was needed. Some stated that changes, based on new understandings in congregations, should take place. Yet other reports "while acknowledging the necessity for inclusiveness in the church as a whole, report honest questions whether inclusiveness is essential on the local level."

Worship. Most responses to worship as described in *A Plan of Union* were positive, especially because of the openness of *A Plan*, the opportunities to become acquainted with other worship traditions, and the place of scripture in the recommendations.

Mission Emphasis: While affirming the emphasis upon mission in *A Plan of Union,* the responses also expressed the "fear that these provisions might reflect a misplaced priority for the church, stressing the 'social' rather than the 'spiritual.'"

Authority: This section combined issues such as the relation of scripture to tradition, the relation of theology and sacrament, and the place of creeds in the life of the church. "On the matter of the locus of authority," the implications team reported, "six out of ten responses approved the Plan's position."

Institutionalism. The greatest number of negative responses to *A Plan of Union* dealt with features that the implications team identified as "institutionalism." While many responses acknowledged the value of eliminating competition between denominations, they did not like the organizational features that *A Plan* had offered. They saw the "hierarchical or pyramiding" of authority as "a death blow to the democratic process of decision-making which will cause the individual to lose an essential locus of identity in an already depersonalized society." Some responses insisted that congregations should have a right to "elect representatives to all higher levels of the church's life." There was strong resistance to provisions in *A Plan* for ownership of property, fearing that they would lead to loss of "individual and congregational freedom."

The Role of Laity. In contrast to the negative responses to institutionalism, the responses to provisions for laity in the Plan were largely positive.

Miscellaneous. Under this heading, the Implications Team included many responses that asked primarily for "clarity, simplicity, [and] brevity." Others asked for "further information." All of the suggestions for improvement, the implications team reported, would be "preserved for the work of future editors in the event the Consultation decides that the Plan shall be rewritten."

A Different Kind of Next Step

When it published *A Plan of Union,"* the Consultation on Church Union was moving forward on a well-focused trajectory: on the basis of substantial agreement on the historic church-dividing issues, the participating churches would set aside their denominational divisions and become one new Protestant church for America, and *A Plan of Union* presented the organizational blueprint for this new church. At the Memphis plenary, however, it had become clear that the churches were unwilling to stay on this trajectory. The implications team identified five courses of action for the delegates in Memphis to consider. Four of these possibilities the team quickly dismissed: (1) to call for a vote on *A Plan of Union;* (2) to begin again and re-write the plan; (3) to discontinue the Consultation immediately; and (4) to phase out the Consultation by transferring important functions to other ecumenical bodies.

The implications team did have a course of action to recommend: that *"the participating churches . . . shift the focus of the Consultation from writing a plan of union at this time to a process of working toward union, reaffirming our commitment to a united church and searching for particular ways of manifesting our unity now."* A member of the implications team who was a scientist by profession provided the metaphor that characterized this proposal. When the hypothesis that has guided a scientist's work turns up negative results, the next step is not to close the laboratory and go home. Rather, the scientist examines the results, noting negative and positive findings, and then modifies the hypothesis or creates a new one. Then, the work can go forward.[6]

The implications team identified four findings, three of which could be listed quickly. (1) The laity want "real representation in the church" and fear "a bureaucratic superstructure." (2) There is much commonality among the churches, especially a common faith and "a common yearning for new life in the church." (3) Unity comes as "a result of study and working together at a common task." The team gave a fuller description to one other finding, which replicated to a considerable degree what has already been described under the second of its ten issues: the importance of the local congregation. "We have learned that there is a personal need for identification with the church in ways that are clear and indisputable, and that the point of identification must be within the most immediately local body."

By the end of their Memphis gathering, the COCU delegates had renewed their determination to move forward in their efforts to "develop a

---

6. *Digest of the Eleventh Meeting,* 179.

full plan of union . . . for a united church—catholic, evangelical, and reformed." They adopted a report entitled "The Way Ahead," with nine steps
that would contribute to the fulfillment of their vision of church union. The
first was that the participating churches "confirm their commitment to the
process of church union and the role of the Consultation itself in guiding
that process."[7]

The most important of the steps, second on the list, instructed COCU's
executive committee (which by another action was significantly enlarged)
"to appoint a commission to rewrite the portions of *A Plan of Union* on
faith, worship, and ministry." This commission was to gather together
"those elements in which there has been general theological consensus" and
give attention to "weaknesses and omissions identified in the study process." When approved by the churches, "at the next plenary if possible," this
revised text would "be submitted to the churches for vote as a theological
basis for working toward mutual recognition of members and ministries
and further development of a plan of union."[8]

Two steps were direct responses to the churches' rejection of the parish
model for the local manifestation of life in the new church. The executive
committee was authorized to appoint a task force "to make a theological
and sociological study of the forms of the church at the local level." The
study was to focus upon the parish "as a means by which to achieve a richer
and more diverse Christian fellowship and liberation from institutional racism" and upon the congregation, which "because of its personal values, is
regarded by many as the locus of Christian identity."[9] The language of this
step indicates that delegates to the Memphis meeting continued to believe
that the character of Christian life at the local level was central to everything
that the churches in the Consultation on Church Union were trying to do.
The Christian communities in the places where people lived and worked
were at the same time manifestations of the church's broken life and the
energizing forces that could shape a new American society.

It was clear to the Memphis delegates, however, that they had not yet
found ways to transform the local forms of church life. This recognition
led them to approve a proposal for "Generating Communities" and the
establishing of an advisory support group to oversee this process. A significant amount of work had already been expended on this effort, as can be
seen in the twenty-seven pages in the *Digest* of the Memphis meeting that
were devoted to two documents on this topic. "A Proposal for Generating

7. Ibid., 53–59.
8. Ibid., 47.
9. Ibid., 54.

Communities" outlined the proposal itself, listed steps in the process, described the responsibilities of the advisory-support group, and laid out a time line for doing this work. The heart of the proposal was that during the next eighteen months thirty generating communities would be organized and that these "covenanting communities" would agree to a three-year minimum agreement.

The second document that had already been prepared was entitled "Congregations Uniting for Mission." This "Working Paper of the Commission on Structures for Mission" intended "to enable leaders in congregations and communities to know the Consultation's intent to be realistic about the present situation and to be realistic about what is needed for the revitalization of the church."[10] After restating the commitment to a uniting church, the document described the predicament of life in their time, which included a critique of the congregation, outlined the realities that had to be faced in contemporary life, described the "style of the Church of Christ Uniting," and characterized eight models for congregations uniting in mission: (1) a cluster of congregations, (2) the uniting of several congregations, (3) the combining of congregations for certain functions, (4) an individual congregation independently pledging itself to the COCU style, (5) a task group, (6) a cadre of professional staff, (7) a long-term task group, and (8) a neo cathedral.

Appearing in both documents was a list of five factors that the "Proposal for Generating Communities" entitled "Marks of Wholeness of the Church." (1) An authentic Church will be responsive to the revelation, judgment, and grace of God as known through the Scriptures and incarnated in Jesus Christ, and will endeavor at every level of its life to authenticate the power of the Gospel through the mission in the world. (2) It will preserve the continuity of its several heritages in grateful recognition of their enriching influences while at the same time fostering maximum openness to further enrichment from other traditions and cultural influences. (3) It will establish norms of an ordered life containing diversity within its unity and openness to change along with elements of continuity. (4) It will strive for inclusiveness in the full participation and representation of all its members, while preserving the unique contributions provided by the diversities of race, age, sex, culture, and economic background. (5) While affirming the ministry of the whole People of God, it will provide for particular vocations in ministry and mission.[11]

10. Ibid., 201.
11. Ibid., 192–93.

Another step in "The Way Forward" committed the Consultation to establish a Commission on Institutional Racism" with responsibilities to examine the current life of the churches, develop strategies for "compensatory action to deal with institutional racism in our present divided churches," affirm the "presence of the black experience and the experience of other ethnic minorities and their role in dealing with institutional racism," and to develop plans and programs that would "equip the constituency to deal with institutional racism as an instrument of injustice for which whites bear special responsibility requiring the development of a new white consciousness of the same depth and magnitude as the problem itself."[12]

The next step on the list was that a document entitled "Guidelines for Interim Eucharistic Fellowship" should be "confirmed and commended to the member communions for distribution to the churches as they seek to grow together as a community of faith."[13] A guiding principle of this thirteen-page document was that eucharistic sharing was "an effective sign of reconciliation when its participants have committed themselves to an inclusive fellowship of faith and action." The "Guidelines" noted a broad range of consensus statements in the United States and abroad that discussed the Eucharist in the life of the Church. The document stated that many of the details of these gatherings would be determined locally. In all cases, however, the diversity of participating churches and the relationship of worship and service in the community were to be affirmed. The Guidelines provided suggestions for planning these liturgies, discussed "practical and pastoral issues," and stated a list of understandings of the Lord's Supper that were widely held by Christians.

Despite the positive character of the Guidelines, the document contained a set of questions that were prompted by the realization that the churches rarely participated in opportunities for shared eucharistic life that already existed. The four Methodist churches in the Consultation, and Presbyterians, United Church of Christ, and Disciples "have a theoretical relationship of open communion . . . [and] Episcopalians can participate in special ecumenical Eucharists." Then came the questions: "If this is so, then why have we rarely received Holy Communion together? Why has not this open communion led to more decisive forms of church unity and common mission? How can the diversities in communion practices be appreciated and seen as contributing to a deeper meaning of the sacrament?"[14]

12. Ibid., 55.
13. Ibid.
14. Ibid., 223–24.

During this proactive period of the Consultation's activities, its leaders may not have recognized the importance of these questions. Despite all of the work on finding new life together, work that continued in COCU for three more decades and was the focus of many other forms of ecumenical endeavor, the conditions that these questions address continued to be largely unanswered.

One of the most instructive documents in the *Digest* of the Memphis assembly, however, had little to do with theology, church order, and the renewal of life in church and world. Rather, it was a one-page diagram entitled "COCU Organizational Chart 1972–73."[15] It consisted of several sets of linked ovals. Across the top, eight of these ovals represented the churches that were participating in the Consultation at that time. The center was occupied by ovals representing the Plenary Assembly, Executive Committee, Secretariat, Chief Denominational Executives, and two subsidiary groups: Finance and Executive Services. Other ovals, some freestanding and others clustered, represented COCU commissions, task forces, and relationships with other organizations. Although the complexity and comprehensiveness of the Commission's work was evident in the 270-page *Digest* of the Memphis meeting, this simple organizational diagram portrays the reality with forceful clarity.

COCU's hopeful new spirit was especially evident during the plenary Eucharist that was celebrated on the evening of the Memphis assembly's last full day of work. The preacher was Vinton R. Anderson, a bishop of the AME Church who for several years chaired COCU's Commission on Worship. Presiding was George G. Beazley Jr., head of the Disciples delegation and COCU's outgoing president, flanked by clergy representing the COCU churches. Since 1968, the plenaries had used the liturgy developed by COCU's commission on worship, which was more contemporary in language and style than most services published in the worship books of the participating churches. Even so, these assembly celebrations had seemed stiff and formal; although theologically adequate, they lacked experiential force.

The Memphis Eucharist broke new ground. The setting was First Baptist Church Beale Street, the oldest African American brick church in the city. Music was led by "The Messengers," a vocal group from Memphis, sponsored by Holiday Inns of America. Overseeing the liturgy, on behalf of COCU's worship commission, was one of its liveliest and most skilled members, Presbyterian Horace Allen, Jr., who taught worship at the United Methodist-related School of Theology at Boston University. During the offertory, a large basket filled with small loaves of bread, especially prepared

---

15. Ibid., 265.

for the occasion, was brought to the altar. Sensitive to Episcopal convictions that the bread needed to be consecrated, presiding minister George Beazley made sure that he touched every loaf. At the close of the service, this large amount of consecrated bread and a copious supply of wine remained for "reverent disposal." One Episcopal delegate proposed that the way to do this was to take these emblems to the downstairs hall where the worshipers had gathered for refreshments provided by members of the host congregation. All who cared to could include the bread and wine in their informal communion with one another, along with the sweet cakes and coffee.

It seemed to many that the evening's multicultural and multiracial Eucharist and fellowship were harbingers of a new church for a new America. That night people once again could believe that the Consultation on Church Union, with God's help, would be able to create a new American church.

10

The Interdependence of Unity and Mission

A theology of social redemption is the task of our divided churches.
—JOHN H. SATTERWHITE

AT THE CONSULTATION'S NEXT plenary in Cincinnati (November 4–8, 1974), a year and a half following the Memphis gathering, the challenges facing the churches became increasingly apparent. "A new detachment of ecumenical pioneers" had come to the meeting with morale that proved to be "unexpectedly high," veteran COCU leader Ronald E. Osborn noted.[1] One reason for their good spirits was that the United Presbyterian Church had returned to the Consultation. Delegates, stand-by alternates, associate delegates from member churches, observer-consultants from other churches and church councils, staff and seconded staff, and other guests and participants brought the number of participants to nearly 300 people. Three-fourths of the voting delegates were attending either their first or second plenary assembly, and the number of women had increased significantly as had the black representation, although "other ethnic minorities were sparse."

Osborn compared COCU with "some political conventions, legislatures, and general bodies of member churches" by showing a "positive response to the pressures of the past decade for more equitable representation of various groups within American society." The gain in representation of various constituencies, however, had resulted in "a drastic reduction in the proportion of academicians, particularly of scholars whose discipline is theology . . . In contrast with ecumenical ventures a decade or two ago, when

1. Osborn, "Moving Yet and Never Stopping," 198–209.

121

theologians largely set the agenda, the Consultation now communicates the pragmatic flavor of a large denominational board—set to a practical task which has some theological implications."

Death, retirement, rotation of office, or resignation had removed some of the Consultation's most important leaders, including Eugene Carson Blake, Robert F. Gibson Jr., Albert C. Outler, George G. Beazley Jr. and David Colwell. COCU's coterie of visionaries, who had dreamed of realizing a united church within a decade, had been replaced by people who came to Cincinnati "to do a job, to try to take one more step toward the goal." For the most part strangers to one another, the Cincinnati delegates tended to huddle within their denominational groups and the occasions for informal contact at meals and on other occasions did little to change this pattern. This plenary "seemed to operate more on general Christian commitment and a decent respect for one another, but less on personal affection among the participants, than some which have preceded it."

The Consultation had also experienced a change in executive leadership. After six years as the Consultation's general secretary, Paul Crow, had resigned in order to succeed George Beazley, who had died unexpectedly in 1973, as chief ecumenical officer of the Christian Church (Disciples of Christ). In that new position, however, he would continue active in the Consultation's work. Taking Crow's place in COCU's executive leadership was Gerald F. Moede, United Methodist minister, scholar, and seasoned leader of the worldwide ecumenical movement. He had earned his doctorate at the University of Basil in Switzerland, served as college professor and pastor in the United States, and for seven years on the secretariat of the Commission on Faith and Order of the World Council of Churches in Geneva, Switzerland. Moede's doctoral dissertation, published in 1964 with the title *The Office of Bishop in Methodism,* indicated his keen interest in one of the central issues that the Consultation intended to resolve.

Moede had shown his understanding of COCU's work by writing an analysis of the outline for *A Plan of Union* that he had sent to Paul Crow following the 1969 Atlanta plenary. He gave particular attention to the outline's treatment of matters related to race, gender, and status, clearly indicating his full support of the direction that COCU was moving. He also discussed issues related to the ministry, especially the office of bishop. Moede closed his letter to Crow by commenting on new understandings of "catholicity" and "apostolicity," that had become talking points among the churches. The Uppsala assembly of the World Council of Churches "made it clear that ethical heresy is as much a denial of catholicity as the creedal variety."[2] Join-

2. Gerald F. Moede to Paul A. Crow Jr., ca. 1969.

ing Moede in the Princeton office was John H. Satterwhite of the African Methodist Episcopal Zion Church who came to COCU from the faculty of Wesley Theological Seminary where he taught ecumenics.

Dutifully Working at the Pragmatic Task

Osborn proposed that *inertia* rather than commitment to the dream may have been the factor that kept many of the COCU delegates focused on the process. "At Cincinnati they plugged away in workmanlike fashion, with only rare moments of elation, but with the same dutiful, rather weary efficiency they bring to the rest of their church work." Expressing this determination to keep moving was the work of the five commissions and task forces, in addition to the commission on worship, that were discussing the issues facing the Consultation: Structures for Mission, Revision of the Theological Basis in *A Plan of Mission,* Generating Communities, Institutional Racism, and Interim Eucharistic Fellowship.

In addition, the assembly authorized COCU's executive committee to enlist a new working group—a task force on women—to address sexism as a divisive force in society and the churches. This group, which would include women and men in its membership, was to gather theological and sociological resources by and for women and bring them to the attention of the Consultation and its commissions.

The Consultation's long-standing and semi-autonomous commission on worship also reported on its work. Speaking on the commission's behalf, Lois Stair (United Presbyterian Church) discussed the development of an ecumenical marriage rite that would be useful to Protestants and Catholics alike. Lewis Briner (United Presbyterian Church) presented a variant of the three-year lectionary that had been developed by the Roman Catholic Church as one of the liturgical reforms initiated by Vatican II. Encouraged by the urgings of Massey H. Shepherd Jr., at meetings of COCU's commission on worship, Protestant churches that were developing new worship materials had set aside their own lectionary projects and were developing variations of the Catholic table of readings, Already under way were Episcopal, Lutheran, and Presbyterian versions. As the United Methodist Church contemplated developing still another version, James F. White, a United Methodist professor of worship, and Hoyt Hickman, the church's executive for worship in its Nashville office, proposed that COCU develop a consensus version that could be used by all of the Protestant churches interested in using the Catholic lectionary. Together, they developed a set of guidelines for this consensus version and a draft lectionary. The document that the commission on worship brought to the plenary assembly summarized the criteria and provided the initial version of the resulting table of readings.[3]

The commission on worship had also completed work on a second liturgy, *An Order for the Celebration of Holy Baptism with Commentary*, which continued the work it had begun in 1968 with its eucharistic liturgy. In their interpretation of the new liturgy, commission members explained that this document would assist the churches in "forming a consensus on baptism rather than being a document which reflects consensus already achieved." The fact that much of the initial drafting had been done by H. Boone Porter, an Episcopalian, and Keith Watkins representing the Disciples of Christ, was in itself an indication that this new document was reaching beyond conventional understandings in the COCU churches. One factor that was shaping the worship commission's work was the Roman Catholic Church's post-Vatican II emphasis upon reforming the whole process of Christian initiation—Baptism, Confirmation, and Eucharist. The document that embodied this new understanding was published (in its official Latin version) in January 1972, but the ideas that it contained were already widely known and discussed. The Council was determined to develop initiatory practices for a church living in a "dechristianized" society. The purpose of the initiatory reforms, Catholic scholar Aidan Kavanagh wrote in his 1978 book on this subject, was "less to give liturgical recipes than to shift the Church's initiatory polity from one conventional norm centering on infant baptism to the more traditional norm centering on adults."[4]

The introduction to *Holy Baptism*, entitled "Entrance into the Family of Christ, A Commentary on Baptism," highlighted three new forces that were shaping discussions about baptism. The first was the ambiguous practice in churches that did not baptize infants but who recognized that children born into Christian homes were "by virtue of that birth a participant in the faith community." Second, there was growing "dissatisfaction with the tradition of delaying admission to communion for a decade or more following baptism" as was common practice in churches that baptized infants. This practice also tended to transfer importance from baptism to confirmation. Third, was the "changing mood in all lands where Christianity had been dominant, and especially in the technologically advanced nations." Even in these nations, the church was finding itself in "a missionary situation" with the result that "even a rite that uses such a natural product as water as the bearer of symbolic import is being questioned."[5] The liturgy could be

3. Commission on Worship, *A Lectionary*.
4. Kavanagh, *The Shape of Baptism*, 106.
5. Commision on Worship, *An Order of Holy Baptism*, 10–12.

ministered to infants and people old enough to speak for themselves, and it was considered to be "a complete rite, containing baptism in water, the invocation of the Holy Spirit with laying on of hands, and Holy Communion." It was assumed that when "administered under properly authorized circumstances" the action of "the laying on of hands (and/or anointing) will constitute confirmation."[6]

Structures for Mission: This commission was chaired by Isaiah Scipio Jr., of the Christian Methodist Episcopal Church. A veteran of World War II with a doctorate from the University of Southern California School of Theology, he had served under Martin L. King Jr., as president of the Western Christian Leadership Conference, and for two years he had been president of the Greater Flint, Michigan, Council of Churches. During his COCU years, Scipio was general secretary of his church's board of missions, supervising work in Liberia, Ghana, Nigeria, West Africa, Haiti and Jamaica.[7] The commission's task, he reported, was "to identify the locuses of power in the churches and determine how they might be utilized for the church union processes." The commission had examined middle judicatories, which Scipio defined as "whatever expression of the Church in your denomination is located between the congregation and the national church."

The report and discussion revealed a serious degree of tension between middle judicatories and congregations on the one side and national denominational structures on the other. The discussion groups at the plenary generated sixteen comments about middle judicatories, one of which was especially revealing: "We must take seriously the power components and curial (guild) interests of middle judicatory entities and leadership and explore these more thoroughly in relationship with national power structures."[8] Especially important in this statement is the open and unambiguous use of the word power. Occasionally, power had been acknowledged and evaluated in churchly literature, with Paul H. Harrison's classic book *Authority and Power in the Free Church Tradition* as a notable example. In the guarded conversations that so often took place in ecumenical gatherings, however, including COCU, the exercise of power and the desire to be able to do so were often obscured.

The reports of two working groups could easily have been dismissed as further examples of what Osborn had described as examples of plugging away in workmanlike fashion. Speaking for the task force on interim

6. Ibid., 23.

7. Biographical information about Isaiah Scipio Jr. is taken from a statement by Dale E. Kildee posted at http://capitolwords.org/date/2004/02/26/E260_honoring-rev-dr-isaiah-scipio-jr/.

8. "Appendix III," *Digest of the Twelfth Plenary Meeting, Supplement,* 56.

eucharistic fellowships, Jerry Boney (PCUS), reported that only a few of these gatherings had taken place, including one in Richmond, Virginia, where Boney taught (at Union Theological Seminary) and Robert F. Gibson Jr, the bishop of Virginia for the Episcopal Church and one of the Consultation's most prominent leaders, had his office.

In its six-page report, the generating communities commission stated the goal of establishing 30 experimental communities, which were intended to be attempts by the Consultation to develop new ways of establishing significant new forms for the church to be present in local communities. Since the churches had rejected the proposed parish plan, something else would have to be developed. The commission repeated the five guidelines for selecting communities that had been adopted at the Memphis plenary assembly in 1973, provided the language for the covenant that participants would make with one another, and listed ten "marks of wholeness" that would be sought in each generating community. The commission acknowledged, however, that it would be difficult to achieve all of the "marks of wholeness" in any one generating community.

This difficulty was increased significantly by decisions made during the Cincinnati plenary assembly. As John E. Brandon, an AME pastor and educator who was serving as COCU's associate general secretary, later wrote, delegates "modified the criteria by which generating communities were to be selected when it directed that energies of the COCU Commission on Generating Communities were to be directed first toward communities in which one or more congregations of the predominantly black denominations were present and in seeking to organize generating communities, at least one of these must be included."[9] This decision limited the number of generating communities, Brandon observed, because the black denominations were not present in some of the places where generating communities had been proposed. Another reason was that it was not possible for already existing groups "to include a predominantly black church for the sake of the experiment if they had not earlier been participants."[10] Once this decision had been made, only one additional generating community was added to the active list. Instead of thirty generating communities, only four were developed. Three of the communities, Brandon reported, "were racially inclusive of blacks and a fourth struggled unsuccessfully to become so."[11]

As he reflected upon this decision a decade later, Brandon observed that the "Consultation learned that there may be times in the life of the

9. Brandon, "Three Black Methodist Churches," 21.
10. Ibid., 23.
11. Ibid.

Church when in particular situations, it will be necessary to choose between commitments to a particular form of church union and commitments to social justice and change. There may be times when it will be necessary to choose between reconciliation of denominations and reconciliation of races." When faced with the choice between establishing a larger number of new communities that were not inclusive, and a fewer number that were, the Consultation chose the latter, thus confirming its commitment "not to perpetuate the institutional racism of present denominations."[12]

What may not have been apparent at the time was that this action concerning generating communities was one of the steps in the process by which issues related to *institutional racism* came to be a major—and perhaps the dominant—focus of attention in the remaining years of COCU's concerted drive to create a new American church. Furthermore, because this decision decimated COCU's efforts to explore new forms for the church in local communities, other questions and possibilities were largely left unexplored. By default, COCU's new American church would continue the traditional pattern of local congregations. The local forms of these churches would remain unchanged and with many of their problems, including institutional racism, unresolved.

During this same period, Brandon also provided staff coordination of the interim eucharistic fellowships, with fourteen locations on the list that COCU recognized. These gatherings, Brandon reports, were "less formally organized" compared with the generating communities and seemed able to bring people together at a deeper level and contributed toward developing "a greater spirit of cooperation on community issues." Quite apart from issues of race and culture, some of these sacramental gatherings kept alive the classic causes of division because of different understandings of ministry and eucharistic theology. Even when Episcopalians could not "be part of the eucharistic celebration," however, they still could be "devotionally present."[13]

Christian Unity and Racial Justice

The Consultation's major interest in the issues of race, culture, and Christian unity came to its sharpest focus in the work of the commission on institutional racism. It was chaired by William P. Thompson, a formidable Presbyterian ruling elder, who had succeeded Eugene Carson Blake as his church's stated clerk. Thompson told the delegates that the report had been drafted by Robert Lear (who served the Consultation as a communications

12. Ibid., 21–22.
13. Ibid., 24–27.

officer) and the definition of "compensatory action" had been written by Leon Watts of the AMEZ Church. The Cincinnati plenary assembly dedicated an entire day to matters presented by this commission, including an address by Paul Lehmann, professor of theology and ethics at Union Theological Seminary in New York. Lehman insisted that "human renewal is the test case of the renewal of the Church, and in human renewal the Church is renewed." This emphasis, he believed, would help the churches avoid what he called "ecumenical narcissism," which could take two forms: a "preoccupation with structures, with orders, with institutional matters," and a "charismatic movement" which mistakes "enthusiasm for renewal." Although he expressed reservations about some aspects of its work, Lehman declared his reasons for believing that the commission on institutional racism was such an important "aspect of the Church of Christ Uniting and a sign that COCU has begun to come in sight of the obedience of faith."[14]

Summarizing the commission's report, William Thompson noted that institutional racism was not the sole concern of the Consultation but instead was but one of the barriers inhibiting their life together. He called attention to Yoshio Fukuyama's address at the 1973 Memphis plenary assembly, which had led to changing the phrase "compensatory treatment" to "compensatory action," which was to be understood as "two-way." While acknowledging that economic disparity between whites and blacks was a major factor to be addressed, the commission stated that racism had resulted in deprivation in all churches. Because of their experience of deprivation and unjust treatment, black churches had developed understandings of the gospel that were much needed by white churches. Furthermore, the strategies of compensatory action, including distribution of financial resources, needed to be done in ways in which both "majorities and minorities" were involved. As a step in this direction, the commission on institutional racism had selected eight target areas to be the center of attention in the immediate future: colleges and seminaries, curriculum development, church camps, overseas mission, communications, church extension, pensions, and ventures at the local level. The last two pages of the report contained a list of six recommendations for action.

Although many of the delegates supported the evolution of this language in the commission's report, others dissented sharply. In contrast with the cool, administrative prose in the document, the debate recorded in the plenary's minutes was heated and rhetorical. Some of the delegates were insisting that the change in terminology was obscuring the historical fact

14. Lehmann, "The Unity of the Church in the Struggle for Justice," 267.

that the real problem was white racism, the systematic oppression of black people by white people. Compensatory action and the emphasis upon reconciliation as the goal did not take the place of reparations—actual compensation of black people as a way of making up for all that they had been denied. One of the sharpest objections was offered by AME scholar and pastor Charles S. Spivey Jr., who forcefully declared that there was "no such thing" as two-way action. "The black churches have little ability or interest in working the other side of the street. There is no concept in this report of black theology or the black experience in the Christian Church. Where are the white churches who are willing to share their resources with black congregations?"[15]

In their business session dealing with this report, the delegates offered a succession of motions to revise and enlarge the document that they would accept and refer to the churches, giving little weight to Cynthia Wedel's observation that they were developing something that would be impossible to accomplish. Some delegates insisted that issues of power, money, and politics had to be dealt with realistically.

An especially clear expression of the mood of delegates was expressed in an action that would revise the commission's report to take into account these factors: (1)the issue for concern is white racism; (2) the consequence of white racism for the presumed beneficiaries which they must face and for which they need the assistance of the victim of racist practices; (3) the diminution of focus from reparations to "compensatory action" by apparent retreat from the call for restitution—the correction of obvious inequities as manifestations of good intention and commitment as the condition for the "two-way" action called for; and (4) a more explicit explication of what is meant by "joint ministry to overcome racism."[16]

Unfortunately, the spirited discussion and parliamentary process marginalized and overlooked one of the important elements in the written report that the commission on institutional racism had prepared for the plenary gathering—the definition of institutional racism, which it was recommending that the delegates adopt "as a guide for all Consultation activity." It was drafted by one of the commission's members, Leon W. Watts, Jr., a minister in the AMEZ Church, who had received the PhD degee from Union Theological Seminary of New York City, with special emphasis on Black Theology. Immediately following his graduation, he received an

15. Charles Spivey, "Digest of the Twelfth Meeting," *Twelfth Plenary Meeting, Supplement*, 25.

16. "Minutes of the Twelfth Meeting of the Consultation on Church Union," *Digest of the Twelfth Meeting, Supplement*, 40.

appointment as Associate Professor of Theology and Practical Theology at Yale Divinity School where he was to teach for seventeen years.[17]

Institutional Racism: A Definition

In the Consultation on Church Union the phrase "institutional racism" is a conscious attempt to focus upon those structures and policies, implicit and explicit, of the participating denominations which stand over against the unity that we confess and proclaim in the Lord Jesus Christ. The particular focus here is on those practices which exclude or disadvantage on the basis of race. These practices prevent the church from affirming the reconciliation given us in Christ. Since the churches, as will the Church of Christ Uniting, affirm the givenness of that reconciliation, the destruction of institutional racism in all its manifestations is of the highest priority in the Consultation.

To deal with the issue of institutional racism concretely, we have chosen compensatory action (i.e., joint ministry to overcome racism) as the earnest of our life together. In other circumstances compensatory action implies a *one-way* enterprise. However, in this case compensatory action is to be regarded as *two-way*. The *two-way* quality is in the fact that the whole church suffers by the presence of racism in our midst, and the whole church benefits by its elimination. Thus compensatory action is not to be seen as repayment by one part of the church to another, but rather as an attempt by the Consultation to live faithfully the mandate of the Gospel to feed the poor, to give sight to the blind, and to proclaim the good news to those who are oppressed. The barriers erected by racism must be eliminated in order that everyone, everywhere may affirm the Gospel of reconciliation. Compensatory action, then, is one of the means by which we proclaim the Gospel to the good of the whole church.

More specifically, in the context of the Consultation, compensatory action means joint ministry to overcome racism—not in some far off future—but now. Such ministry is proposed to bring the resources of black and white churches alike to bear effectively as remedy for the deprivation which we have all suffered due to racism. The goal of the Consultation is to achieve that inclusiveness which must mark the Church of Christ Uniting.

17. Biographical information comes from http://drleonwwattsiifund.org/biography.html.

Consensus Struggling to Find Expression

The commission on institutional racism was a major new tributary coming into the work of the Consultation on Church Union. The central stream, however, was represented by the commission on theological revision, which had been charged with the responsibility of revising *A Plan of Union*. Chairing this commission was John Deschner, a United Methodist scholar who had done his doctoral studies under Karl Barth and then had come to the faculty of Perkins School of Theology in Dallas, where he focused much of his work on John Wesley. His ecumenical interests were focused in his membership on the Faith and Order Commission of the World Council of Churches.[18] Deschner's sympathy with the new directions that COCU was taking had been made evident in an essay, "Ecclesiological Aspects of the Race Problem," which he had published in *International Review of Mission* in 1970.[19] In acknowledging the widespread interest in issues related to race, Deschner wrote that it was not true "that our theology is sufficient and only our practice at fault . . . A theology capable of speaking only of universal humanity and 'integration' is not yet developed and nuanced enough to shed evangelical light on the race problem which we face today, particularly in the church's own fellowship."

Deschner stated his intention to "demonstrate that the race problem is a faith and order issue at three points, at least: in our understanding of baptism and concrete identity, of the eucharist and a relevant koinonia, and of a flexible yet resilient church order." In baptism, we are renewed in our "racial identities," which are "given their proper place in the universal community of man." More important is that we are "baptized into Christ's identity" and "given a role in Israel's vocation to the nations . . . Henceforth, there is no place for sinful racial pride: there is only place for gratitude in one's 'race' and for racial service, as those indeed who are called to share in His suffering service to the nations." Turning to the Eucharist, Deschner asked, "Can we rightly celebrate the eucharist if our congregation, our ministry, and our liturgy do not visibly manifest the power of Christian unity to reconcile the races? And the practical point is not merely to permit but actively to seek out and facilitate this development."

Deschner criticized the "tight identification of church order and church organization" that characterized the churches of their time. He suggested that they "begin to imagine the kinds of post-denominational

18. In 1975, Deschner became associate moderator and in 1983 moderator of the Commission on Faith and Order of the World Council of Churches. He later chaired the drafting committee that produced *Baptism, Eucharist, and Ministry* (1982).

19. Deschner, "Ecclesiastical Aspects of the Race Problem," 85–95.

diversification and pluralism which must develop if the churches are to be *in* the racial and other struggles of our time." Deschner misjudged the future, however, when he proposed that we "will not move through the coming decade, I think, with these denominational structures intact, and certainly not with the entire apparatus under the initiative and control of 'the church' as at present."

In his statement to the COCU assembly, Deschner reported that the commission had revised chapters I-VII in three ways: they had (1) recast the document in clearer and simpler language and form, (2) responded to theological objections, especially dissatisfaction with the treatment of ministry, the relation of Scripture and tradition, and the way of relating social and spiritual aspects of the plan, and (3) addressed omissions, especially the growing appreciation of the importance of diversity, the recognition of the importance of individual identity and congregational membership, and the need to understand the church-dividing and church-uniting implications of "all whom wealth, privilege, power and color separate." Deschner suggested that the Consultation should be cautious in claiming "an achieved consensus concerning these chapters." Rather, they had "something like a consensus struggling to find expression."[20] He asked that the theology commission's mandate be continued so that it could complete its work of providing a "theological basis for mutual recognition of members and ministries."

Deschner then introduced the commission's recommendation that the Cincinnati plenary approve a new text on the mutual recognition of members and recommend it to their churches for affirmation. This recommendation elicited spirited response from the delegates, in light of which the document was significantly revised and then "accepted" by the COCU assembly. Both versions began with the same lead sentence: "As a witness to the faith that animates our participation in the Consultation on Church Union, we, the ——— Church, confess that all who are baptized into Christ are members of His universal Church and belong to and share in His ministry through the People of God, Father, Son, and Holy Spirit."[21] The commission's draft used this sentence as the springboard for actions that the churches would take in order to begin the process of integrating their respective memberships into a recognizably united body of Christians. It proposed that the churches "pledge" to manifest this membership and ministry in five ways, including more frequent worship together, more effective engagement in mission, and "more determined striving to give greater visible form to the reconciled

20. "Minutes of the Twelfth Meeting," *Digest of the Twelfth Meeting, Supplement,* 13.

21. References to and quotations from the draft statement and the approved document in the following paragraphs are taken from *Digest of the Twelfth Meeting.* The draft statement appears on pp. 50–53 and the approved document on pp. 67–68.

household of God." Then comes an important sentence: "Therefore, we covenant with the other participating churches in the Consultation on Church Union to do everything possible to hasten the day when, together with other churches to whom the Spirit's leading may yet be joined, we all shall be one in a visible fellowship truly catholic, truly evangelical, and truly reformed." The draft statement also lists nine implications of the declaration, wording them as declarations: "Mutual recognition of membership implies . . . "

During the debate, the delegates changed the character of the document, replacing the emphasis upon action with instructions for continued study of what was meant by the mutual recognition of members. The significant shift was evident when the two titles are compared. Whereas the commission's title had been "A *Declaration* of Mutual Recognition of Members," the title of the document that the plenary approved was "*Toward* the Mutual Recognition of Members: An *Affirmation*" (italics added).

The revised and approved document features a section with the heading "An Inquiry about the Implications of This Affirmation," which leads with this sentence: "The Consultation on Church Union believes that the commitment to seek mutual recognition of membership can be a new and creative ecumenical step if each affirming church undertakes an inquiry into the implications of the affirmation, and shares its findings with the other churches in the Consultation." It proposes nine questions intended to "open this inquiry," among which three are especially significant. Question three suggests that mutual recognition of members would mean that "at each celebration of His Eucharistic supper, our Lord's invitation and hospitality are extended to all who, baptized and repentant, draw near with faith." Question five suggests that mutual recognition of membership implies "a new obligation to explore the new possibilities for mutual recognition of the ordained and licensed ministries of both men and women." Questions seven and eight propose the importance of developing "a richer ethnic, cultural and other diversity in our congregations and traditions" and increased efforts to deal with racial and social injustice in the world.

Both versions of the statements on mutual recognition propose a series of actions, and here again, the tone is significantly different. The draft statement recommends that the churches be asked to approve this document "as a commitment . . . to the other participating churches," the result of which would be participation in "a national ecumenical service of mutual recognition of members." In sharp contrast, the adopted statement drops all references to services of reconciliation of members and places full emphasis upon asking each church "to undertake a serious inquiry into the implications of its own affirmation, and to share its findings with the other churches in the Consultation."

This debate may well have been one of the most important in COCU's extended effort to bring about church unity, because it was testing an assertion that was the foundation for their work—that each church recognized the other churches as authentic manifestations of the one, holy, catholic, and apostolic church. If they really believed this, then it would have been possible to recognize one another's members as fully Christian and to modify their ecclesiastical disciplines in order to let this reality be expressed. The hesitation to extend this recognition and to revise internal processes was a sign that that the assertion was only partially true.

The Unity Revival

Despite the caution that the delegates displayed in their handling of the proposal concerning the recognition of members, the fourteenth meeting of the Consultation concluded with a new burst of energy. At its beginning this assembly may have been marked by "the pragmatic flavor of a large denominational board," but by its closing the "fervor for church union took hold of the hearers with cumulative force. Someone said later it was the first 'unity revival' we had ever had at a COCU plenary; all that was lacking was sawdust on the floor. If someone had given an altar call, the aisles would have been crowded."[22]

This renewal of ecumenical passion had been generated, in part, by the interpretive addresses delivered during the assembly. Paul Crow described what he called "the ecology of church union," certain facts which if rightly handled could "liberate our churches to discover that union which the Gospel requires."[23] Collaboration, useful as it might be, was not a substitute for Christian unity because it obscured the focus on Christian community, which was the goal of union in Christ. After describing the "human crisis of staggering proportion" in which they were living, Crow reiterated the vision that had long been at COCU's heart: the "overriding issue of our time is not the survival of our institutions but the survival of the human race on this planet." Referring to the crisis "which looms in America today," he declared that "a united and renewed church is urgently needed in America in order to speak effectively to this moral and historical crisis."

The interdependence of unity and mission was vigorously reasserted by John Satterwhite, COCU's new associate general secretary. "A theology of social redemption is the task of our divided churches," Satterwhite declared, "and it is a responsibility of the COCU process as a repository of nine great

22. Osborn, "Moving Yet and Never Stopping," 205.
23. Crow, "Living Our Way Toward Union," 217ff.

spiritual traditions to see that injustices and oppressions are understood by all church persons." It would not be enough, however, for the Consultation to continue talking about justice and liberation. The churches needed to enter directly into the struggles in order to bring about justice and liberation. "[We] have been commanded to enter into the sufferings of Christ in this world, for behind that Cross, we believe, is the victory of the resurrection."[24]

The climax in the series of revival speeches was the address by COCU's new general secretary. "You might think you are hearing a sermon," Gerald Moede told delegates, and "for this I make no apology." His plan was to "commend organic union as a model of Christian unity" and to share his "dreams of the place of the Consultation within the ecumenical movement," all within the context of New Testament ideas. "What kind of unity does our Lord want us to have?" Moede asked:

> Must it not be unity "in the Apostles' teaching and fellowship, in the breaking of bread and the prayers"—a full unity in faith, in commitment to one another, in worship, in life, all centered in the bread broken together and the cup shared, the communion of the body and Blood of Christ? . . . As long as churches live apart (even if they belong to the same Council or are in full communion with one another) sacramental sharing continues to be the exception rather than the rule; the mutual forgiveness and renewed fellowship that stem from the week-by-week gathering of the people around word and sacrament simply do not occur. Cooperation at all levels among churches is a very positive development, but insofar as it leaves untouched basic issues by which the Church lives its life (faith, worship, sacraments, congregational fellowship) it can not solve the basic problems existing between the churches."[25]

Moede was clear that "our American dependence on, and fascination with, success, wealth, size, fame, and ability-to-do will make this vision difficult to embody." The churches' ability to contend with racism in American society requires that they give further consideration to theological and ecclesial issues such as the relation of liberation and church unity, the "nature of Christian identity conferred in Christian baptism," and the relation of justice to eucharistic fellowship. "The Lord's Supper has traditionally represented the place of reconciliation in the church. But since it has become one of the most obvious places of separation, we have to make a special effort to deal with it holistically." This process, Moede acknowledged, will

24. Satterwhite, "Church Union for Justice and Liberation, 250–56.
25. Moede, "Called Together," 230–31.

include fear and conflict. "But Jesus accepted the necessity of conflict, and yet transcended it on the Cross. He took on himself the cost of conflict. Thus conflicting forces can be overcome in the unity he gives, since he is leading all things to unity in himself."

Delegates to the 1974 Cincinnati plenary assembly may have come as good-spirited but weary church workers ready to do their work with dutiful efficiency, but Moede's sermonic address propelled them back to their ecumenical labors with renewed hope for their churches and the world.

11

The COCU Consensus: In Quest of a Church of Christ Uniting

A sufficient theological basis for covenanting acts
and the uniting process . . .

—SIXTEENTH PLENARY ASSEMBLY

THE "UNITY REVIVAL" MANIFESTED in the 1974 plenary assembly under-girded ecumenical activities of the COCU churches during the next few months and shaped an active docket of work for the Consultation when it gathered for its thirteenth plenary assembly at the Bergamo Conference Center near Dayton, Ohio (November 3–6, 1976). The Consultation's sense of progress was confirmed by the decision of the National Council of Community Churches to become a participating church. This communion was the result a union in 1950 of two fellowships in the Community Church movement and at the time was described as the largest interracial merger of religious bodies in America.[1] Some time after joining the Consultation on Church Union, the church changed its name to International Council of Community Churches.

The Consultation's commissions and task forces (generating communities, interim eucharistic fellowships, institutional racism, women, middle judicatory concerns, and a new commission on persons with disabilities) reported progress in their explorations and activities. COCU was making

1. Http://www.icccusa.com/default.cfm/PID=1.13.

serious efforts to develop new attitudes and practices for churches and their members concerning the issues and opportunities facing the nation.

An imaginative expression of the churches' desire to move closer to one another was the launching of a new COCU-sponsored publication, a Lenten booklet entitled *Liberation and Unity: A Guide for Meditation and Action*.[2] The Consultation was joined in this project by the three black churches, and Associate General Secretary John H. Satterwhite managed the project. The booklet provided a one-page devotional statement for each day in Lent, with more than 50 black pastors and church workers contributing to the project. Publishing the Lenten manual on behalf of the Consultation was the Department of Education of the Christian Methodist Episcopal Church in Memphis. A review of the first issue, published in *Theology Today*, described the meditations as "of uniformly high quality, spiritually sensitive, biblically based, and centered in the classic Christian theological traditions." This review also called attention to two additional features: "the connection between the devotional life and social justice" and "a confessed concern to relate both Lent and Black Theology to church unity."[3]

In 1978 the Consultation's Commission on Worship published *Word, Bread, Cup*, a small manual focused on celebrating the Lord's Supper. It acknowledged the importance of liturgical resources that would be more flexible than those in *An Order of Worship* (published in 1968).[4] The introduction referred to "[r]acial and ethnic minorities, youth and young adult cultures, charismatic and other evangelical movements, the human potential movement, the influence of Eastern religions and cultures, and authentic American folk traditions " as contributors to the new pluralism of the times.[5] Rather than presenting a liturgy as had the earlier publication, this booklet provided a commentary on "the shape of the service," guidelines for developing services, and "illustrative texts." The intention for the publication was "to show both our underlying unity of liturgical form and our rich diversity of expression, both our agreements and our differences."[6] Although *Word, Bread, Cup* represented modest developments in the decade since *An Order of Worship* had been published, it expressed little of the diversity that was described in the introductory statement.

2. *Liberation and Action* continued as an annual publication until the final issue in 2002.

3. "Meditation for Maundy Thursday," 368.

4. The Commission on Worship insisted that the title of this publication be printed in all capital letters and with no punctuation.

5. Commission on Worship, *Word, Bread, Cup*, 4.

6. Ibid., 5.

Actual progress toward the goal of becoming a uniting church was more clearly expressed by the report that eight of the nine COCU churches had accepted the document concerning the mutual recognition of members that the 1974 plenary assembly had approved. In light of these reports, COCU's Executive Committee recommended that the Dayton assembly authorize a consultation on the implications of the mutual recognition of baptism and membership. This consultation was convened two years later (on January 23, 1978) in Fort Worth, Texas.

In preparation for the Fort Worth consultation, Gerald Moede prepared an extended document entitled "Ecumenical Pressure and the Mutual Recognition of Baptism/Membership." His purpose was "to study the findings [on mutual recognition of baptism and membership] thus far revealed, and to ask what these findings imply for the future, to nurture and develop whatever implications have been identified, with the goal in view of bringing the churches to *act* on the insights emerging."[7] Moede described two classic types of the church that had come together in the North American context. In the *church type,* persons were born into citizenship in the political realm and into membership in the one church that was allied with the nation. In the *sect type*, churches were voluntary associations in which the life of the church depended upon the personal service and cooperation of members.

What had emerged, especially in America where freedom of religion is a basic principle, was the *denomination* with characteristics that were drawn from both church and sect models. In some respects, Moede observed, the denomination combines the weakness of each of its predecessors. In all of the COCU churches, he concluded, vestiges of church-type and sect-type remain. Denominations have become more "ecclesiocentric than christocentric" and they have reached an impasse in which they can agree on theology but remain separated because of organizational issues. Drawing upon the language of Catholic theologian Avery Dulles, Moede wrote that the "Church is a manifold entity; it contains both mystical and societal elements; *koinonia* always exists in the form of a *politeia.* What the recognition of baptism/members intends to do is open up what have become exclusive polities by agreeing that we are truly members one of another, based upon our baptism."[8] The challenge is to find a way to be faithful to our communion in the one body of Christ that exists always and everywhere, the body into which we were incorporated by our baptism, without having to deny the variant of Christ's body in which we live. "To find a way of 'double belonging'! This is the need that [mutual recognition of baptism/member-

---

7. Moede, "Ecumenical Pressure," 246.
8. Ibid.

ship] addresses." It could be enabled by joint confirmation services, dual membership, ecumenical baptisms, transformed liturgical rites, simultaneous membership in several congregations, and intermingling of juridical and bureaucratic systems of the churches.

Similar ideas were at work in the commission on worship, which in 1980 published two new liturgies related to baptism and initiation into the church's life. *An Order of Thanksgiving for the Birth or Adoption of a Child* was designed to be used on various occasions related to infancy. In the Preface to the second liturgy, *An Affirmation of the Baptismal Covenant (also called Confirmation),* Moede stated that it could be used on various occasions including common services "in which the young people publicly affirm their faith together, with bishops, or presiding ministers all joining together in the laying on of hands . . . Such 'mingling of members' seems particularly appropriate since each of the churches in the Consultation has accepted the baptism/members of the others."[9]

The First Revision of Chapters I–VII

The most important work of the Dayton plenary assembly was the revision of the theological chapters of *A Plan of Union.* Reporting for the commission given this task was United Methodist theologian John Deschner, who told delegates that the commission had recast the document in clearer and simpler language and form. More important, it had responded to theological objections, especially dissatisfaction with the treatment of ministry, the relation of Scripture and Tradition, and the way of relating social and spiritual aspects of the plan. It had also addressed omissions, especially the growing appreciation of the importance of diversity, the recognition of the importance of individual identity and congregational membership, and the need to understand the church-dividing and church-uniting implications of "all whom wealth, privilege, power and color separate." They had succeeded in making the document shorter, moving from 20,000 words in *A Plan of Union* to 16,500 words in the proposed revision. Deschner concluded his report by explaining that the churches would be asked to approve the statement and consider whether they were "willing to gather around this basis" in order to "develop the implications of the mutual recognition of membership, . . . work toward a mutual recognition of ministries, . . . and to create a revised plan of union for a Church of Christ Uniting."[10]

9. Commission on Worship, *An Order for an Affirmation of the Baptismal Covenant,* preface.

10. Deschner, "A Theological Basis," 23–29.

He explained that the commission had sought to give greater clarity to the ministry of the whole people of God. Furthermore, the document was seeking to bring together the historic episcopate and a constitutional and reformable episcopacy. The undertone of conversation at the plenary, however, indicated that the revised language concerning the ministry was not well received by some of the delegates. Acknowledging their discontent, the delegations of the two Presbyterian churches spent an evening discussing the issues that had come to the surface and subsequently made a joint statement to the assembly, affirming that "we are fully committed to the episcopate as an order of ministry in a form still to be defined by the Consultation on Church Union. This has been our constant position since the adoption [in Dallas in 1966] of the *Principles of Church Union.*"[11] A potential crisis on ministry, Gerald Moede later wrote, had been averted.[12]

Discussion and debate concerning the draft revision of *A Plan of Union* dominated the assembly. Moede noted that more than 500 written suggestions were received and worked through at the meeting. Many of them were debated in plenary sessions, some were incorporated as editorial revisions, and some were saved for future work.[13] At the close of debate on the commission's draft revision, the Dayton plenary assembly adopted a resolution stating that it "commends the document, *In Quest of a Church of Christ Uniting,* to the participating churches with the request that it be received as a statement of emerging theological consensus for study and response, and for guidance in furthering the mutual recognition of members and working toward mutual recognition of ministers."[14]

The plenary asked that the appropriate bodies in each of the churches send to the COCU offices "any suggestions, proposed revisions, additions or deletions to Chapter VII (on the ministry) which that church recommends." The date by which these responses were to be received was November 1977. One by one, the churches responded, but not until early 1979, two and a half years after the revised draft had been released, could the Consultation hold a plenary assembly to consider the reports from the churches. This they did in their fourteenth meeting, in Cincinnati on March 6–9, 1979. All of the churches except for the Christian Methodist Episcopal Church had submitted reports, which varied in length, from three pages to thirty-five

---

11. *Digest of the Thirteenth Plenary Meeting of COCU*, 58.

12. Moede, "The Consultation on Church Union," 10.

13. Ibid., 7.

14. *Digest of the Thirteenth Meeting*, 51.

pages, and in character, from succinct summaries of the church's considered opinion to point-by-point comments on the entire text.[15]

Each church reviewed the consensus statement from the perspective of its own tradition, which it valued and believed could contribute constructively to the uniting church. The AMEZ statement illustrated this church-centered position: "The African Methodist Episcopal Zion Church . . . holds herself as a model for inclusiveness, void of racial, sexual, and denominational bias albeit, not in practice, the ideals are set before us as goals to be achieved."[16] Less evident in the church responses are acknowledgments that their respective traditions were insufficient at some point and needed the contributions that would be brought from other traditions that would be part of the union. Even less evident is any acknowledgment that the churches believed that *In Quest* offered the basis for creating a stronger church than any of the participating churches could be on its own. There is an undertone of waning interest in the union effort, which the AME report stated clearly: "This response from the A.M.E. Church to 'an emerging theological consensus' is really a last-ditch effort to be faithful to its involvement in the Consultation on Church Union." The theological consensus needed to "be inclusive of 'Liberation Theology,' and not overwhelmingly influenced by European thought."[17]

The reports made it clear that one of COCU's central principles was in trouble—the principle that the uniting church would accept the fact of the historic episcopate and be a church with such a ministry but that no theological explanation would be given or required. The Episcopal Church stated that the catholic principle required more than the fact of ordination by bishops in apostolic succession. The sacramental character of the bishop, as distinguished from administrative function, had to be maintained, and the bishop's necessary functions in the church had to include confirmation in addition to ordination. Methodist churches focused attention on the necessity of the very administrative practices that the Episcopal response denigrated.

The joint Presbyterian report came close to rejecting agreements about the episcopal office that had been part of the Consultation's plan from the beginning. Their document stated that "the episcopal character of the presbytery" might well be respected in a form of unity, which would maintain

---

15. "Responses to *In Quest of a Church of Christ Uniting*," published as Part IV of *Digest of the Fifteenth Meeting*, 201–98.

16. Ibid., 206.

17. Ibid., 203.

freedom and diversity in the Church.[18] Their report cited "two main concerns" that were present in the majority of all-Presbyterian study groups. "(1) Why have union anyway? We have nice relations with other denominations and isn't unity in the spirit the important thing? (2) Save us from bishops and a hierarchy of command; we thought we got away from Rome."[19]

Reservations concerning the office of bishop also came from churches with congregational polity—the Christian Church (Disciples of Christ), National Council of Community Churches, and the United Church of Christ. Some segments of these churches were willing to accept the ministry of bishops, but only within a context in which this ministry was grounded in an understanding of the church in which presbyters, elders, and laity were important modes of leadership in ecclesial affairs. These churches were uneasy about hierarchical control by bishops and the loss of meaningful participation in church governance by conferences, presbyteries, and congregations. Some respondents were convinced that episcopal and congregational forms of governance were incompatible and they were unwilling to give up their free-church way of life and accept a bishop-led pattern of church organization.

The responses to provisions for worship, sacraments, and creeds differed widely. Disciples and Episcopalians, who were polar opposites in some ways, seemed much alike in their serious regard for classic theologies of Eucharist and Baptism. Both were interested in affirming the importance of the long tradition of the Church as a primary factor in shaping the continuing practice of the church. The Episcopal response assumed that its practice already was consistent with the tradition and that its responsibility was to assure that COCU preserved the necessary elements of catholicity. In contrast, Disciples discussed ways in which their own doctrine and practice either were consistent with or in contrast to the grand tradition. They saw the provisions of *In Quest* as challenges that could lead to new understanding and practice. With respect to the historic creeds, Episcopalians insisted that they must be understood to be authoritative, while Disciples indicated a readiness to use creeds liturgically and as teaching instruments.

There was general agreement that the "church dividing issues" related to race, gender, and social status, now labeled "theological alerts" had to be understood as theological issues along side of the traditional issues of ecclesiology and sacramental theology. Yet, the churches were only in the early stages of recognizing the implications of this redefinition or believing that this theologizing of the alerts would be sufficient to transform the character

18. Ibid, 252.
19. Ibid., 240.

of their churches or of American life. More work would have to be done on the alerts to give these issues their place in shaping a new church.

Although the responses indicated that the structure of the new church would have to become something different from what had originally been proposed, there was little indication as to what that new form might be. The one clear statement was provided by the Episcopal Church when it included the text of a resolution that had been adopted by its 1979 General Convention. In brief, the statement declared that the "visible unity we seek will be one eucharistic fellowship" and the uniting church "will recognize itself as a communion of Communions, based upon acknowledgment of catholicity and apostolicity." Beyond this core, the Episcopal Church could "not yet see" the shape of collegiality or other factors that would mark this communion of Communions. One result of this statement, according to William A. Norgren, assistant ecumenical officer of the Episcopal Church, was that it "gets the superchurch idea off our backs. It relieves the Churches of having to create one organization and concentrate on the dialogues and the sharing that can be built." [20]

The Second Revision: A Consensus Near at Hand

At this critical moment in COCU's history, a reconstituted theology commission took up the work. John Deschner had stepped down as chair of the commission, in part because of his increasingly prominent role in the Commission on Faith and Order of the World Council of Churches. Appointed to be his successor was Lewis S. Mudge, a theologian from a prominent Presbyterian family. From his teaching post at Amherst College, he had been called to be the dean at San Francisco Theological Seminary, in San Anselmo, California. [21] The membership of the commission also was changing. New members included persons who were unfamiliar with COCU's quest and others who seemed as interested in reaffirming their own church's identity as they were in revising a document that would transcend denominational particularity. Weekends of "relationship-building" had to be added to the commission's schedule. [22]

20. The text of the resolution plus extended discussion of the convention setting where it was adopted are contained in a document entitled "Nature of the Unity We Seek 1979." Norgren's second sentence would read better if it were expanded with the words "and allows them to concentrate . . ." Episcopal News Service: Press Release #79198 (http://www.episcopalarchives.org/cgi-bin/ENS/ENSpress_release.pl?pr_number=79198).

21. Online obituary notice: http://www.ncccusa.org/news/090916lewmudge.html.

22. James O. Duke, pers. comm.

It easily could have been assumed that at this stage in the Consultation's life the theology commission's task was clear and relatively straightforward: to revise theological material on which the churches were already largely agreed, and to complete a document on which the churches would move forward to create a new American church. A more realistic assessment, however, would develop during the next four years when the theology commission did its most concentrated work. The cautious responses to the Deschner-led commission's initiative concerning the mutual recognition of membership could have been interpreted as signs of passive resistance among the churches. Under Mudge's leadership, the commission would have to analyze the responses, identify the factors that these churches were resisting, and restate the theological consensus in ways that would lead to action by the churches.

Another challenge for the commission was to take into account the continuing theological discussion among churches around the world. A major element in the new ecumenism was the expanding series of bilateral conversations in which churches were addressing theological issues that long had separated them from one another. Foremost among them were the bilateral conversations of the Catholic Church with representatives of church families around the world, including churches of the Consultation. A similar pattern developed between other church traditions, including Lutherans with Reformed and with Anglicans (Episcopalians), and Anglicans with Orthodox.[23] The bilaterals explored a wide range of theological topics. Some of them dealt with long-standing doctrinal causes of division, such as justification by faith. Other topics were understandings and practices of the church, ministry, and sacraments.

In these conversations representatives of the churches sought to find areas of theological agreement and to define as carefully as possible where agreement had not yet been reached. COCU's theology commission, however, carried a responsibility that the bilaterals did not, which was to provide a way for the churches to move from agreement to union. The bilaterals required time, energy, and financial resources, which the participating churches had to bear, and this in a period of diminishing strength. The burden of this challenge affected COCU's executive committee and made it

---

23. A comprehensive collection of papers from bilateral conversations is deposited in the Burke Library Archives, Columbia University Libraries, Union Theological Seminary, under the title "American Bilateral Conversation Records, 1932–1975" http://library.columbia.edu/content/dam/libraryweb/locations/burke/fa/wab/ldpd_4492686.pdf.

increasingly difficult for this committee "to coordinate the various tentacles and initiatives of the enterprise" that COCU had become.[24]

Another aspect of ecumenical theological engagement was of more immediate importance to the theology commission: the agreements that the Commission on Faith and Order of the World Council of Churches was bringing together as the culmination of a fifty-year period of intense theological discussion among churches of the world. Documents of major importance were being prepared for discussion at Faith and Order's meeting in Lima, Peru, in 1982, after which they would be published with the title *Baptism, Eucharist and Ministry* (often referred to as *BEM*). The purpose for the emerging ecumenical document was not to provide detailed theological discussions of the topics it treated. Instead, it concentrated attention "on those aspects of the theme that have been directly or indirectly related to the problems of mutual recognition leading to unity." Some churches, such as the Roman Catholic, that were not members of the World Council were, however, members of the Commission on Faith and Order, which gave *BEM* a remarkably comprehensive character. COCU's theology commission "deliberately tracked the responses" of the churches to *BEM* and to other unity dialogues. "It was generally, tacitly, agreed that nothing was to be contrary to Faith and Order ecumenical agreements. New (our own) proposals, if any, would—or should—press to take advantage of openings and initiatives of most ecumenical promise in current discussion."[25]

An increasingly important aspect of the theology commission's docket of work was continued theological redefinition of topics that earlier periods of ecumenical endeavor had described as "church-dividing" issues. The title of one of the most important books in the opening years of the twentieth century—*The Social Sources of Denominationalism* by H. Richard Niebuhr—had made the point, that factors such as place of origin, social standing, class, ethnicity, and race clearly separated people into distinct and sometimes antagonistic churches. Consistently, these factors had been understood as non-theological rather than theological. Theology, according to the prevailing understanding, dealt with factors such as the ministry, sacraments, and church order. With increasing forcefulness, however, COCU's task forces and working groups had been pushing to a new level of understanding. Rather than being elements of custom and social structure, these divisions contradicted theological understandings of humanity in general and of the church in particular. Furthermore, some of COCU's seminal theological studies and addresses had been exploring this kind of

24. James O. Duke, pers. comm.
25. Ibid.

theological redefinition. What remained to be done, however, was a two-fold task: to rewrite the theological consensus so that the alerts were now incorporated as factors fully parallel with other factors long understood to be theological; and to present these new understandings in such a way that the churches would be led to act upon them.

Fortunately, the commission members were basically agreed. James O. Duke, a Disciples member of the commission, writes that "although time-consuming . . . revising the whole document in light of the alerts was a welcome and quite readily-handled task." The greater challenge facing the Consultation as a whole "was the question of whether the churches would ever live up to their theological commitments in actual practice."[26]

In his first report to a COCU plenary assembly, at its fourteenth meeting in Cincinnati (March 6-9, 1979), Mudge acknowledged that much work would have to be done in order to accommodate the churches' concerns as expressed in their responses to the revised document. Even so, he insisted, the consensus the churches thought they had achieved was not in danger. While some revising could be worked on soon, other sections of the work would have to be done in concert with other COCU entities, especially the commission on church order. Mudge noted that there were "a number of divergent proposals for altering the emphasis of the document, and to help delegates understand this aspect of their task he offered three "sample issues" as illustrations. [27]

The first question was how they should incorporate matters related to "Discipline, Orthopraxy, and the 'Alerts.'" Should the commission bring into "the main text of the consensus our convictions about the potentially church-dividing issues of racism, sexism, institutionalism and congregational exclusivism?" Support for doing so was provided by reports to the plenary assembly from the task force of persons with disabilities and the women's task force. Writing for the women's task force, United Methodist executive Jeanne Audrey Powers stated that "it was indisputable to participants" in the conference that issues of language were now in the forefront not only in the work of feminists but of "leading creative theologians (both male and female) who believe that 'God-talk, the essence of their discipline,' is crucial to how they reflect on our faith. She also stated that "the Consultation on Church Union provided the first arena for this encounter to take place *across denominations* and that it was centered totally in the issue of the

26. Ibid.

27. Mudge, "Report of the Theology Commission," *Digest of the Fourteenth Meeting*, 177–97.

unity of the Church as the Church speaks its own faith through the liturgy marked a major advance for our churches as a whole."[28]

Mudge's second sample issue was the fact that the churches appeared to hold two views of ministry. The issue, he proposed, was not so much a matter of polity but of the mindset that people bring to the debate. One approach begins with "the constitutional structure in which ministry operates" and deals with matters of power and decision-making. The other approach begins with the personal charisma or sacramentality of the minister, and here questions arise about "how the minister represents, images, or enacts the truth or reality out of which the church lives." Because the functions of ministers were directly connected to matters of polity that were assigned to COCU's commission on church order, it was clearly understood that revisions of Chapter VII would take place in close coordination with that commission. Mudge summarized the third sample issue within the churches' responses with these questions: "What is meant by 'Sufficient Agreement'? Agreement on What?"

The theology commission had already done a significant body of work in order to revise *In Quest,* and its report to the Cincinnati meeting included a 23-page redraft of Chapter VII on the ministry, which it offered as "an illustration of the commission's thinking" and "a promise of what might be achieved with another two years of theological labor." Unexpectedly, all ten churches and the discussion groups responded favorably to the draft. Momentum developed in the denominational caucuses and the COCU executive committee to "accelerate the process." Instead of waiting until 1981 or 1982 to complete the draft, the assembly decided, it would hold an adjourned session only a few months later to consider a further revision of Chapter VII. As soon as that chapter could be completed, the consensus statement in its entirety would be "sent to the churches as a theological basis for the future stages toward a united and uniting church."

"By this action at Cincinnati in 1979," Paul Crow reported, "COCU's work and expectations [were] accelerated and a new surge of enthusiasm [was] evident among the delegates and the churches." He placed this decision in the context of international bilateral conversations between churches, such as Anglicans and Roman Catholics, and the Commission on Faith and Order of the World Council of Churches. A "consensus on ministry and other theological issues is near at hand. Indeed, we already have enough agreement to justify far more unity than we have yet expressed in COCU or elsewhere."[29]

28. *Digest of the Fourteenth Meeting, First Session,* 198.
29. Crow, "COCU and the Sparks of the Spirit."

Adoption of the theological basis for unity

Ten months later, January 22-24, 1980, COCU delegates reassembled in Cincinnati for the adjourned session of the fourteenth plenary assembly. Although their primary task was to consider the revised draft on ministry, they devoted part of their time to commemorating COCU's beginning two decades earlier. In his summary of the Consultation's history, James I. McCord expressed his hope that the anticipated agreement on ministry would be a landmark for the ecumenical movement everywhere."[30] In his reflections on his sermon that had launched the Consultation, Eugene Carson Blake told the assembly that he had included the episcopacy in his proposal not only for the benefit of the Episcopal Church but because he was hoping for an even wider union. He quoted from a statement that the World Presbyterian Alliance had issued in 1959 at the four hundredth anniversary of Calvinism. This worldwide body extended an invitation "to all who would, with us, put their traditions and systems under the judgment of Christ, seeking his correction, and ready to relinquish what he does not approve." Presbyterian and Reformed churches were ready to lay on the altar "all that we claim" for our churches. "With the whole Church we hold ourselves alert for the surprises . . . and new forms with which an eternally recreating God can startle us while he secures his Church."[31]

The primary purpose of the adjourned session was to examine a revised draft of chapter VII on the ministry. The Theology Commission had provided the text, which delegates debated at length, both in denominational meetings and in plenary assembly. By the end of their gathering, they reached agreement and adopted a resolution that commended Chapter VII on the Ministry, along with Chapters I through VI, to the participating churches "with the request that it be received for study and response as a statement of emerging theological consensus and for guidance for furthering the mutual recognition of ministers." The resolution asked the churches to submit "proposed revisions, additions, or deletions" by December 31, 1981, which gave them nearly two years to examine the document.

The revised draft included a preamble in which the Consultation carefully stated the limited character of the consensus that had been achieved, especially in reference to the ministry. "The understanding of ministry here proposed does not presuppose that our goal must be pursued in a particular manner, nor that the unity we seek must take a particular form. Rather, maintaining both diversity and freedom within the perspectives outlined

30. McCord, "How We Began," *Digest of the Fourteenth Meeting,* 7.
31. Blake as quoted by Moede in *The Consultation on Church Union,* 18.

here, we seek together to enter fully and organically into God's promise of covenant faithfulness to the one People of God in each place, searching for the form or forms of church life which will be most faithful to that calling."[32]

During the adjourned session, the delegates continued their efforts to define the process of covenanting that would provide the process leading to visible union and characterize the nature of the new church. They also focused attention on the issues under study by commissions and task forces dealing with generating communities, interim eucharistic fellowships, persons with disabilities, the place of women in the church, and worship.

Despite the evidences that the theological document was coming together in a way that the churches could affirm, it took two more tries to complete the process. At the Consultation's fifteenth plenary assembly in Louisville (March 7-12, 1982), Lewis Mudge reported that most of the traditional theological disagreements, even those dealing with ministry, had been bridged. They still were seeking to incorporate the issues that the Consultation now had added to its list of theological issues, matters dealing with race, gender, power, and physical condition. "We must show," the theology commission's report stated, "that belief is so directly articulated by conduct that right conduct and right belief must be understood as two aspects of one reality."[33]

These processes came together in the Consultation's sixteenth plenary assembly, which met in Baltimore, Maryland, November 26-30, 1984. At this meeting, the delegates' intentions are clearly stated in prefatory statements by Gerald F. Moede, COCU's general secretary, and Lewis S. Mudge, chair of the theology commission. The document's three-page "Forward" offers still another explanation of how the 55-page final draft should be understood. This document represented the churches' determination to be faithful to the biblical injunction that Christians should be of one mind and spirit. It was noted that the twenty-two year process that had led to this consensus statement was paralleled in the larger Christian world by discussions that had led the Faith and Order Commission of the World Council of Churches to develop *Baptism, Eucharist and Ministry*. Although the COCU materials do not mention the fact, John Deschner, who had chaired COCU's theology commission during the first revision of Chapters I-VII, had carried major responsibility for developing Faith and Order's document. Furthermore, Lewis Mudge had served simultaneously on the COCU and Faith and Order commissions.

32. *Digest of Fourteenth Meeting*, 38.
33. *Digest of the Fifteenth Meeting*, 78.

Despite the significant amount of work the theology commission had done to revise and perfect this document, delegates to the assembly continued the process, discussing and revising the draft during business sessions on Tuesday and Wednesday mornings and Thursday afternoon. On Friday morning, the last session of the assembly, delegates continued to work on this document, dealing with minor editorial suggestions, questions for clarification, and proposals for revisions of meaning. Discussion of the draft came to its conclusion when George M. Pike, president of the Consultation, read the proposed resolution of transmittal:

> RESOLVED: that the 16th Plenary of the Consultation on Church Union approves this text and asks the participating churches, by formal action, to recognize in it
>
> 1) an expression, in the matters with which it deals, of the Apostolic faith, order, worship, and witness of the Church,
>
> 2) an anticipation of the Church Uniting which the participating bodies, by the power of the Holy Spirit, wish to become, and
>
> 3) a sufficient theological basis for the covenanting acts and the uniting process proposed at this time by the Consultation.[34]

Pike called for a roll call by delegations. Each of the nine participation churches voted *yes*. The minutes record that the vote of the Christian Church (Disciples of Christ) was announced by the youngest member of the delegation and that the vote of the Episcopal Church included "additional comments about ordination." George Pike declared that the vote was unanimous and the resolution was adopted. "The Plenary began singing 'Amen, Amen.' Following the passing of the peace and the embracing of many delegates, Gerald Moede led in singing "Now Thank We All Our God."[35]

> Now thank we all our God With heart and hands and voices,
>
> Who wondrous things hath done, In whom His world rejoices;
>
> Who from our mothers' arms, Hath blessed us on our way
>
> With countless gifts of love, And still is ours today.

After twenty-two years of work, representatives of nine Protestant churches historically representing the central core of American culture and public life stood united on a theological foundation that they earnestly

34. Consultation on Church Union, *COCU Consensus*, 2.

35. "Minutes," *Digest of the Sixteenth Meeting*, 89.

hoped their churches would claim. The hymn, often sung in all of their churches, expressed a joyful sense of past achievement and future promise. The positive action concerning their theological consensus, however, had been possible only because of the work being done at the same time under the leadership of COCU's commission on church order and the commission on worship. Even with their agreement on theology, the churches still had to solve the issues related to the form that this new form of Christian unity would take, and here these commissions were pointing in a new direction.

COCU at the Turning Point

One person who clearly understood the change that was taking place among the COCU churches was John Deschner, former chair of the theology commission. He began his address to the Baltimore Assembly by declaring that "there is no other place in American Christianity where the ecumenical situation of the churches is so clearly visible, and the hope of the churches so patiently and creatively cared for as in this Consultation." This meeting marked a turning point in three ways, Deschner continued. For twenty-five years, COCU had been "the delegated center" for thinking about the formation of a uniting church. By approving the theological consensus, the Consultation had placed that responsibility back upon the churches. They had shifted from an external ecumenism to an internal ecumenism, from "a COCU-centered to a church-centered next step in the quest for a Church of Christ Uniting."[36]

The churches were turning away from COCU and toward one another. "The way ahead is not a decision of each church about COCU, but about the other churches: Does our church recognize the ministries of the other *churches* as apostolic? Does COCU's work help our church acknowledge the other *churches* as 'authentic parts of the One, Holy, Catholic and Apostolic Church of Jesus Christ?'" The third aspect of this turning point was that the churches were being asked to adopt a greater seriousness in their endeavor. Henceforth, they would be asked not to consult and cooperate with one another but to covenant to create a new kind of union. Deschner's metaphor was that COCU had served as the marriage broker. "It has even drafted out for them how to pop the question. An engagement ring is the next step, and that has to happen between the churches."

Deschner then reinforced two distinctive aspects of COCU's work by placing it in the world context. Although the "catholic" constituency in the Consultation was small, in world Christianity "well over two-thirds of

36. Deschner, "COCU at the Turning Point," 21–30.

the Christian community" are part of "catholicism" spelled with a small "c." COCU was declaring that each church and the new united church that would emerge all had to become truly catholic, truly evangelical and truly reformed. The North American character of the Consultation also placed the Consultation in a minority position since a majority of the world's Christians "now live in the Third World, where the concern for justice and liberation, not the traditions of Europe and America dominate the scene." Without the "Alerts," the issues of justice that had become part of COCU's theological concern, the Consultation's activities and documents would be "irrelevant to the cause of church unity today and tomorrow."

During its twenty-five-year history, the Consultation had accomplished significant work, Deschner continued, which he summarized under five headings. Perhaps most important was the basic idea, that the new church would from the beginning be catholic, evangelical, and reformed, with bishops in apostolic succession. The representative character of the Consultation was also important. It embraced catholic, protestant, and free church traditions and a full range of polities, episcopal, presbyterial, and congregational. The entry of the three black Methodist churches had "changed the character of virtually every issue." COCU's theological work, especially in its early years, was impressive. Deschner pointed to the mutual recognition of membership in one baptism, interim eucharistic fellowships, and the theological "Alerts" as representative of another achievement: each one moved the churches toward new relations with one another and demonstrated that "COCU has opted for an ecumenism oriented toward the future, not simply on the past." The final achievement in Deschner's list was that at a time of deep disappointment, when the 1970 plan was rejected, COCU had invented an "open-ended, provisional, taking-one-step-at-a-time-together method, which dissolved fears of massive dislocations, and kept our attention fixed on the real and important things."

In his concluding comments, Deschner referred once again to their vision of the Church of Christ Uniting. "The churches, when they grasp their own truest identity, really want this." In this statement, Deschner was laying aside the "unity for the sake of mission" justification that had taken up so much of the Consultation's time and attention. Instead, he focused explicitly upon the deeper reason, the reason close to the heart of the desire for unity, which was that in its union across the historic divisions the church would become its true self.

12

Unity in Diversity:
Churches in Covenant Communion

Pledging to Walk Together Until We Are Visibly United in Christ . . .

EVEN THOUGH THE CONSULTATION on Church Union had affirmed the theological chapters of *A Plan of Union* in 1970, it had taken another fourteen years to complete *The COCU Consensus*. In 1984, the Consultation completed the document that it hoped the COCU churches could affirm as "an expression" of "the great Apostolic tradition" that they "hold in common."[1] What would it take, delegates may well have been asking, to complete the rest of *A Plan of Union*? What new approach to expressing their unity could be developed to replace the quasi-constitutional approach to organic union that the churches had rejected in 1970? The search for a new way had begun at COCU's 1973 meeting when the implications team proposed that the churches should free themselves "from the patterns of past unions" and search for "the way in which we can make real in our generation the unity which has been given to us by Christ."[2] The assembly then authorized the executive committee to form a new commission that would focus attention on various projects that would be involved in "living our way toward unity." Paul Crow was asked to chair the commission, thus assuring the executive committee that the new commission would stay on focus.

1. *The COCU Consensus*, 2.

2. "The Significance of the Responses to A Plan of Union," *Digest of Eleventh Meeting*, 183.

Covenanting as a New Possibility

As they began their work, the church order commissioners were able to consider developments in Wales and England as models for the Consultation. In Wales, a group of churches formed a joint committee on covenanting in 1975. This body developed a document which emphasized that the churches held much in common and were called to repentance for perpetuating their division. It proposed a covenant with seven affirmations, each with a specific intention that would give "integrity to the affirmation." Later developments encouraged the churches to worship regularly together, establish planning committees to encourage local unity relations, and continue the theological work that needed to be done. Similar activities took place in England, beginning in 1974, resulting in the publication two years later of a document entitled *Visible Unity: Ten Propositions.* This model included a liturgical service of covenanting in which official declarations of the churches were laid on the table and the churches sought "God's pardon for past disobedience and his help to fulfill their vows." This model continued the theme that had become commonplace in ecumenical circles, which was that unity and mission are inseparably bound together.

The idea of covenanting was introduced into COCU's docket of discussion by Gerald Moede in an address to the 1979 plenary assembly in Cincinnati (March 6-9, 1979). Citing Albert Outler's 1969 paper, "The Mingling of Ministries," Moede noted that by accepting one another's baptisms, the churches already had expressed a limited degree of communion in sacred things. Moede asked "whether the current practice of the churches has not become too rigid, falling behind theological agreement already reached."[3] He invoked a second paper by Outler in which the Methodist historian had proposed that the basic question for COCU was how the ministerial orders each minister carried could "become more widely and fully representative in the household of faith, without repudiating the intention of those who ordained me, my own exercise of them in good faith, and the fact that they have been authenticated . . . by the Holy Spirit?" Drawing upon Catholic theologian Henri Nouwen, Moede proposed that "*compassion* is at the core of the authority of the minister." By focusing upon compassion—"leadership in the way of the cross"—the Consultation could work toward agreement on the challenging issues of episcopacy and the ministry of the laity "as epitomized in a person like the Presbyterian elder."

Moede then turned his attention to what he called the *morphe* of the Church of Christ Uniting, the "bones and muscles of the body," that

3. Moede, "Members, Ministers, and Morphe of the One Body," 209–29.

COCU was envisioning. He restated the over-arching principle: that "at every *place,* local, regional, and national, there will be Eucharistic fellowship, free mobility of ministerial leadership and members, joint planning and implementation of mission, and some kind of joint decision-making and shared oversight." Moede listed five elements in this ideal. The "center must be related to the parts in a biblical fashion." "Diversities are to be encouraged, not ironed out." Episcope (the ministry of overseeing the church's life) must develop in a manner that is "primarily pastoral . . . and that intentionally interprets law by grace and not vice versa." Using his personal health history as an analogy, Moede stated that the churches suffered from a disconnect between the head that wills "unified and cohesive action" and the nerves and muscles so that "all movement [becomes] random and eventually totally impossible." What the churches needed was "a certain living relationship between the shared oversight we have just mentioned and free autonomy." What would be the "*carrier,* the enabler of further development" as the COCU churches moved toward visible unity? "The biblical covenantal principle," he proposed. "If the churches are seriously resolved to accept one another as partners and move toward a greater unity, then a way can be found, and *shall* be found."

It would take time, however, for the implications of Moede's proposal to be developed so that the COCU churches could move forward. In 1981, two years after Moede's Cincinnati speech, the Presbyterian seminary in Austin, Texas, devoted an entire issue of the *Austin Seminary Bulletin* to the idea of covenant, exploring it from several standpoints: the Old and New Testaments, church history, as an ecumenical theme, and in relationship to theological understandings of ethical relations in the modern world. Consultation leaders Lewis Mudge and Paul Crow contributed papers to the journal.

A few months later, at the 1982 plenary assembly in St. Louis, Robert S. Paul delivered Bible lectures entitled "The Cost of Covenant." A British Congregationalist, who since 1958 had taught at the Hartford Seminary Foundation, Paul had attended the first assembly of the World Council of Churches and served as the associate director of the Graduate School of Ecumenical Studies in Switzerland. His essay in the *Austin Seminary Bulletin* described the role of covenant in the federalist theology of New England Congregationalism, but three of his conclusions were pointed toward the Consultation on Church Union: its emphasis that faith involves both belief (doctrine) and action (ethics); its insistence that because our essential covenant is with God we are also brought into covenant with one another and therefore cannot avoid an ecumenical commitment; and its insistence that the covenant with God brings the church into essential relationship to human society and to the whole of God's creation.[4]

Near the close of his final COCU Bible lecture, Paul described six ideas that he believed "to be particularly pertinent to our situation," drawing these points largely from the passage in Mark's gospel that describes the instituting of the Eucharist.[5] It was important that the churches regain "table fellowship," because "worship and the eucharist [are] at the very center of our endeavor, not because we wish to brush social involvement and ethics aside, or give them a relative importance to the ecclesiastical things that churches enjoy doing, but *because ethics and social concern begin here.*" The death of our Lord, Paul continued, was "the seal of God's *eternal covenant—*what God *always* intends when he draws people into covenant, that they should be his people, and that he should be their God." When we go to communion, Paul asked, "what is it we take to ourselves when we accept the cup? 'This is my blood, the blood of the covenant, which is poured out for many.' . . . Jesus put it into human terms as the representative human being, and now the Church is called to put it into communal terms for all people."

None of Paul's predecessors, not even Eugene Carson Blake, had said it any more forcefully: "*Our* covenant is important because before a skeptical twentieth century will listen to what we have to say about peace and the Good News in Jesus Christ, it needs to be seen that those Christians really do love one another. This is the new wine for which our Lord waits to partake in his Kingdom." Unity and mission were inextricably combined.

While Robert Paul's Bible lectures provided a theology of covenant, COCU's Commission on Church Order described the elements that necessarily belonged to the covenantal relationship.[6] For the churches participating in the Consultation on Church Union, covenanting would begin with "*claiming our emerging theological consensus.*" Each participating church would be asked, "whether it believes the emerging consensus is sufficient as a basis to enter anew into God's covenant." The immediate corollary would be the "m*utual recognizing of our churches.*" This recognition would be established by liturgical acts in which the churches would acknowledge that persons baptized/confirmed in any of the participating churches had thereby been baptized/confirmed into "Christ's Holy Church." To accept the validity of baptism in a church means that the validity of that church is also

---

4. Paul, "The Covenant in Church History," 38–50.

5. Ibid., 31–35. The six points are taken directly from Paul's text, although some of the discussion related to each point is not included.

6. "Commission on Church, Order," *Digest of the Fifteenth Meeting,* 105–17.

being accepted. People baptized in one of these churches "would not receive baptism/confirmation again to become a member of another communion."

The next action, *"reconciling our ministries,"* would be more difficult to accomplish. That this be done was important because the ministry of each church was a primary means of continuity with the Christian tradition and with denominational heritage. The commission noted that church unions elsewhere had followed a two-stage process that began with mutual acceptance, confession, and an act of covenanting in a new body with a mutually accepted ministry. This would be followed by a process that would allow each of the ministries thus brought together "to offer to all the others its own spiritual gifts and apostolic authority. None of the ministries thus mingled would have forfeited its own distinctive heritage, and all would gain a greater fullness. Basic to all this: we will be recognizing each other as we are now, but only in the light of what we pray we may become together."

Another action recommended by the Commission on Church Order confirmed recommendations that COCU was already seeking to do: *"initiating eucharistic fellowship."* The Lord's Supper would be shared on a regular basis by local congregations and by Covenanting Councils at national and regional levels. The next element on the list, *"exercising social and personal mission,"* was consistent with COCU's long-standing principle that as the churches engaged in mission in the world they "would make decisions together."

The final point on the list provided by the church order commission was the one that would move the Consultation dramatically forward: *Commissioning Apostolic Councils at national, regional and local places.* These councils would be the key element at every level of the church's life for this joint decision-making. The process would start with a national liturgical event which, among other actions, would inaugurate an *"apostolic collegium,"* the primary purpose of which would be "to exercise (and manifest) a collective oversight (*episcope*) of the covenanting process as the member churches move forward year by year into deeper relationships with Christ and one another. The focus of this Council would be overseeing such ministerial actions as baptizing, confirming, and ordaining together." To show that this course of action was consistent with ideas already present in church union discussions, the church order commission presented material from four efforts around the world: *Groupe des Dombes* (an annual gathering of Catholic and Protestant church leaders to discuss matters related to the faith and order of the churches), Anglican Consultative Council, the Trinidad response to "Ten Propositions of the *United Reformed Church,"* and the *Lima Agreement of WCC Faith and Order."*

By the time that delegates had completed their 1982 meeting, they were agreed that the ideas presented by the church order commission provided a way for their churches to continue moving toward their goal of a visibly united church. They strengthened one of the six elements in the commission's list. Covenanting would include both *recognizing* one another's ministries and *reconciling* them. They affirmed a resolution that "affirms covenanting as the appropriate way ahead in the quest for visible unity in a Church truly catholic, truly evangelical, and truly reformed. This can only be described as a transforming experience." The resolution included two important themes that the church order commission had presented: "joyful obedience to God's covenant" and "sincere contrition for the divisions that continue to separate our churches."[7]

Liturgies for Covenanting

To this point in its process, the Consultation on Church Union was depending upon its theology and church order commissions to develop ideas, draft documents for consideration, and lead the assembly delegates in their work. In 1982, however, a third working group, the Consultation's long-standing commission on worship, came to a new place of prominence. Members of the worship commission presumed that liturgical actions actually change the state of being of the participants, pointing to the marriage rite as an example. While the license issued by civil government authorized two people to be married, their new relationship and social entity were brought into being by the wedding ceremony itself. With respect to covenanting, the critical actions by which the churches and their ministries would come into a new relationship would be the liturgies of reconciliation in which they participated.

The efficacy of liturgical actions, the worship commission proposed, was central to uniting the separated ministries. Despite similarities in self-understanding and functions in the churches, the ministries were divided because of differences in how they had been ordained. The conclusion seemed to be self-evident: divisions that had been brought into being by liturgical actions could only be overcome by new liturgical actions.

Although the worship commission had maintained close contact with the theology and church order commissions, it had been working on its own timetable. Speaking to the 1982 plenary assembly on behalf of the worship commission, Horace Allen acknowledged "a certain discontinuity" between the rite that the worship commission had developed and the reports of the

7. *Digest of the Fifteenth Meeting*, 119.

other two commissions.[8] At this point, the commission had developed two draft liturgies, a national service to be done once and a regional service to be celebrated in many places over the country. Both liturgies included a subtitle describing what they were planned to do. The national service was "An Order for Declaring Covenant, Reconciling Ministries, and Celebrating the Lord's Supper." The regional service used a similar subtitle, replacing the word *declaring* with the word *affirming*.[9]

The drafts focused attention upon the reconciliation of ministries because the commission on worship assumed, as did the other commissions at this time, that covenanting marked "the beginning of an interim period of indefinite length." Quoting the theology commission's Lewis Mudge, Allen compared the covenanting moment with "throwing a bridge over a chasm." The interim period "will be accompanied by certain anomalies, especially to the juridical mind." Certain aspects of the life of the churches would not be fully reconciled and integrated. The laity already have been reconciled, he proposed, in the acceptance of mutual membership that their churches had already affirmed. Now, the focus needed to be on reconciling "the minister of *epicopé*." Each church would name persons from its own life who would participate. "That provides us with the essential office," Allen told the delegates, "both in mission and for the continuing function of ordination." The churches would not proceed immediately to reconcile the presbyterate and diaconate since to do so might provide "obstacles either juridically too great, or liturgically too complex to do at one moment."

The draft liturgies included three "signs," which the commission on worship explained in notes published with the liturgical texts. The clasping of hands was "a ceremony of greeting, welcome, and friendship," which in Christian tradition was understood to be a sign of peace. It was used "to conclude the liturgy in which the churches publicly declare their recognition of one another and as the preparation for the reconciling of their separated ministries." The laying on of hands, the commission noted, had several meanings in scripture, including "blessing, healing, reconciling, confirming, ordaining, and setting apart for sacrifice." It had long been associated with baptism, confirmation, ordination, and healing, "and all of these meanings come to mind as the sign is used in the service for reconciling ministries." In the draft liturgy, this sign was used in a complex manner. Each person named by the churches "for the exercise of ordaining responsibility" would

8. Horace Allen, Jr., "Remarks by Commission Members," *Digest of the Sixteenth Meeting*, 137–40. Allen was a Presbyterian liturgical scholar, who taught worship at Boston University's School of Theology and at that time was serving as president of the North American Academy of Liturgy.

9. "Liturgies for Covenanting," *Digest of the Sixteenth Meeting*, 271–86.

silently lay hands on each of those whom the churches had put forward for this ministry until all have received the sign from the others. "In this way the richness associated with the historic episcopate will be conjoined with the richness of ministries which have handed on the apostolic tradition through other forms and signs."[10] The Eucharist, which was the third sign, expressed "the fullness of Christian communion with the risen Christ" and with "the host of witnesses in every time and place who also give themselves to God through Christ by the Holy Spirit."[11]

The importance of the worship commission's word was highlighted at the 1984 COCU plenary assembly when John Deschner told delegates that the "truly fresh element" in their gathering was "the work of the *Worship Commission* in imagining an act of worship that cannot yet be." The commission's key insight, that covenanting is an act of worship, is brilliant, Deschner declared. "We don't make covenants, biblically speaking, simply with one another, but with God; and we don't make any covenant with God that we don't first receive." Why the churches had not understood earlier in the Consultation's life "that our most relevant and compelling action as a Consultation on Church Union could be simply such a united act of worship: a covenanting service, where, with all necessary preparations behind us, and with the utmost seriousness of commitment, and fully understanding what we are doing, and with many appropriate visible signs, we ask God's forgiveness together, and we receive God's promise together, and we say to God together, in the presence of one another, that we make covenant: i.e., that we make a commitment to God and to each other to persevere in actualizing of the Church of Christ Uniting."[12]

One More Time Around

At the sixteenth plenary assembly in Baltimore (November 26–30, 1984), the Consultation completed its work on its theological document, "*The COCU Consensus*," and sent it to the churches. It also debated revised drafts of "Covenanting toward Unity" and "Liturgies for Covenanting." The delegates, however, were not yet satisfied with these documents and authorized and instructed the two commissions (church order and worship) to continue their work in preparation for the next plenary assembly. This plenary assembly, one of the most important in COCU's history, took place in New Orleans, December 5-9, 1988.

10. Ibid., 278.
11. Ibid., 271.
12. Deschner, "COCU at the Turning Point," 23.

Speaking on behalf of the church order commission, Paul Crow referred to the wide range of comments they had received from the churches and from individuals.[13] In addition, the commission had initiated approximately twenty ecumenical gatherings around the country, many of them extending over two days. The result was what Crow described as "a surprisingly clear profile of the attitudes of Christian leaders across the land with respect to the 1984 Covenanting draft." There was "a near universal recognition of our churches' essential unity in Christ," coupled with "a pervasive dissatisfaction with entrepreneurial denominationalism in America." Christian leaders also registered "a near universal rejection of the idea that merged structures would be efficacious in furthering true unity among the churches," and they gave "a strong sense of affirmation of the essential idea of Covenanting as the way ahead in church unity." Because of the flexibility in the draft, "relatively little anxiety was expressed in regard to the proposed ministry of the bishop." Church leaders felt that the 1984 draft expressed a "pre-occupation" with national concerns at the expense of local concerns, especially in reference to the place of laity.

Two features of the draft had received "very close attention" from nearly all respondents: the method for mutual recognition and reconciliation of ministers and the provisions for establishing councils of oversight. Concerns focused upon the authority given these councils and upon "the quasi-constitutional (i.e., institutional) character" given these councils. From 1986 through 1988, the Church Order Commission had prepared eight full revisions of its text and in the summer of 1988 had circulated a fully revised text among "all known participants" of the scheduled seventeenth plenary assembly.

In presenting the work of the Worship Commission, Vinton R. Anderson noted that he had served as chair for fifteen years. He introduced Horace Allen to provide the detailed interpretation of how the commission had responded to the comments from the churches. In his remarks, Allen called attention to the work of another Presbyterian member of the commission, Lewis Briner who had long served as its vice chair and Alan Detscher who represented the Bishops' Committee on the Liturgy of the Roman Catholic Church. Allen reiterated three pillars or dimensions of church union: "theological (the churches receive and voice together the faith of the church through the ages), governmental (the governing bodies of the churches consider and act on commonly developed proposals for Christian unity), and liturgical (the churches' unity is declared and confirmed

---

13. Crow, "Report of the Church Order Commission," *Digest of the Seventeenth Meeting*, 63–67.

in corporate acts of worship." The COCU churches had moved away from the idea of organic unity, he proposed, and instead were seeking to reconcile their ordained ministries while "maintaining the distinctiveness of our denominational traditions polity-wise and liturgy-wise." He proposed that they were contemplating a form of "autocephaly," a pattern that was well known among Orthodox Churches but "has never before been an option in western Christianity . . . namely: a harmony of churches which have their own self-government, but are fully in communion with one another."[14]

At this stage in his presentation, Allen turned his attention to the revised liturgies. Rather than explain revisions that the worship commission had written into the texts, he used his pedagogical skills to help the assembly understand their shape, the sequence and meaning of their eight "blocks of material," the "chunks" which were present in all three liturgies, national, regional, and local: introductory and penitential rites, service of the word, covenant/baptismal affirmation, reconciling bishops, reconciling ministers of word and sacrament, reconciling deacons and ordained ministers of governance (which for some of the participants clearly referred to the office of ruling elder), inaugurating councils, and Holy Communion. Allen and Vinton Anderson then read and demonstrated the reconciliation of ministers with ordaining responsibility so that delegates could "hear and see what it would look like and feel like." He also explained the worship commission's suggestions for how these services would be scheduled and performed.

The most challenging element in the liturgies was the portion in the National Service entitled "Reconciling Ministers with Ordaining Responsibilities." Each covenanting church was to present "a person whom it has named for the exercise of ordaining responsibility." The representatives of the churches would present persons "to be received by all as bishops in the Church of God."[15]

> They have confessed the Christian faith and have been baptized.
> They have heard God's call and been ordained by their churches
> to the ministry of word, sacrament, and order. In their own
> churches they have exercised a ministry of apostolic oversight.

14. Allen, "Report of the Worship Commission," *Digest of the Seventeenth Meeting,* 107–17. Allen also referred to the first of his own papers to be published, a commentary on Eugene Carson Blake's Grace Cathedral sermon. This paper, "One Visibly Catholic Church," had been published in *Theology Today* in 1961.

15. References and quotations in the following paragraphs are taken from "A National Service," in Consultation on Church Union, *Churches in Covenant Communion,* 47ff.

A "Declaration of Intention" is then stated by a leader of the service:

> It is our intention, within this covenant which we have made with each other, that each of these bishops, now being reconciled by a mutual laying on of hands and prayer, will recognize and receive the ministry and tradition of the others. Our purpose is that these ministers become reconciled, that they may henceforth serve together as representative pastoral ministers of oversight, unity and continuity in the Church, fulfilling the ministry of bishop as expressed in the theological consensus affirmed by our churches.

The ministers to be reconciled renew their ministerial vows in a litany prayer. Then the sign of reconciliation is given. Each of these ministers with ordaining responsibility lays his or her hands upon each of the others in silence. "When all have received this sign of reconciliation," the rubric states, "the covenanting bishops offer this prayer":

> We give you thanks, O God,
>
> for calling us into this new covenant.
>
> Complete in us your gifts,
>
> received and exercised in our separation,
>
> that we may now minister together as bishops
>
> in your church.
>
> Give us grace to manifest
>
> and set forth the unity of your church,
>
> proclaim the Christian faith,
>
> maintain worship in spirit and in truth,
>
> feed the flock of Christ,
>
> and in all things care for your church.

The next portion of the service bore the title "Reconciling Presbyterial Ministers of Word and Sacrament." It followed the same pattern as the liturgy for bishops. In the prayer that these ministers said in unison, they asked God to "complete in us your gifts, received and exercised in our separation, that we may now minister together as presbyters in your church." Following a "hymn invoking the Holy Spirit," the "signs of reconciliation" are given and received.

> *During the singing of this hymn, stations are formed, each containing one bishop and a lay person. Each presbyter goes to one of these stations to receive, first from the bishop and then from the lay person, the signs of reconciliation for wider ministry. The sign*

of reconciliation given by the bishop is the placing of the hand of blessing upon the head in silence. The sign of reconciliation given by the lay person is the hand of fellowship or the holy kiss. As the reconciled presbyters return to their places, they greet one another and other members of the assembly in the love, joy, and peace of Christ (italics in original).

Despite the mature form of the drafts before them, delegates brought questions and recommendations, and the schedule provided blocks of time for plenary debate, discussion by working groups, drafting time for the two commissions, and denominational caucuses. The last working session of the seventeenth assembly, Friday morning, December 9, 1988, was dedicated to final reports from the two commissions and voting by the delegations on the previously circulated resolution by which the Consultation would transmit its document *Churches in Covenant Communion* to the churches. The transmittal resolution requested that each church by formal action:[16]

1. Approve this text as the definitive agreement for joining with other participating churches in covenant communion, including the acts sufficient to enable it,

2. Declare its willingness to enter into a relationship of covenant communion with the member churches of the Consultation on Church Union and other churches which similarly approve this agreement and *The COCU Consensus* which is its theological basis, sealed by the proposed inaugural liturgies, and

3. Begin to identify for itself such steps and procedures as may be necessary to prepare for the reconciliation of ordained ministries and for entering into covenant communion as set forth in this document.

All nine of the participating churches voted to approve the resolution, although Edward W. Jones, speaking for the Episcopal Church, said that his delegation welcomed "the opportunity to commend" this document to their church, but added that "the way of reception" would challenge their church and that they would have to commit themselves to interpretation not only of the document itself but also "the entire aim of the Consultation on Church Union."[17] The assembly sang "Now Thank We All Our God" and passed the

---

16. *Digest of the Seventeenth Meeting,* 40.

17. The votes and statements by representatives are in *Digest of the Seventeenth Meeting,* 30–33.

peace to one another (at considerable length, the minutes report). The assembly concluded its time together by celebrating Holy Communion.

The Consultation also adopted a resolution in which it declared that the understanding of covenanting in the revised text of *Churches in Covenant Communion: The Church of Christ Uniting* was the definitive definition and took precedence over previous definitions including those in *The COCU Consensus* (1984). Early the next year the Consultation published its completed draft in a hundred-page book entitled *Churches in Covenant Communion: The Church of Christ Uniting*. Its "Forward" notes that the most significant change from earlier drafts "has to do with the way that the goal of the covenanting process is now stated." In 1984, covenanting was described as "an interim step on the way toward becoming one church." Even this idea, however, had been unacceptable to the churches. They were resisting "any commitment to an eventual merger of church structures." Church union was not "the consolidation of forms and structures," but instead it was what "the early church referred to as 'communion in sacred things.' This means becoming one in faith, sacraments, ministry, and mission. This kind of unity is visible and organic, whether or not organizational structures are consolidated."[18]

After twenty-eight years "of patient and persistent labor by the representatives of the churches, the initial suggestion which was put forward for a new form of church union—one that would be truly catholic, truly evangelical, and truly reformed—now finds embodiment in this document . . . together with its theological basis set forth earlier and itself a part of the proposal."[19]

Later this same year, the Consultation's staff published the two definitive documents—*Churches in Covenant Communion* and *The COCU Consensus*—under one cover. Everything the churches needed to make their decisions was right there, convenient and accessible to everyone. Increasingly, the question was whether anyone would pay it any heed.

18. Consultation on Church Union, *Churches in Covenant Communion*, 2.
19. Ibid., 3.

PART THREE

Reshaping the Ecumenical Vision (1989–2002)

13

From COCU to Churches Uniting in Christ

Like a Grain of Wheat, COCU Falls into the Earth and Dies.

WHEN THE COCU DELEGATES left the seventeenth plenary assembly in 1988, they knew that it would take several years—perhaps a decade—for their churches to study and act upon the two documents that the Consultation had created. In 1995, seven years into the cycle, COCU's newly appointed general secretary, Daniell C. Hamby, gave an optimistic assessment of how the process was unfolding. "What is opening up for the Church of Christ Uniting is anything but cold. Indeed, it is beginning to sizzle . . . [The] dream of a Church which is truly reformed, truly catholic, and truly evangelical is being realized. And the question we must now face is how we will welcome the reality of a Church of Christ Uniting in the year 2000."[1] Less confident, however, was Edward W. Jones, Episcopal bishop of Indianapolis and leader in his church's ecumenical endeavors. His church's interest in COCU, he wrote in 1995, had begun to wane as early as 1967, and his purpose now was "to interpret the Episcopal Church's unreadiness to move as quickly as others may have wished to move."[2]

This slowing down of the COCU process was much in the mind of Vivian U. Robinson when she addressed the Consultation's eighteenth plenary assembly that met in St. Louis January 20–24, 1999. A member of the Christian Methodist Episcopal Church, Robinson had earned her PhD

1. Hamby, "The Winter Is Past!," 51–59. The quotation combines sentences from pp. 51 and 59.

2. Jones, "Episcopalians and the Consultation on Church Union," 61–73.

degree at the University of Nebraska and spent many years on the faculty of Paine College. She was elected president of the Consultation in 1988, and to her surprise this two-year term had stretched to a full decade. In her opening remarks, she used lines from a hymn by Charles Wesley:

> What troubles have we seen, what mighty conflicts past,
> Fightings without and fears within since we assembled last!

She closed her statement with lines from an African-American gospel song:

> We don't feel no way tired.
> We've come too far from where we started from.
> Nobody told us the road would be easy.

But we don't believe God brought us this far to leave us.

During this decade, COCU's staff and executive committee had met twice a year, organized task groups, and appointed "Covenanting Enablers" whose "task was to work with the denominations to help them approve" the COCU documents. There had been two full-time general secretaries during this period, David W. A. Taylor and Daniell C. Hamby, and two interims, J. Ralph Shotwell and Lewis H. Lancaster Jr. "Our expectations," Robinson reported, "were that in ten years all the member churches would have acted on the covenant communion proposal and we would be in the final preparations for the Church of Christ Uniting." Instead, eight of the nine churches had "voted favorably on the two definitive texts that open the way to "full communion in sacred things."[3] Although Robinson did not mention the fact, several of these actions had included reservations, which meant that this plenary assembly would have to confront important questions concerning COCU's future.[4]

The Responses by the Churches

In its report to the churches, the 1988 plenary assembly asked them to respond with formal actions on three aspects of the plan to create the Church of Christ Uniting. Each church was asked to approve *Churches in Covenant Communion* as a sufficient basis for joining with other churches in this new

3. Robinson, "Reflections of the President," 35–39.

4. In his statement to the assembly, the acting general secretary, Lewis H. Lancaster Jr., stated that seven churches had acted favorably, another had not yet found a constitutional way to move forward, and still another would not take action until the following year ("General Secretary's Report," *Digest of the Eighteenth Meeting,* 40–43).

covenanted relationship. Each church was asked to declare its willingness to enter into this relation with other churches that had approved the document and the theological basis that was expressed in *The COCU Consensus*. Each church was asked to begin to identify for itself the steps and procedures that would be necessary to prepare for reconciliation of ministries and for entering into the covenanted communion.

The *United Methodist Church* provided straightforward, unambiguous responses to these three requests. By action of its 1988 General Conference, the church affirmed that it recognized in *The COCU Consensus* an expression of "the apostolic faith, order, worship, and witness of the church." The United Methodist Church recognized in this same document "an anticipation of the Church Uniting," and also recognized "a sufficient theological basis for the covenanting acts" that they anticipated would be proposed by COCU in 1992. The church's 1996 General Conference resolved to make certain changes in its *Book of Discipline*, declared its willingness to "enter into a relationship of Covenant Communion" with other churches (in COCU and others that would agree to these documents), and instructed its Council of Bishops to take leadership in the processes that would lead to their church's entry into the Church of Christ Uniting.[5]

A shorter, but similarly specific response came from the *United Church of Christ*. Its 1989 General Synod declared that *The COCU Consensus* was a sufficient basis for covenanting actions and its 1995 General Synod approved *Churches in Covenant Communion* and declared its willingness to enter into this new relationship with the other eight churches.[6] In the statement sent to the Consultation on Church Union, the United Church of Christ indicated that the church had not received guidance on how to act if fewer than the nine participating churches should choose to enter. They also reported that their church had entered into full communion with the Christian Church (Disciples of Christ) and had approved *A Formula of Agreement* that brought them into full communion with the Evangelical Lutheran Church, the Presbyterian Church (U.S.A.) and the Reformed Church of America.[7]

Even more concise was the report given by the *Christian Methodist Episcopal Church*. Its 1994 General Conference declared the church's "willingness to enter into covenant communion with the other members of COCU." Its statement reporting this action, however, included a cautionary

5. "United Methodist Church Statement," *Digest of the Eighteenth Meeting*, 31–34.

6. The "Recommended Action" of the United Church of Christ was taken at its Twentieth General Synod and can be found in the Minutes of that gathering on pages 143–46.

7. "United Church of Christ Statement," *Digest of the Eighteenth Meeting*, 30.

comment: "We continue to have some concerns about the trust level among the churches of COCU, and we have hopes for a common mission in regard to racism."[8]

The *African Methodist Episcopal Church* also provided a clear statement of approval. The 45th Session of its General Conference (no date given) affirmed the covenanting proposal and resolved that it agreed "to enter into covenant communion with the other churches. A "whereas" clause prior to the resolutions, however, quoted lines from *Churches in Covenant Communion* which declared that "each church will retain its own autonomy, its own name and identity, including its own form of church government and worship, its own pattern of ministerial placement, and its own confessional and international relationships."[9]

The *Christian Church (Disciples of Christ)* reported the action of its 1995 General Assembly that committed the Disciples to continuing in the process of covenanting. It specifically approved the *Churches in Covenant Communion* as sufficient for moving forward, declared its willingness to enter into this relationship, and stated its intention to identify steps and procedures that would be needed. The Disciples statement, however, stated three unresolved challenges: defining the place of the office of the elder (a lay ministry) in the proposal's threefold ministry, finding a way for Disciples to accept the personal historic episcopate, and making sure that covenanting councils would not become another layer of bureaucracy.[10]

A more ambivalent, although still favorable, report was submitted by the *African Methodist Episcopal Zion Church,* as can be seen in two sentences that conveyed the core of this church's report: "The African Methodist Episcopal Zion Church will continue our study of the covenanting process at the grassroots level through our local churches of the various documents and materials. The African Methodist Episcopal Zion Church is committed to the Consultation on Church Union" (action taken at the 45th Quadrennial Session in 1996).[11]

The *International Council of Community Churches* also provided an ambiguous report which it presented in four stages. First, the ICCC affirmed "the language for leadership" that had emerged in the Community Church

8. "Christian Methodist Episcopal Church Report," *Digest of the Eighteenth Meeting,* 18.

9. "African Methodist Episcopal Church Resolution," *Digest of the Eighteenth Meeting,* 11–12.

10. "Christian Church (Disciples of Christ) Resolution," *Digest of the Eighteenth Meeting,* 15–16.

11. African Methodist Episcopal Zion Church Report," *Digest of the Eighteenth Meeting,* 13–14.

Movement, and it would continue to use that language while seeking "to understand how these reflect and parallel the biblical terms of bishop, presbyter, and deacon." Second, it would continue to affirm the "free church traditions which we see in local congregations" and the individual conscience and "power to interpret and determine the use of creeds." Third, it affirmed that its actions to move into covenant communion would "contribute to our commitment to openness, appreciation, cooperation with all God-centered religious groups." Fourth, the ICCC affirmed its "ongoing faith journey and democratic processes leading to unity in diversity for all God's people."[12]

The *Presbyterian Church (U.S.A.)* reported that it was positive toward continuing with the other COCU churches but was encountering difficulties in taking the appropriate steps. Its 1988 General Assembly had recognized *The COCU Consensus* as a sufficient basis for moving forward in covenanting acts including the reconciliation of ministers. Its 1993 General Assembly had taken similar action with respect to *Churches in Covenant Communion* and had initiated a process to draft changes in the church's *Constitution* that would be necessary in order to take these steps. Their church, however, also was experiencing opposition to the recognition of any office of 'bishop' within the Presbyterian Church (U.S.A.). Many Presbyterians insisted that "our corporate approach to *episcope* [is] the equivalent of the office of bishop" and should be "so considered by partner churches." The church's 1996 General Assembly had passed a set of amendments intended to facilitate its participation in the covenanting process, but a majority of presbyteries had rejected them.

Even so, the Presbyterian Church (U.S.A.) was committed to working "through the Consultation on Church Union toward racial reconciliation, mutual reconciliation of ministries, regular celebration of the sacrament of the Lord's Supper, and engagement together in Christ's mission to the world." The report also indicated that progress toward the goal of full communion among the participating churches could be enhanced by studying *A Formula of Agreement* which proposed full communion between the Evangelical Lutheran Church in America, the Reformed Church in America, the United Church of Christ, and the Presbyterian Church (U.S.A.)[13]

The *Episcopal Church* reported that in its 1994 General Convention their church said that "we are 'not ready' to enter into covenant communion, and we also expressed a number of 'reservations' about both *The COCU Consensus* and *Churches in Covenant Communion*." The Episcopal

12. "International Council of Community Churches Report," *Digest of the Eighteenth Meeting*, 23–24.

13. "Presbyterian Church (U.S.A.) Report to the 18th COCU Plenary," *Digest of the Eighteenth Meeting*, 25–29.

Church, however, intended to remain in the conversation with the other COCU churches, send a delegation to the current plenary assembly, and study COCU documents in the light of the Chicago-Lambeth Quadrilateral in order to see what actions their church could take in its 2000 General Convention. Several factors had caused the Episcopal Church to take this increasingly cautious posture toward the Consultation on Church Union. Among them was the continuing struggle between "the catholic and protestant dimensions of American Episcopalianism" and the fact that "some of our best energy went towards those churches most like us liturgically," especially the Evangelical Lutheran Church in America. Five "guiding principles" had emerged for the Episcopal Church with respect to its continuing participation in the Consultation on Church Union. It would continue with COCU to fight racism, seek to develop a common catechesis for baptism, encourage the other churches to "affirm the major elements of *Baptism, Eucharist and Ministry* (published by the World Council of Churches), give special emphasis to bilateral agreements, and seek to develop ever more significant relations between their churches.[14]

Searching for a Way Forward

Since the churches had given such ambiguous responses to the documents that were to bring them into a new covenantal relationship, the 1999 plenary assembly (St. Louis, January 20–25, 1999) would have to determine what to do next. President Robinson identified three questions. Should the COCU churches give up the multilateral character of their project and instead develop a series of bilateral agreements? Should they redefine their goal as cooperation in mission and delay the commitment to becoming "one church in faith, sacraments, and ministry?" How could COCU's vision be redefined in order "to attract the ecumenical energy of the churches?"[15]

A drafting committee was appointed to develop proposals that the delegates could use in order to develop a suitable course of action. Chosen to chair this committee was Michael K. Kinnamon, professor of theology at Lexington Theological Seminary. Earlier in his career, Kinnamon had served as Executive Secretary of the World Council of Churches' Commission on Faith and Order Commission. During that period of time, Faith and Order completed the consensus statement *Baptism, Eucharist and Ministry*, which it published in 1982 and sent to member churches for official response.

14. "Episcopal Church Report on COCU," *Digest of the Eighteenth Meeting*, 19–22.
15. Robinson, "Reflections of the President on the Past Ten Years," 35–39.

The drafting team prepared recommendations that the delegates could debate in open assembly despite sometimes tense confrontations that took place privately. By the close of the assembly, they prepared a report recommending that the churches terminate the Consultation on Church Union and create a new relationship, which they entitled Churches Uniting in Christ (CUIC), to continue the search for greater unity. The delegates at the plenary assembly hoped that all nine COCU churches would enter into this new entity and that other churches, especially the newly formed Evangelical Lutheran Church in America, would be drawn into closer participation. They proposed that the transformation of COCU's *Church of Christ Uniting* into *Churches Uniting in Christ* take place during the Week of Prayer for Christian Unity in 2002, only three years after the conclusion of the eighteenth plenary assembly, which would be COCU's final meeting. The heart of this proposal was a list of nine "visible marks of Churches Uniting in Christ":

1. Mutual recognition of each other as authentic expressions of the one Church of Jesus Christ;

2. Mutual recognition of members in one Baptism;

3. Mutual recognition of ordained ministry;

4. Mutual recognition that each church affirms the apostolic faith of Scripture and Tradition which is expressed in the Apostles' and Nicene Creeds and that each seeks to give witness to the apostolic faith in its life and mission;

5. Provision for celebration of the Eucharist together with intentional regularity;

6. Engagement together in Christ's mission on a regular and intentional basis, especially a shared mission to combat racism;

7. Intentional commitment to promote unity with wholeness and to oppose all marginalization and exclusion in church and society based on such things as race, age, gender, forms of disability, sexual orientation, and class;

8. An ongoing process of theological dialogue, with special focus on racism, reconciliation of ministries, and other topics that the churches had identified; and

9. Appropriate structures of accountability and appropriate means for consultation and decision making.[16]

16. "Report of the Eighteenth Plenary of the Consultation on Church Union," *Digest*

The plenary assembly also adopted a document entitled *"A Call to Christian Commitment and Action to Combat Racism,"* which asserts that there is "an irrefutable link between the churches' search for unity in faith, sacraments, and ministry and the struggle to overcome racism in the churches and the human community." After calling attention to the connection between racism and power, *A Call* makes a foreboding observation: "Unless significant initiatives are taken to counter current conditions and trends, racism—especially white racism—will continue to corrupt our national and ecclesiastical aspirations for a society that truly incarnates 'liberty and justice for all.'" The document calls upon the churches to make and implement nine "strategic commitments." Some of them were exhortations to continue making the theological case against racism and to deepen the churches' understanding of this issue. Other items noted specific actions that could be taken, such as claiming observances on Martin Luther King Jr., Day as occasions for dialogue leading to systemic change. The churches were to search out racism in their own structures and procedures and to renew their "commitment to the struggle for equal human rights through advocacy."[17]

In order to keep the process moving forward following its adjournment, the plenary assembly authorized the Consultation's executive committee to oversee next steps, one of which was to secure new executive leadership for its work during this period. It negotiated an agreement with Michael Kinnamon to serve as part-time General Secretary of the Consultation and Gordon White to serve as part-time Associate General Secretary. White opened the COCU office in Massachusetts and took care of administrative work while Kinnamon directed COCU's activities and did most of the traveling. During his time in his executive position, Kinnamon did not visit the Massachusetts office, and the two executives communicated largely by phone and electronic media.

Kinnamon soon concluded that the Episcopal Church was not willing to enter Churches Uniting in Christ if the mutual recognition of ministry remained on the list of visible marks. At the request of COCU's Executive Committee, Kinnamon (CCDC), J. Robert Wright (EC), and Lewis Mudge (PCUSA) met to find a way to move forward.[18] Following the lead of this working group, COCU's executive committee revised the report that the plenary assembly had adopted by removing the recognition of ordained

---

of the Eighteenth Meeting, 109–11.

17. "Call to Christian Commitment and Action to Combat Racism," *Digest of the Eighteenth Meeting* 119–22.

18. Michael Kinnamon, personal communication.

ministries from the list of visible marks for the Church of Christ Uniting and rearranging the remaining eight marks so that "an ongoing process of theological dialogue" concluded the list. Their intention was "not to remove the objective of a reconciled ministry, but to set its accomplishment within the context of a new covenanted relationship." They also developed several paragraphs that would serve as the framework and starting point for these discussions about ministry.[19]

The decision to remove recognition of ministries from the list was criticized by some COCU participants, including former general secretaries Paul Crow and Gerald Moede, as "giving away the store." By so doing, the Executive Committee had removed one of COCU's most important objectives. After several months of work, the Executive Committee issued "A Recommendation for the Future" in which it confirmed the plenary's hope that Churches Uniting in Christ, could be inaugurated during the Week of Prayer for Christian Unity in 2002 and that "the reconciliation of ministry can be accomplished by the time of the Week of Prayer for Christian Unity in 2007."[20]

COCU leaders decided the new relationship would be inaugurated by an act of worship—a liturgy of Word and Sacrament—in which the churches would confess the sin of division, ask for healing and reconciliation, make solemn promises to God and one another, and then take a subsequent step that would demonstrate their commitment to work for justice and mercy in the world around them. A special committee, chaired by Keith Watkins, long-time member of COCU's commission on worship, drafted the liturgies.

COCU Becomes CUIC

The Consultation on Church Union came once again to Memphis, Tennessee, for its final plenary assembly from January 18–21, 2002. It was fitting that Michael Kinnamon, who had served as COCU's general secretary since the previous assembly, deliver the keynote address, in which he outlined his "Reflections on Where We Have Been and Where We are Headed as Churches Uniting in Christ." He listed seven "driving principles," all of which he said follow from one assumption: "Because we have communion with Christ, we also have communion with one another . . . Diverse as we are, says *The COCU Consensus,* by reasons of race, sex, physical or mental

19. "'Recommendation to the Churches,' by the Executive Committee of COCU," *Digest of the Eighteenth Meeting*, v–xiii. Background information received from Michael K. Kinnamon, pers. comm.

20. "A Recommendation for the Future," *Digest of the Eighteenth Meeting,* v–vii.

condition, language, politic, or vocation, we belong to one another by baptism into the one body of Christ."[21]

On January 19, 2002, a congregation of approximately six hundred people crowded into St. Mary's Episcopal Cathedral in Memphis, Tennessee, for a service of Word and Sacrament marking the conclusion of the Consultation on Church Union. Since the sermon that had initiated the Consultation forty years earlier had been preached in another cathedral of the Episcopal Church, it seemed appropriate that COCU's final act occur in a similar space. The liturgy was adapted from the "An Order of Worship for the Proclamation of the Word of God and the Celebration of the Lord's Supper"—the COCU Liturgy published in 1968. In her sermon, "There Is Still Room," Kathryn Bannister referred to the early Christians who met in homes sharing meals and living as "sojourners anticipating the coming of Christ. They extended hospitality that transcended barriers of ethnicity and culture and resisted the social stratification of their time. All this sharing across barriers was, for them, proof of the truth of Christianity. Anything less and the church would be inauthentic."[22]

The next afternoon, on the day commemorating the assassination of Martin Luther King Jr., an even larger congregation, perhaps as many as 1,000 congregants, gathered at Mt. Olive Cathedral of the Christian Methodist Episcopal Church for a second service of Word and Sacrament entitled the "National Act of Worship Inaugurating Churches Uniting in Christ."[23] During the Prayer of Confession early in the service, representatives from each church named one way in which their church manifested the sin of division. Then the assembly prayed:

> We confess that we are diminished by pride and separation.
> We acknowledge the sinful divisions of our churches
> which keep our ministries unreconciled.
> We admit our failures in our mission of justice and love.
> We confess that we support systems of racism and other
> oppression that despoil your incarnate image and violate creation.

McKinley Young climaxed his sermon by declaring that God had brought them to this "epiphanal moment. It's our discovery of Christ's presence in a new way, bringing together the fragmented and the disjointed; healing the broken, restoring the downtrodden, raising the dead, and enlivening those whose life and joy has been diminished by racism and sin;

21. Kinnamon, "We Have Come This Far By Faith," 1–9.

22. Bannister, "There Is Still Room," 11–16.

23. "National Act of Worship," 42–51.

calling us to a new order and to a new understanding of what it means to be disciples of the Most High."[24]

Coming between the service of the Word and the service of the Table, was an element entitled "Inaugurating a New Relationship" which included recitation of the Nicene Creed, a series of declarations that the people made to one another, and concise prayers of the people. "With gratitude to God," worshipers affirmed "the one baptism that makes our members one people in Jesus Christ; the apostolic faith as expressed in Scripture and Tradition that marks our churches as authentic expressions of the one church of Jesus Christ; the one ministry, called by the Holy Spirit, that unites us in worship and mission." In a unison declaration, the worshipers made eight promises, which consisted of the "eight fundamental assumptions" from earlier plenary documents slightly recast in liturgical language. They promised to conduct regional festivals of thanksgiving, celebrate the Eucharist together with intentional regularity, and join in overcoming racism. In theological dialogue they would reform their separate churches until they were fully catholic, fully evangelical, and fully reformed. They would continue the process that would provide the foundation for the mutual recognition and reconciliation of ministries of the churches. The sign of this new relationship was the exchanging of the peace of Christ that followed the promises. The inaugural act was completed with the prayers of the people:

> *Leader:* Holy God, the earth you created in beauty now languishes in pain, waiting for its redemption.
> The peoples of the earth whom you created
> to live in peace and joy
> now experience violence and despair.
> Transform us and our *Churches Uniting in Christ*
> that we may become ministers to this world and its people.

> *People*: Make us bold in our struggle against cruelty.
> Give us courage and endurance to accept no peace
> where there is oppression, and to work for justice,
> God's Shalom, and the common good.
> Help us speak to the conscience
> of our country and its institutions.
> Use us to heal the brokenness in life.
> Renew our joy so that all creation can sing
> the glad songs with which the world began.

24. Young, "An Ecumenical Epiphany," 17–22.

During the offering and preparation of the table for the Eucharist, representatives of the churches brought "symbols from each participating church—historic documents, chalice and paten, shield or logo, and objects from a mission of justice and mercy." The Invocation of the Holy Spirit, which was the concluding section of the eucharistic prayer, gave clear expression to the focus on mission that had come to be the distinctive characteristic of the new relationship that these churches would have with one another:

> *Leader:* Holy God, send your Holy Spirit upon us and these gifts,
>> that all who eat and drink at this table
>> may be one body and one people,
>> a living sacrifice in Jesus Christ.
>> Through this meal unite us with the risen Christ
>> so that we may give ourselves for the life of the world.
>> Through us bring good news to the poor
>> release to the captives,
>> recovery of sight to the blind,
>> and freedom to the oppressed.
>> Give us the power to work for justice
>> that all the world may be filled with peace and joy.
>> This sacrifice of praise and thanksgiving we offer you,
>> eternal God, through Jesus Christ,
>> in the unity of the Holy Spirit,
>>> one God for ever and ever.
>
> *All:* **Amen.**

The next morning, most of the congregants came together again, but this time on the streets of Memphis. Joined by many others from the city, they walked in procession from City Hall to the Lorraine Motel, now known as the National Civil Rights Museum. They were commemorating Martin Luther King Jr., who had been gunned down on the balcony of that motel thirty-four years earlier. They also were remembering the march that religious leaders of the city had made on the day after Dr. King's assassination. Ministers, priests, and rabbis had gathered at St. Mary's Cathedral for their own memorial and to protest the mayor's unwillingness to settle the labor dispute that had led the sanitary workers to strike and had shut down garbage collection for fifty-three days. On April 4, 1968, they had made their own march on City Hall. William Dimmick, Dean of St. Mary's, had picked up the Cathedral's gold processional cross and in an impromptu move, led the march. In honor of the courage shown that day, the current dean of St. Mary's, C. B. Baker, led the Churches Uniting in Christ as they marched. She carried the same cross, which was appearing in a public procession for the first time since that earlier, tempestuous march in 1968. Another leader of the parade was Willie W. Herenton, the first African American mayor of Memphis, who had been part of the garbage workers' march on the day of King's death.

When people had gathered in the street facing the second floor balcony where Dr. King had died, representatives of the churches that would enter into the new relationship made brief statements. As their first act, these nine leaders of *Churches Uniting in Christ* signed a document entitled *Appeal to the Churches "To Seek God's Beloved Community."* In this appeal, they affirmed that "love, repentance and forgiveness are powerful sources of unity," and they rejected "the values of distrust, envy and personal institutional survival." They affirmed that "Christ died for *all* people" and that "we are *all* children of God, made in the divine image, and accountable for our individual and collective actions." They concluded their statement with this sentence:

> Our appeal to you is to join in the audacious and prophetic quest to incarnate this vision and, with God's help, renew our faith, proclaim the good news, unite our churches and heal the nation.[25]

After forty years of diligent work, the Consultation on Church Union had, like a grain of wheat, fallen into the earth and died (John 12:24). As delegates started on their journeys home, many prayed—unsure how their prayers would be answered—that the COCU seed would bear much fruit.

---

25. "Appeal to the Churches," 27–29.

14

Remembering the Church
that Never Came To Be

Learning from COCU's Forty-Year History . . .

THE CONSULTATION ON CHURCH Union concluded its work with its vision of a new church for America unfulfilled. Along with other church union enterprises in the twentieth century—the Philadelphia Plan of the 1920s, the Federal Union Plan of the 1940s, and the Greenwich Plan of the 1950s—the COCU Plan of the 1980s left the ecumenical Protestant churches in America organizationally divided and their members and ministers still encumbered from participating in sacramental life across ecclesial boundaries. During an era when the "separate but equal" system in America's public school systems was being dismantled, the nation's Protestant churches continued to be organized in systems that were predominantly white or black. The churches maintained themselves as denominational systems in which each church, locally and nationally, acted as though it were the one church, whole and complete, for its community and the nation.

If one conclusion can be derived from this history, it is that the century-long pursuit of multilateral church mergers can no longer be regarded as an effective way to achieve Christian unity in the United States. It is hard to imagine any combination of theological and social factors, save the virtual collapse of existing ecclesial systems, that could inspire a new effort to achieve a comprehensive American plan of church union in the decades immediately before us.

A second conclusion can also be drawn, that the softer mode of church union, the covenanted communion that COCU adopted in its final period, lacks the structural connections that keep the churches together until they experience and manifest the unity that their covenants profess. While this second approach has the right rhetoric, it lacks the gears underneath that transform speech into action. Even though the Consultation on Church Union does not provide a pattern for overcoming the church's shattered form, this forty-year history is a case study that warrants study and reflection. There is much for the churches to learn from the most comprehensive effort to unite separated churches in American history.

What the COCU Churches Tried To Do

The way to begin is by recounting the objectives that the leaders of the Consultation on Church Union pursued throughout the movement's history. Although they evolved as theological reflections deepened and conditions in the world and the churches changed, five objectives consistently energized COCU's work.

Establish "full communion" among the churches, their members, and ministries. From COCU's beginning, full communion included "a mutual recognition of Baptism and a sharing of the Lord's Supper, allowing for an exchangeability of members; a mutual recognition and availability of ordained ministers to the service of all members of churches in full communion, subject only but always to the disciplinary regulations of the other churches."[1] Throughout the Consultation's history, most of its churches received members from the other churches on the basis of their baptism in the other church, received members from other churches at Holy Communion, and recognized the ordinations that had been performed in the other churches. Even so, these churches tended to live as separated communities of faith, rarely sharing in sacramental relations with one another. By means of their relations in the Consultation on Church Union, they hoped to resolve theological and practical barriers and establish fuller sacramental communion.

Overcome theological and disciplinary factors that divide the churches' ministries into separate systems. The most important theological barrier to this full communion was the inability of the churches to recognize and accept one another's ordained ministers who functioned as the guardians of tradition and the leaders of the community of faith. Although they functioned

1. This language comes from a later, non-COCU source: Norgren and Rusch, *Toward Full Communion*, 17.

in similar ways—leading worship, preaching, administering the sacraments, participating in governance, and leading in mission—the ministries of these churches existed within separate institutional systems. Some ministers were ordained "in apostolic succession" and others were not. Some were described in language that was primarily pastoral and sacramental, while others were described in ways that were largely organizational and institutional. Some ministry systems assigned primary authority to individuals—to bishops; others assigned this authority to groups—presbyteries or conferences. Methodist churches had bishops, as did the Episcopal Church, but the Methodist episcopacy had evolved within the American context and emphasized the administrative character of the office as much or more than the sacramental. The authority and responsibilities of Methodist bishops were exercised within a system that required collaboration with conferences of laity and ordained elders in local and regional settings, which gave the office some of the characteristics that also were found in Presbyterian and United Church of Christ governing systems.[2] The Consultation intended to unite these ministries despite their historic causes of separation and varied patterns of operation.

Heal the breach between Reformed and Anglican branches of the Protestant Reformation. Although COCU leaders would have welcomed full participation by the Lutheran branch of the Reformation, the membership of the Consultation consisted of churches from the Reformation heritage that were largely shaped by the theology and ecclesiology associated with John Calvin and his associates. This heritage was deeply rooted but separately developed in the Church of England and the Kirk of Scotland and later was implanted as a central feature in major American denominations, especially the Episcopal Church, the Methodist Churches, the Presbyterian Churches, the United Church of Christ, and the Christian Church (Disciples of Christ). Conflict between these branches of the Reformation focused, in part, on the means of maintaining continuity with the apostolic Tradition. The Anglican branch depended upon bishops and the Presbyterian-Congregationalist branch depended upon designated bodies of elders and pastors. The challenge facing COCU was to harmonize these two systems.

Strengthen the churches' engagement in mission in the American context. Throughout the earlier decades of the twentieth century, in Europe, Britain, and North America, one of the primary themes of inter-church discussion had been that the needs of the world required a united Christianity. COCU leaders, beginning with Eugene Carson Blake, cited this purpose as

---

2. For a thorough discussion of the evolution of the Methodist episcopal system, see Moede, *The Office of Bishop in Methodism.*

a primary reason for the new unity movement. Since the close of World War II, however, the tenor of the times had been changing. During the 1950s, the return to normalcy that had marked the ending of hostilities wound down and new pressures were emerging across the United States. In communities across the country, and at the national level, early leaders of the Consultation churches developed active outreach ministries in their communities, worked closely with their counterparts in other Protestant denominations, and developed new levels of understanding and appreciation of members in other churches. COCU hoped to strike down the divisive barriers so that the churches, united into one body, could minister with greater effectiveness.

Often COCU's focus on mission paralleled themes that were being discussed in ecumenical documents around the world, especially economic, ethical, and justice-related topics. Early in COCU's work, however, the participating churches found that their focus was shifting to American issues, especially those related to gender, race, ethnicity, and social status. They came to realize that in these matters their churches were as much in need of reform as was the rest of the society. With the entry of the historic black Methodist churches into the Consultation, there was reason to believe that the united church would be even more effective in mission than had originally been anticipated.

Reshape the denominations into a new Protestant church. Although they worked with increasing levels of harmony with other church leaders and through councils of churches, many COCU leaders were convinced that the denominational system was an ineffective way of addressing the nation's needs. They believed that leadership and resources were dissipated because their denominational systems had become an historical anachronism rather than serving as a useful pattern for mission. The conclusion was that by coming together in a new, post-denominational Protestant church, which would be present in communities everywhere, they would become more effective in bringing the gospel to bear upon the new challenges facing the nation and its people. Furthermore, in communities across the land the members of their churches already were experiencing a trans-denominational sense of identity with one another. This tacit unity, however, needed to become real in the structural life of the churches at regional and national levels.

Why COCU Seemed So Promising

Although the participating churches held differing degrees of enthusiasm for the Consultation on Church Union, the venture seemed promising, and during its first decade people could believe that the vision of unity would be transformed into a new American church that embodied catholic, evangelical, and reformed features.

The four churches in the original proposal were, in fact, much alike. Initial statements, beginning with the sermon by Eugene Carson Blake, emphasized this similarity in theology, ecclesiology, and sacramental life. Although not stated, the leaders of the movement also assumed that their churches represented similar cultural values and enjoyed similar locations in American life. In many communities, the four churches that Blake had named were aligned with community patterns of business, education, and community organization. Even with the addition of the Christian Church (Disciples of Christ) and the Evangelical United Brethren Church, this cultural and American homogeneity remained largely intact. During mid-century, virtually all members of the legislative, executive, and judicial branches of government across the United States, and leaders in business and education and cultural institutions, held at least nominal membership in one of the ecumenical Protestant churches.[3]

In an early COCU essay, sociologist Paul H. Harrison wrote that these churches were being forced by social forces into patterns that were increasingly similar despite their significant differences in theological explanations. After describing "powerful grassroots trends" to limit the exercise of power by church officials (regardless of their formal titles and positions), Harrison also outlined the "movement to increase efficiency of organization, to render more effective the decision and policy-making process, to reduce competition between denominational agencies, and to rationalize the total organization of the denomination." This latter tendency "is in profound accord with the present striving for church union. So long as a majority of churchmen wish to maintain a vital relationship with the world in terms of missionary, evangelistic, social action, and educational goals the centralizing tendency will continue." Later in this same essay, however, Harrison described the continuing "preference for or a commitment to symbols, traditional terminologies, and interpretive formulae," that superseded the drive toward unity.[4]

The ecumenical movement around the world pushed toward action. Five factors can be identified: (1) a tradition beginning in the 1930s that connected a united church with the conviction that the Christian message was the best hope for overcoming destructive ideologies (such as fascism and materialism) and moving modern culture toward its fulfillment; (2) the

---

3. Hollinger, *After Cloven Tongues of Fire*, 22.

4. Harrison, "Sociological Analysis of the Participating Communions," 108, 119.

post-World War II conciliar movement, culminating in the creation of the World Council of Churches in 1948, that brought Christians of many traditions together for sustained theological discussion and concerted action; (3) the example of national church unions, especially the United Church of Canada and the Church of South India, that combined differing ecclesiologies into new patterns of churchly life; (4) movements in the Roman Catholic Church, epitomized in the Second Vatican Council, that moved Christian unity forward on the docket of discussion for all churches; and (5) the liturgical movement that from the 1960s onward encouraged American churches to revise their worship books and hymnals according to ecumenically based theological and cultural criteria.

The proposal to unite these churches quickly caught fire. The dramatic scope of the proposed union captured the imagination of the public, as can be seen in the coverage given the Consultation by leading newspapers and news magazines. Responding to this interest, the participating churches invested substantial resources of personnel, time, and church funds in the endeavor. A wide range of church leaders became interested in the Consultation's work, including church executives, pastors, scholars in the seminaries and universities, opinion leaders in the popular religious press, and renewalists at a time when dramatic changes in the character of church life were taking place. Furthermore, as COCU's work gave increased attention to new issues, especially those related to gender and race, new constituencies became involved in its work.

The churches reached agreements on traditionally divisive issues more quickly than had been expected. The result was that a set of principles was published that provided the basis for moving forward quickly in drafting documents on which the churches could unite. Even though COCU had already become more complex and the issues more challenging, the Consultation neared the conclusion of its first decade with strong reasons to believe that its hopes would be realized and a new American church would come into being within its second decade.

Why COCU Lost Momentum

Even during the late 1960s, however, some of the participating churches were becoming uneasy about the process in which they were engaged. In 1964, when COCU was still in its formative stages, a small group of prominent Methodists expressed significant disagreements with basic features in the Consultation's activities. Writing in 1995, Episcopal bishop Edward W. Jones noted that his church had developed misgivings as early as 1967. In

1972, Eugene Carson Blake's United Presbyterian Church withdrew briefly from the Consultation. Even so, the Consultation continued to receive substantial support from the participating churches. During the 1970s and 1980s, the confidence that the new church would soon come into being diminished. Goals were revised and the vision of melding the participating churches into one new church was set aside. "Covenant communion," which the churches developed as their revised mode of manifesting unity, was far different from the united church for America that had been anticipated in COCU's first years. Among the reasons for this loss of confidence are the following.

As the number of participating churches increased, the theological issues under discussion became more complex and the structural challenges of reconfiguring American Protestantism became more difficult to resolve. One of the first actions of the four initiating churches was to invite the three churches that were already in union conversations with a COCU church to join the Consultation, and two of them accepted the invitation. One of them, the Christian Church (Disciples of Christ) differed from the others in its use of lay elders to preside at the communion service and its emphasis upon believer baptism as the norm for this sacrament. More significant variations were introduced by the entry of three African American Methodist Churches. While they strengthened the weight of Wesleyan theology and spirituality, they also brought their own variants of the Methodist connectional system. They sharpened COCU's recognition of the nation's history of racial injustice, a history that was deeply imbedded in the churches as much as it was in society as a whole. These churches also made it necessary that the new church order its life so that people of color would be able to maintain the dignity and freedom of action that they had enjoyed in their separated churches.

Key ideas in the original proposal came into question or failed to be confirmed in practice. One of these ideas was the claim that the four churches in the original proposal were already so much alike that very little stood in the way of their coming together in a new church. It was to become increasingly evident that catholic and reformed/evangelical visions of the church were not easily blended together. In bilateral conversations with Lutherans, the Episcopal Church acknowledged that their two churches were closely parallel "sacramental eucharistic communities" holding similar attitudes toward the classical dogmatic tradition and the nature of ministry. Despite significant differences with respect to ordination, Lutherans and Episcopalians were willing temporarily to set aside certain disciplinary regulations in order to establish a new relationship.[5] In contrast, the reformed/evangelical churches in the Consultation had become Word-centered, rational communities despite the determination of their sixteenth-century founders, especially John Calvin, to maintain a balance between Word and Sacrament. To the Episcopal Church, the other COCU churches seemed so different from itself that Episcopalians were unwilling to make the same concessions with them that they would make with the Evangelical Lutheran Church in America.

A second COCU idea that was not confirmed during the Consultation's later years was that historical precedent is sufficient grounds for continuing and extending a practice in a united church, with the corollary that if the practice is deeply enough rooted, it is not necessary to agree on the theological explanation. This reasoning seemed to have resolved debates over the forms of baptism, the result being that both infant and adult baptism would be practiced in the Church of Christ Uniting, but with the understanding that no one would have to practice a form that went contrary to his or her conscience. With respect to ordination in apostolic succession, however, the idea failed. The closer that COCU came to a time of decision, the greater was the unwillingness of the churches to move forward on the basis of precedent alone. Until the theological justification could be agreed upon, churches would not agree to new patterns of ministry. A particular clear statement of this point of view was offered by Episcopal theologian Richard A. Norris Jr., who had served on COCU's theology commission for fourteen years. "I went into it with great enthusiasm and even hope; but in the end I came to feel not just that I disagreed with this or that aspect of the proposals doctrinal or organizational, but more, that the issues had not been explored deeply enough to make agreements real and disagreements fruitful."[6]

Traditional loyalties, prejudices, and animosities proved to be more enduring than had been anticipated. Methodists were determined to keep their connectional system, churches with congregational polity were loathe to change to a tighter connectional system, Presbyterians became increasingly determined to maintain their practice of the corporate episcopacy,[7]

---

5. During much of COCU's history, Anglican and Lutheran churches in the United States and abroad were engaged in serious theological discussions seeking to resolve differences between them. The most important result in the United States was the new relationship between the Episcopal Church and the Evangelical Lutheran Church of America that the General Convention of the Episcopal Church approved in 1997. See Norgren and Rusch, *Toward Full Communion.*

6. Corney, "The Reverend Canon Richard A. Norris, Jr.," 421.

7. Small, "Ecclesial Identity," 3–5.

Disciples, especially in areas where traditional culture remained deeply ingrained, were determined to maintain lay presidency at the Eucharist, and Episcopalians made it clear that even though they were willing, under certain conditions, to suspend temporarily their insistence upon apostolic succession, they would not take that action to bring about unity with COCU churches.[8] In the years since COCU was discontinued, none of its churches has taken important steps to change its theology and polity in order to manifest the patterns described in the documents that outlined what the Church of Christ Uniting would be like. The "insidious character of denominations and denominational life," writes the Disciples' Robert K. Welsh, "resists all forms of change, even within a denomination . . . Theology issues are often identified to mask that reality and dynamic."[9]

Structural changes in American society, including the Civil Rights Movement, changes in sexual mores, the rise of secularism, and the changing balance of ecumenical and evangelical churches worked against the COCU endeavor. During the 1950s, radical changes were taking place all across American society. Foundational to the changes was the post-modern emphasis upon individualism rather than wholeness. Regardless of a church's formal polity, the localized and individualized factors have been increasingly determinative of church policy. In this period of rapid social change, while the Consultation was championing many of the transformations that were taking place in American society, it was trying to remake a new church based upon a model of church union that had been crafted in an earlier era. Despite its efforts to adapt its program to new social conditions, the Consultation seemed unable to accommodate the new challenges. As soon as the intention to unite into one new church was set aside, the COCU churches, white and black, settled back into their previous cultural, social, and theological modes of behavior.

The ecumenical movement was changing shape. One of the early expressions of Catholic-Protestant rapprochement following the second Vatican Council was increased ecumenical vigor, particularly at local levels. These expectations gradually faded, however, and at the same time local interest in other ecumenical activities, including COCU, waned. The denominations' diminished interest in COCU and their growing interest in bilateral conversations led, in the minds of some, to a renewed confessionalism in the ecumenical movement. On the basis of his work as a prominent UCC leader

---

8. One of the provisions of the Lutheran Episcopal "Concordat of Agreement" was that the Episcopal Church would temporarily suspend, for Lutheran pastors only, its requirement that celebrants at the Eucharist had to have been ordained in the apostolic succession.

9. Robert K. Welsh, pers. comm.

during this period, John H. Thomas, has observed that churches have increasingly replaced the ecumenical question, "what new thing can we claim together to bear witness to the gospel in our time and place?" with "what confessional commitment must we defend in order to preserve critical elements of our identity?"[10] Bilateral conversations are proving to be effective ways to resolve theologically defined separations and move past ancient disputes. Since agreements are expressed primarily in agreed statements, however, giving only modest attention to new structures of inter-church relationship, this form of ecumenical activity gives the appearance of significant progress but does not carry with it the necessity of changing church practice. Thomas also notes that church councils at the local, regional, and national levels have been losing strength. One impact upon the COCU churches was that as the councils, which had been "rich venues for helping COCU convene judicatory and congregational leadership, lost strength, COCU was left without a key partner."

COCU's Achievements

Even though the Consultation on Church union was unable to bring its participating churches into The Church of Christ Uniting, this forty-year endeavor by the nation's ecumenical Protestant churches at the center of American culture made valuable contributions to the churches and the nation.

These ecumenical Protestant churches were "culture changers," and the Consultation on Church Union was one of the instruments they used to reshape American life. From the 1940s onward, and especially in the 1960s, the leaders of these churches, writes historian David A. Hollinger, "led millions of American Protestants in directions demanded by the changing circumstances of their times and by their own theological traditions. These ecumenical leaders took a series of risks, asking their constituency to follow them in antiracist, anti-imperialistic, feminist and multicultural directions that were understandably resisted by large segments of the white public, especially in the Protestant-intensive southern states." It is clear to Hollinger that the dramatic shift in American religious life, away from the ecumenical communions and to the evangelical churches that defended the old ways, is in large part the result of the culture-changing actions by leaders of the dominant denominations.[11] If we honor the new patterns of American life,

10. John H. Thomas, pers.comm.

11. David A. Hollinger, in an interview with Amy Frykholm, *Christian Century,* July 11, 2012. See also Hollinger, *After Cloven Tongues of Fire.*

it is right that we understand the principles and actions that the churches used to make these changes, including their labors within the Consultation on Church Union.

The Consultation on Church Union served as a laboratory for testing some ideas and practices that were vigorously promoted among the churches. Every generation has to develop its own modes of evaluation, but the ideas which COCU examined continue to be important. One example is the way that the Consultation clarified the place of the worshiping congregation in the life of the church. During the 1960s and thereafter, some of the strongest prophetic voices were people such as academician Gibson Winter and social activist Stephen C. Rose both of whom were convinced that local congregations were bastions of homogeneous people determined to use their churches to provide religious justification for their way of life. Persuaded by this line of thought, the drafters of COCU's 1970 *A Plan of Union* proposed a new mode of local organization for the churches, a system that cut across the sectors of urban life, as Winter had recommended, and was marked by criteria for faithful practice that Rose had described in his much-discussed book *The Grass Roots Church.* During the next period of time, however, COCU's parish plan was resoundingly rejected by all of the churches. It became clear that the local unit of the church consists of people who come together for worship and nurture on a regular and continuing basis. Although local congregations often become self-centered and ingrown, the resolution of this problem, COCU concluded, was renewal of their sacramental and theological life rather than replacement of the congregations by impersonal, bureaucratic, mission-centered parishes.

COCU's commission on worship developed ecumenically informed liturgies for the Lord's Supper, Baptism and Confirmation, and an ecumenical version of the Roman Catholic Church's three-year lectionary. No matter how they may differ in the detail of faith and life, most churches include two patterns of sacramental worship in their public activity: the celebration of the Lord's Supper, often referred to as the Eucharist, and the celebration of Baptism. These sacraments are rooted in the ministry of Jesus and have anchored much of the liturgical, theological, and missional activities of churches everywhere. Despite basic similarities in meaning and form, the churches have developed many different ways of celebrating these constituent actions of church life. Discussions within COCU's commission on worship led to the publication of a series of liturgical texts that it presented to the Consultation churches for review and, upon approval, for trial use. The purpose was to provide models that the churches could use as they continued their separate processes of liturgical reform.

During a sixteen-year period, the worship commission completed work on seven documents: *An Order of Worship* (1968); *An Order for the Celebration of Holy Baptism* (1973); *A Lectionary* (1974; reprinted in 1975 and 1978); *Word, Bread, Cup* (1978); *An Order for an Affirmation of the Baptismal Covenant* (1980); *An Order of Thanksgiving for the Birth or Adoption of a Child* (1980); and *The Sacrament of the Lord's Supper: A New Text* (1984). Several characteristics mark these publications. (1) They were shaped by the theological and pastoral consensus concerning worship that was emerging within the worldwide liturgical movement. (2) They were adapted to forms and phrasing from new liturgies already in use or under development in the participating churches. (3) They made use of insights and materials that were being developed according to Vatican II initiatives for renewing worship. (4) They adopted contemporary and vernacular patterns of speech and set aside traditional and archaic language that had long been in use. (5) They represented liturgical understandings that sometimes were ahead of the policies and practices that were under discussion in the other sections of the Consultation on Church Union. (6) They were prepared in the hope that they would be used by the churches in the process of moving together into a new mode of union in sacramental life.

Although the liturgies failed to win widespread use, they provided a way for worship experts to develop some of their ideas about the theology, language, and culture of worship in the mid-twentieth century. The new prayer books subsequently published by the churches benefited from what the editors had learned while developing the COCU liturgies. Work on the lectionary was continued by the more broadly based and sharply focused Consultation on Common Texts and resulted in *The Revised Common Lectionary* which came into widespread use in churches around the world.

The Consultation on Church Union created a theological consensus that could guide its churches into a new way of life that would make them more complete than they have been or can hope to be by maintaining their separate identities. Individually the COCU churches recognized, and sometimes acknowledged publicly, that they fell short of what the church should be. They recognized that with God's help, and in close communion with one another, they could be transformed into a corporate body that more fully embodied the church's true character. With some degree of seriousness, they indicated their readiness to begin making theological, sacramental, and structural changes that their churches needed to accomplish. Once the push to create a new united church lost its force, however, the existing patterns of faith and practice, especially those related to polity, remained in place. "Instead of building on shared riches found in our diverse traditions and welcoming the gift of others into our particular church family," Thomas E. Dipko, a prominent United Church of Christ ecumenical leader, has observed, "we became (as church institutions) even more resistant to 'change.' However, at the same time, our members moved with comfort and relative ease from one church tradition to another and experienced the 'reception' of these gifts individually. That sounds contradictory precisely because it is!"[12]

At one level of life in the COCU churches, this new consensus continued to pull the communions forward. It had been redefined so that in addition to classical issues of ecclesiology it included societal factors related to gender, race and ethnicity, and social standing. In this aspect of their lives, the COCU churches have continued their efforts to change their own systems and to keep American society moving toward justice and freedom for all people.

The COCU movement for Christian unity demonstrated the difference between voluntary cooperation and binding commitment in effecting institutional change. The participating churches were familiar with councils of churches, coordinating councils, and joint mission projects through which they addressed specific theological, social, and cultural challenges. The practical advantage of voluntary cooperation was that it required only moderate levels of commitment to a cause and to the other participants. It was always possible to withdraw or withhold support for some aspect of what a council proposed to do. In contrast, binding commitments were drawn up in such a way that the parties were required to stay involved even when they would have preferred to withdraw. They had to show up, pay their assessments, and make the required changes in their own accustomed ways of doing things.

Through much of its life, the Consultation on Church Union held organic union as its objective. Churches would yield their sovereignty and independent existence in order to become part of a larger ecclesial identity. When the churches concluded that the attempt at organizational merger had faltered, they adopted the idea of covenanting toward union, first as a major step toward permanent union and later as the replacement for corporate unity. During the covenanting process, however, the churches showed little willingness to accept binding commitments that would keep them in the relationship until the agreed changes had been accomplished. As the time drew near when they would need to make these commitments, their readiness to stay together faltered. Covenanting had little chance to succeed because other than moral incentive and good will, it had little power to hold the churches together until they could establish stronger bonds of unity.

The discussion revolving around the Consultation on Church Union and the new American church that it hoped to create contributed to the continuing

12. Thomas E. Dipko, pers. comm.

debate concerning the relationship of religion and culture. Early in COCU's life, some of its critics questioned whether it was appropriate to develop a new church that would be so closely intertwined with the cultural, social, and political structures of the nation. As Canadian theologian Douglas John Hall has written, the establishment of religion in the United States was more deeply ingrained than in Europe. In the old world, it was on the level of intertwined institutions whereas in the new world the establishment had to do with ideas, morality, and cultural forms.[13] To create a united, and therefore stronger, ecclesial partner in this dominant culture was not only questionable on theological grounds but it seemed capable of threatening the actuality of the separation of church and state. Although I do not remember reading the idea expressed this way in the COCU literature, the Consultation helped many people recognize that the institutional amalgamation of America's dominant churches could have threatened the American commitment to freedom of religion. It certainly would have complicated the inevitable process of disestablishing the ecumenical Protestant churches from their cherished role as validators of the vision of American exceptionalism.

During COCU's history, its own sense of how the new church would be related to American life gradually changed. Early COCU leaders assumed, perhaps unwittingly, that the new church would continue to occupy the center of American religious, cultural, and political life. This new ecclesial body would become the version of the church that expressed the distinctive character of Christianity in the United States. During COCU's forty-year history, however, the historic Reformation churches lost their preeminence and other patterns of Christian presence became increasingly dominant. Even in a new united form, a later COCU generation realized, the new church they hoped to create would be only one among several American churches that sought to represent the nation's central religious values. Recognizing this change of perspective, one reviewer of the manuscript suggested that a better title for the book would use the indefinite article *An* instead of the definite article *The*. The new title would have been: *An American Church That Might Have Been.*[14] Although I considered making the change, the original title has been retained. It more adequately expresses the spirit that permeated the Consultation during its most distinctive period of work. These visionary leaders intended to create *The American Church*.

The danger that a few COCU critics sensed can be seen with greater clarity a generation later in the alliance between ideologically conservative politicians and theologically conservative church leaders who in recent

---

13. Hall, *The End of Christendom*, 31.

14. My thanks to Thomas E. Dipko for suggesting the change in the title.

years have described themselves as the Moral Majority. The current inter-penetration of religious conviction and political power, whether the religion be Christianity in the United States, Judaism in Israel, or Islam in other places, is a severe threat to freedom, peace, and human well-being—and to the integrity of religion itself. By giving careful attention to the Consultation on Church Union, it may be possible to understand more clearly the benefits and dangers of identifying religion and national identity.

Despite the many achievements brought about by the Consultation on Church Union, the churches continue to be divided from one another. The challenge to develop a more adequate historical embodiment of the one, holy, catholic, and apostolic church remains.

15

Still Needed—A New Church
for a New Nation

Toward A Post-COCU Configuration of
Ecumenical Protestantism in America . . .

SINCE THE 1960S, AMERICAN society has become more complex than even
the most visionary leaders of mid-century renewal movements, including
the Consultation on Church Union, could have imaged. Among the contributing factors are: (1) the shifting balance between the once dominant
Anglo-European culture and the formerly subordinate cultures, especially
African-American and Hispanic; (2) the lessening of confidence in Western
patterns of thought that emphasize the scientific-historical world view, and
the rising impact of systems that grow out of the experience of women and
people of color; (3) the increasing distance between elite members of the
society and the growing majority of the population that feels loss and oppression; (4) diminishing confidence in traditional institutions, including
government, the universities, and the churches; (5) the alliance of conservative political and religious systems; and (6) religious pluralism that is
rapidly diminishing the once dominant function of Protestant churches in
American life.

The most obvious result for the ecumenical Protestant churches is that
they have lost their preeminence and confidence. So too with their related
institutions: church councils, theological faculties, and organizations such
as the Consultation on Church Union and its successor Churches Uniting
in Christ. A new cohort of visionaries has emerged whose members assume that the old ways are disappearing (perhaps not rapidly enough). New

modes of being the church are developing that are intended to be suitable for the postmodern, post-Christian era which we have entered.

Despite these changes in America's intellectual, political, and religious culture, the churches that trace their heritage to the Reformation inspired by Luther, Calvin, Cranmer and others have a continuing role in American life. The ecumenical Protestant churches order their lives so that they will be faithful to the past, attentive to the present, and oriented toward a future that is consistent with the Holy Commonwealth that Jesus proclaimed. The need for this kind of historic Protestant presence in this post-Christendom era is intensified by the fact that strident, politically and culturally conservative versions of church-sponsored activity have become such a dominant and divisive force in public affairs.

The denominationally structured pattern of church life that has been characteristic of the ecumenical Protestant churches, however, no longer serves as an effective carrier of the Christian vision or transmitter of its constructive social power. Cooperation in church councils and other consortia provides only a partial remedy to the negative effects of the churches' divided pattern of co-existence. Councils can function only as denominations exist and therefore are in themselves manifestations of the structural pathology of American church life. Now needed is an ecclesial form that heals the shattered condition of the historic Protestant churches and binds them together more tightly so that their members and ministers are interconnected and thus able to function as one body in Christ.

To their credit, these churches continue to engage in ecumenically oriented activities. They participate in councils of churches; the heads of communion and other officers and administrators of the churches maintain harmonious and constructive relationships. Churches Uniting in Christ stays alive, although with such a modest degree of activity that some observers predict its demise. The churches push forward in bilateral conversations over theological issues, and agreements to enter into full communion are negotiated, although with little evidence that the churches follow through on developing new levels of actual communion with one another. Local efforts to come together, such as interchurch services during Lent, take place here and there. Baptized Christians move with ever-greater freedom from one denomination to another. The "double belonging" that Gerald Moede encouraged is sometimes practiced, but it has developed little enthusiasm among church members. Theological education takes place in seminaries that are genuinely ecumenical in faculty and student body, but clergy are still ordained in one church rather than in some broader configuration of a post-denominational church. As they move forward into a new period of life, the ecumenical Protestant churches can continue and accelerate these limited efforts to manifest and advance already existing evidences of their oneness in Christ.

As they continue their efforts to reshape the form of ecumenical Protestantism in America, these churches will do well to hold fast the vision that defined the Consultation on Church Union from its earliest days: that they become a visibly united church that is truly catholic, truly evangelical, and truly reformed. During the thirty-year period between the launching of the Consultation and the completion of its major documents (1962–1992), the participating churches revised and broadened their understanding of these three characteristics. In times of stress, one church or another, momentarily seemed to step away from some part of this vision, but COCU as a whole continued steadfastly to uphold this vision of the new church it hoped would come to be. This vision was the central element in the heritage that the Consultation bequeathed to its successor organization, Churches Uniting in Christ. In these post-COCU years, the ecumenical Protestant churches—with the list broadened to include all of the communions that fall within this broad category—will stay focused for their future together so long as this vision is their guiding principle.

A second inheritance from the Consultation on Church Union also will be important as ecumenical Protestantism moves toward a new configuration. *A Church of Christ Uniting* will seek to portray in its congregational life, corporate structures, and mission in the world the new humanity that the biblical record describes—a humanity in which gender, social status, and race and ethnicity no longer divide because "we are all one in Christ" (Gal 3:28). The rapid changes in American society, especially those generated by immigration, mean that programs to combat racism in the COCU churches need to be redefined and re-patterned. The importance of the emphasis on overcoming racism, which came to define COCU, however, will remain at the center of a reconstructed ecumenical Protestantism.

A third inheritance from the Consultation on Church Union will also be important as these churches move toward a new configuration: the focus upon contributing directly to ministries in the community that are marked by wisdom, mercy, and justice. Eucharist, union, and mission are linked together, although the relationship between them is more subtle than the blunt causal connection—unity leads to mission in the world—that characterized early COCU literature. At the same time that COCU was getting started Alfred Shands published a book, *The Liturgical Movement and the Local Church,* in which he interpreted the relationship between eucharistic worship and the renewed activity of parish churches in their communities. "Liturgy is the canvas on which the parish learns graphically what it means to be the Church," Shands wrote. "As long as we go on thinking that we are a collection of individuals, little of significance can happen. Yet when we realize that we have been joined together to embody the self-offering of Christ as exemplified in the liturgy, then mission begins. The mission of the church is to be the *Body*, the *group* joined together in Christ. It is the community, the cell, the team which bears the responsibility for carrying on the mission."[1] An ever-closer linkage of Eucharist, unity, and mission will characterize the ecumenical Protestantism that is coming into being.

One more factor from the COCU experience can also be continued in a new form of ecumenical Protestantism in America: the importance of attending to the soul of the nation in which "it lives and moves and has its being." Theologians, historians, and sociologists offer many ways of describing how religion and society are intertwined; and they are right in presenting their strong judgments upon some of the ways that this relationship has functioned. In this nation's history, several religious traditions have contributed to the construction of the central core of its culture, but more influential than most is the one that the ecumenical Protestant churches represent. They have shaped some of the nation's strongest characteristics, as well as some that are now recognized as being insufficient and misguided. The nation is increasingly diversified, and part of that diversity is the increasing variety of faith and values-based traditions that now shape the character of the nation. Because classic Protestantism is accustomed to participation in the culture-shaping activities of the nation, a united and visible ecumenical Protestant church will continue to participate actively in the processes by which this society changes and matures in the years ahead.

October 31, 2017, marks the 500th anniversary of Martin Luther's action that led to the shattering of the unity of the Western Church and the emergence of the divided form of Christianity we have known for generations. We are entering a time of radical change that may be similar in its scope to the Reformation initiated by Luther, Calvin, Cranmer, and their colleagues. The churches that emerged out of the Reformation and embraced the humanism and nationalism that were also developing during those generations will continue on, but in a less dominant, more collegial form. Newer ecclesial networks, many of them anchored by independent evangelical or charismatic congregations, seem likely to extend their influence in the United States as well as around the world. Other faith traditions are becoming naturalized so that they too can become full partners in shaping the inner spirit and public patterns of our culture. Ecumenical Protestantism has much to offer in this transformed era and all who have been

1. Shands, *The Liturgical Movement*, 35.

part of this form of the Christian tradition will continue to have important roles to play.

The basic challenge facing the ecumenical Protestant churches, if they are to be responsible in the coming years, is deeply theological: to discern in one another's churches the marks of authentic Christian faith and affirm the validity of one another's churches despite their many variations. This challenge can be phrased in a series of questions. Are the ecumenical Protestant churches able to accept one another as real churches, which are blessed by God even in their divided state of being? Are the members of one another's churches, who were baptized by whatever form in those churches, Christians in the full sense of the word, and therefore fully qualified to receive the sacramental bread and wine whenever they are presented in remembrance of Christ? Are the sacraments of Holy Communion celebrated in one another's churches truly remembrances of Christ despite the variations of liturgical form, theological language, and ministerial order? Are the ministers in one another's churches fully ministers on the basis of their ordinations, irregular as they may seem to have been? Is the Christian faith confessed in worship and practiced in life in these churches authentic, anchored in the apostolic tradition, and oriented toward life in the world?

When the churches give positive answers to these questions about one another, then they are in a position to move together as equals in the eyes of God and of one another. Even though our systems differ and need to be harmonized, a new form of Christianity can arise only when the churches discontinue their long habits of judging the past and establish a new habit of refusing to insist upon remedial action to make up for the alleged deficiencies of some of these practices. The churches cannot require that people be rebaptized in a more "complete" way or "confirmed" by a second rite if the baptisms once administered really made them Christians. They cannot reordain or regularize ministers who previously were received into ministry by prayer and the laying on of hands and whose ministries have been blessed by the Holy Spirit and received by the people they serve. The churches cannot insist that ministers rewrite the prayers of remembrance and consecration spoken for past generations in churches all around the country in order to guarantee retroactively that Jesus was truly remembered in these celebrations at the communion table.

For a new church catholic, evangelical, and reformed to come into being, certain anomalies will be necessary. Some of the old ways of thinking and acting will have to be suspended for a time—and maybe forever—as churches acknowledge that Christ has already made all believers into one body. Only as they come together in absolute humility and in full confidence that Jesus is present will their divisions soften and their experiences of unity become ever stronger.

The ecumenical challenge continues. With church leaders of generations in the past, and especially with those who labored in the Consultation on Church Union, we continue to pray that we will become more fully the church which is built on the one foundation, Jesus Christ himself, and which has been "built into a spiritual house, to be a holy priesthood, to offer spiritual sacrifices acceptable to God through Jesus Christ." Coming together in a new way, our churches may yet fulfill the description offered by a scripture writer long ago: "But you are a chosen race, a royal priesthood, a holy nation, God's own people, in order that you may proclaim the mighty acts of him who called you out of darkness into his marvelous light" (1 Pet 2:5, 9).

APPENDICES

A Proposal Toward the Reunion of Christ's Church

Eugene Carson Blake
Grace Cathedral
San Francisco, California
December 4, 1960

TEXT: ROMANS 15:5–7

"Now the God of patience and consolation grant you to be like-minded one toward another according to Christ Jesus! That ye may with one mind and with one mouth glorify God, even the Father of our Lord Jesus Christ. Wherefore receive ye one another as Christ also received us to the glory of God."

THIS IS A SIGNIFICANT occasion. When I received the gracious invitation from your Dean and Bishop to preach in this pulpit, on this particular morning, it became clear to me at once that the occasion demanded not only as good a sermon as God might enable me to prepare and preach, but also a sermon that would deal with the unity of the Church of Jesus Christ realistically—neither glossing over divisions with politeness nor covering them with optimistic generalities.

Led, I pray by the Holy Spirit, I propose to the Protestant Episcopal Church that it together with The United Presbyterian Church in the United States of America invite The Methodist Church and the United Church of Christ to form with us a plan of church union both catholic and reformed on the basis of the principles I shall later in this sermon suggest. Any other

Churches which find that they can accept both the principles and plan would also be warmly invited to unite with us.

I hasten to make it clear that at this stage this is not an official proposal. My position as Stated Clerk of my Church's General Assembly gives me no authority to make such a proposal officially on behalf of my Church. I speak this morning as one of the ministers of my Church privileged and required to preach under the Word of God. I speak as a minister especially privileged (and therefore under a special requirement) especially privileged to have represented my communion for the past nine years in many formal and informal relationships with other communions both inside and outside the ecumenical movement. I speak as one minister of Jesus Christ who believes that God requires us to break through the barriers of nearly 500 years of history, to attempt under God to transcend the separate traditions of our Churches, and to find a way together to unite them so that manifesting the unity given us by our Lord Jesus Christ, His Church may be renewed for its mission to our nation and to the world "that the world may believe."

Before setting forth the basic principles of the union which I propose, it is, I think, important to make clear the compelling considerations that have moved me to believe that union ought now to be sought by us and to clear away some possible misunderstandings of reasons and motives for seeking it.

First of all I am moved by the conviction that Jesus Christ, whom all of us confess as our divine Lord and Saviour, wills that His Church be one. This does not mean that His Church must be uniform, authoritarian, or a single mammoth organization. But it does mean that our separate organizations, however much we sincerely try to cooperate in councils, present a tragically divided Church to a tragically divided world. Our divided state makes almost unbelievable our common Christian claim that Jesus Christ is Lord and that He is the Prince of Peace. The goal of any unity or union in which we ought to be interested was clearly stated by the Central Committee of the World Council of Churches last summer. The unity sought is primarily a local unity, "one which brings all in each place who confess Jesus Christ as Lord into a fully committed fellowship with one another." The World Council statement emphasized that the unity sought "is not one of uniformity nor a monolithic power structure." The point of church reunion is not to be found chiefly in national or international organization; it is found most fundamentally in local communion and common witness in all the places where men live.

In October, I was at a political dinner at which I had been invited to give the invocation. A gentleman introduced himself to me as we were waiting to go in to the tables and asked me what Church I represented. When I told him, he said, "My wife is a Presbyterian. I am an Episcopalian. We go happily to each other's churches. Why don't you church officials do something about bringing our churches together?" Many such ordinary Christians wonder why we continue to be divided.

In the *Christian Century* last January, Bishop Pike wrote, " . . . of this I am sure: The Holy Ghost is on our side whenever we break through the barriers between Christian bodies. He will increasingly provide guidance to show the ways in which we can defeat the complacent obstinacy of our national Church bodies in this regard."

And I am sure that Bishop Pike agrees with me that there are many complacencies in local churches among members and ministers that must be disturbed by the Holy Ghost if Christ's will for His Church is to be accomplished in our time and place. For although many American church members are ready to criticize their church leaders for inaction, I fear that just as many are complacently happy in the divided state of the Church.

Another clear reason for moving toward the union of American Churches at this time came home to me with compelling force during the presidential campaign this fall. The religious issue was, you will remember, quite generally discussed even though all the high level politicians attempted to avoid it as much as possible. Now that the election has been decided and nobody really knows how much the religious question figured in the result, I recall the issue to remind you that one result is clear. Every Christian Church, Protestant, Orthodox, Anglican, and Roman Catholic has been weakened by it. Never before have so many Americans agreed that the Christian churches, divided as they are, cannot be trusted to bring to the American people an objective and authentic word of God on a political issue. Americans more than ever see the churches of Jesus Christ as competing social groups pulling and hauling, propagandizing and pressuring for their own organizational advantages.

And this is at a time when the United States of America finds itself at a pinnacle of world power and leadership—needing for herself and the whole free world that kind of spiritual vision and inspiration that only the Church of Jesus Christ, renewed and reunited can give. Our culture, our civilization, our world leadership are under the materialistic threat of Marxist communism. But our culture becomes increasingly secular, our civilization becomes increasingly decadent, and our world leadership becomes increasingly confused precisely because their Christian foundations are undermined and eroded. And our divided churches, all more and more sectarian in fact, are all therefore less and less Christian in influence.

Finally I am moved to propose this step of church union this morning because my proposal grows out of the convictions expressed in 1959 by thirty-four leaders of Presbyterian and Reformed Churches, theologians and administrators, from all over the world in an address to their fellow Christians, made on the occasion of the 400th anniversary of the Calvinist Reformation. We said:

"The occasion we celebrate (i.e. the 400th anniversary of the beginnings of Presbyterianism) makes invitations more appropriate than proclamations. We ourselves are ready to accept all invitations from sister churches to that comparison of opinion and experience in which Christians submit themselves afresh to the Lord of the Church. And we issue our own invitations to all who would, with us, *put their traditions and systems under the judgment of Christ*, seeking his correction, and ready to relinquish what he does not approve.

"All that we claim for the Presbyterian and Reformed Churches we would lay on the altar. We offer it all to our fellow Christians for whatever use it may be to the whole Church. With the whole Church we hold ourselves alert for the surprises with which the Lord of history can alter the tempo of our renewal, and for the *new forms* with which an eternally recreating God can startle us while he secures his Church."

In this spirit and out of this conviction, I now propose the principles upon which a church union of the scope I have suggested may be even now possible of achievement under God.

Let me begin by re-emphasizing the requirement that a reunited church must be both reformed and catholic. If at this time we are to begin to bridge over the chasm of the Reformation, those of us who are of the Reformation tradition must recapture an appreciation of all that has been preserved by the catholic parts of the Church, and equally those of the catholic tradition must be willing to accept and take to themselves as of God all that nearly five hundred years of Reformation has contributed to the renewal of Christ's Church.

Let me pause here to be quite sure that all of you understand exactly the sense in which I am using the word *catholic*. In common parlance in America we often talk about "the Catholic Church" and mean "the Roman Catholic Church." That is not the meaning of *catholic* that I here use. At the other extreme all our churches repeat the Apostles' Creed in which we say, "I believe in the Holy Catholic Church." All of us claim to be catholic in the strict sense of confessing that Jesus Christ has established one universal Church in all ages and in all places and that we are at least part of it. Here, however, I have used the word *catholic* in still a third sense when I speak of the "catholic parts of the Church." I refer to those practices and to those understandings of faith and order, of church and sacraments which are catholic in contrast to the protestant or evangelical practices and understandings. I refer specifically, for example, to the Anglo-Catholic or high Church practices and understandings of your own Church. When I say then that the proposal I make is to establish a Church both catholic and reformed, I mean one which unites catholic and reformed understandings and practices in an even broader and deeper way than that already present in your communion.

Such a union as I now propose must have within it the kind of broad and deep agreement which gives promise of much wider union than seems possible at the present moment, looking ultimately to the reunion of the whole of Christ's Church.

First let me list the principles of reunion that are important to all who are of catholic tradition.

1. The reunited Church must have visible and historical continuity with the Church of all ages before and after the Reformation. This will include a ministry which by its orders and ordination is recognized as widely as possible by all other Christian bodies. To this end, I propose that, without adopting any particular theory of historic succession, the reunited Church shall provide at its inception for the consecration of all its bishops by bishops and presbyters both in the apostolic succession and out of it from all over the world from all Christian churches which would authorize or permit them to take part.

I propose further that the whole ministry of the uniting Churches would then be unified at solemn services at which the bishops and representative ministers from each Church would, in humble dependence on God, act and pray that the Holy Spirit would supply to all and through all what each has to contribute and whatever each may need of the fullness of Christ's grace, commission and authority for the exercise of a new larger ministry in this wider visible manifestation of Christ's Holy and Catholic Church. You will note that this proposal implies no questioning of the reality of any previous consecration or ordination, nor any questioning of their having been blessed and used by God. It does imply that a renewal of our obedience to Jesus Christ in this visible uniting of His Church can be the occasion of fresh indwelling of the Holy Spirit and a new *charisma* for us all.

I mention first this principle of visible and historical continuity not because it is necessarily the most important to the catholic Christian but because it is the only basis on which a broad reunion can take place, and because it is and will continue to be the most difficult catholic conviction for evangelicals to understand and to accept. My proposal is simply to cut the Gordian knot of hundreds of years of controversy by establishing in the united Church an historic ministry recognized by all without doubt or scruple. The necessary safeguards and controls of such a ministry will become clear when I am listing the principles of reunion that catholic-minded Christians must grant to evangelicals if there is to be reunion between them.

2. The reunited Church must clearly confess the historic trinitarian faith received from the Apostles and set forth in the Apostles' and Nicene Creeds. Here there is no real issue between the Presbyterian and Episcopal Churches. The difference that must be bridged is the issue between those in all our Churches who stand for a corporate confession of historic faith and those who fear that any required confession is too restrictive. A quarter of a century ago this would have been a sharper issue and more difficult to bridge. The tendency of the Presbyterian Church to be over-legalistic and of the Episcopal Church to be over-traditional have been modified by renewed theological and biblical understanding in our time. Equally the tendency in some of the so-called free Churches to suppose that no belief, that no confession of the faith, was necessary has given way to a general recognition of the necessity of corporate and individual confession of Christian faith as against the secular, humanistic, and atheistic ideologies of our times.

3. The reunited Church must administer the two sacraments, instituted by Christ, the Lord's Supper (or Holy Communion, or Eucharist) and Baptism. These must be understood truly as Means of Grace by which God's grace and presence are made available to His people. It will not be necessary, I trust, for a precise doctrinal agreement to be reached about the mode of operation of the sacraments so long as the proper catholic concern for their reality is protected so that, with the Word, the Sacrament is recognized as a true means of grace and not merely a symbolic memorial.

Much more could be said. Doubtless there are those of catholic tradition who would like even at this stage to add precise points to protect their consciences and convictions. The above, however, are the basic points and seem to me to be enough to be listed as basic principles if we are willing to add one more word. It must be agreed that every attempt will be made by those drawing up an actual plan of union to include within it those essentials of catholic practice and faith that will enable those of that persuasion to worship and witness joyfully and in good conscience within the fellowship of the united Church.

And now let me list the principles of reunion that are important to all who are of the reformation tradition:

1. The reunited Church must accept the principle of continuing reformation under the Word of God by the guidance of the Holy Spirit. A few years ago I would have felt that here was an issue on which no possible agreement could be reached. The reformation Churches have traditionally found their authority for faith and life in the Scriptures alone. So long as the wording *sola scriptura* is required, no bridge can be made between catholic and evangelical. But it is now clear in ecumenical conversations that Protestants generally have come to recognize the right place of tradition, just as catholics have generally become aware of the rightness of judging all tradition by the Scriptures as interpreted to the Church by the Holy Spirit.

The point that the Reformation tradition does require from a reunited Church is that God speaking through the Scriptures, must be able to reform the Church from age to age. While the Bible is not a law book or a collection of proof texts, it is God's instrument to speak His Saving Word to Christians and to the Church. If the catholic must insist on taking the sacraments more seriously than some protestants have sometimes done, so protestants in the reunited Church must insist on catholics fully accepting the reformation principle that God has revealed and can reveal Himself and His will more and more fully through the Holy Scriptures. The reunited Church must keep Word and Sacrament equally and intimately united in understanding and appreciation.

2. The reunited Church must be truly democratic in its government, recognizing that the whole people of God are Christ's Church, that all Christians are Christ's ministers even though some in the Church are separated and ordained to the ministry of word and sacrament. You will have noticed that in the first catholic principle which I mentioned I proposed that the traditional three-fold ministry in the apostolic succession be established in the reunited Church. If evangelical protestants are to enter such a Church with joy and in conscience there are several subsidiary points that must be made clear in the government and ethos of the reunited Church.

Episcopal churches should recognize that it will be with great reluctance that Presbyterians and Congregationalists will accept bishops in the structure of the Church. I should say, however, that there are many aspects of Episcopacy that American Presbyterians and other non-Episcopal Churches more and more generally recognize as valuable and needed. We Presbyterians for example need pastors of pastors quite desperately, and we know it. But we don't need an aristocratic or authoritarian hierarchy, and we don't believe a reunited Church does either. Furthermore Congregationalists and Presbyterians need to recognize how much of democracy is now practiced in American Episcopal churches. In this diocese I remind you that presbyteries have been already established.

On the positive side we Presbyterians would offer to the reunited Church the office of the ordained ruling elder, elected by the people in their congregations to share fully and equally in the government of the church. It will be important for all entering this union to attempt creatively to develop a new form of government that avoids the monarchical, clerical, and authoritarian tendencies that have been historically the dangers of episcopal church government. Equally this new form of government must avoid the bureaucratic dangers that appear to be the chief threat of non-episcopal churches. It is the essence of Protestant concern, however, that decisions should generally be made by ordered groups of men under the guidance of the Holy Spirit rather than by a man who has personal authority to impose on others his decision or judgment.

While Protestants more and more recognize that a *catholic* understanding of the sacraments does not necessarily imply a clerical control of the church nor the priestly abuses that introduced fear and magic into the medieval church and chiefly caused the Reformation, nevertheless they hold the conviction as strongly as ever that clericalism and priestly control of the church must be guarded against by a government of the church in which lay people and ministers share equally.

It will be further important to continue to protect in the united Church the responsible freedom of congregations including the election of their pastors and the responsible freedom of ministers to answer the call of God received through the free action of the people. I may say that this ought to present no great problem since all our Churches are largely *congregational* in this respect. At the same time I would hope that all of those entering into such a union as I here propose would be concerned also to find a way in the context of such freedom to preserve the Methodist ability to find some place of employment of his gifts for every minister who is in good and regular standing. If the reunited Church is to have a dedicated and competent ministry, we must find a better way than any of us has yet found to recruit, educate, and employ a ministry avoiding on the one hand professionalism and on the other that kind of equalitarianism which produces disorder and anarchy in the Church.

3. The reunited Church must seek in a new way to recapture the brotherhood and sense of fellowship of all its members and ministers. Let me illustrate what I mean by a series of suggestions of what might appear on the surface to be minor matters but which if creatively resolved in the reunited Church would not only remove many protestant misgivings but would, I believe,

strengthen the witness of the Church to the world. Since it appears to be necessary to have certain inequalities in status in the Church as between members and officers, and as among deacons, presbyters, and bishops, let us make certain that the more status a member or minister has the more simple be his dress and attitude. Let us seek to make it evident in every possible way that in the Church the greatest is the servant of all. "My brother" is a better form of Christian address than "your grace." A simple cassock is generally a better Christian garb for the highest member of the clergy than cope and miter. And must there be grades of reverends, very, right, most, etc.? Do there even need to be any reverends at all? It is actually provided explicitly in the Union Plan of Ceylon that a Bishop shall not be addressed as "My Lord." It would be my hope that those planning for a reunited Church would take the occasion to find many ways to exhibit to each other and to the world that we take seriously our Lord's word, "You know that those who are supposed to rule over the Gentiles lord it over them and their great men exercise authority over them. But it shall not be so among you; but whoever would be great among you must be your servant."

Clearly connected with this will be such matters as finding a way to avoid too great inequities in ministers' salaries, in the richness or grandeur of ecclesiastical establishments, lest the poor be alienated or the world conclude that luxury has sapped the soul of the Church. I speak in the full recognition of the spiritual value of this great Church and the rightness of completing it in beauty. Yet I speak for simplicity and brotherhood as ever being the requirement of Christ's Church.

4. Finally the reunited Church must find the way to include within its catholicity (and because of it) a wide diversity of theological formulations of the faith and a variety of worship and liturgy including worship that is non-liturgical.

The great confessions of the Reformation must have their place in the confession, teaching, and history of the reunited Church just as do the ecumenical agreements of the undivided Church. I would hope that such a Reformation confession as the Heidelburg Catechism, partly because of its Lutheran elements, might be lifted up in some acceptable formula as having a proper place in the confession of the whole Church. And further, the reunited Church should, as led by the Holy Spirit under the Word, from time to time seek to confess its united faith to the world in new formulations appropriate to its place and time. Our two Churches, however, need to appreciate better than they have the fact that direct and joyful experience of Jesus Christ as John Wesley knew it can be restricted too much by overreliance on creedal formulas. Our two Churches need to appreciate better than they have the liberating and creative inspiration of the Holy Spirit in the theological freedom of the congregational churches at their best.

Thus the united Church must avoid that kind of legalistic formulation of doctrine which on the ground of expressing unity of faith in fact produces a sterile uniformity which breeds alternately neglect and schism.

In worship there is great value in a commonly used, loved, and recognized liturgy. But such liturgy ought not to be imposed by authority or to be made binding upon the Holy Spirit or the congregations. More and more it would be our hope that in such a Church, as is here proposed, there would be developed common ways of worship both historic and freshly inspired. But history proves too well that imposed liturgy like imposed formulation of doctrine often destroys the very unity it is designed to strengthen.

Again there are many more things that those of the evangelical tradition in all our Churches would doubtless like at this stage to add as precise points to protect their consciences and convictions. The above, however, seem to be the essential and basic points which such a union as I propose would require if here again we are willing to add one more word. We must agree that every attempt will be made by those drawing up the plan of union to include within it those essentials of reformation faith and practice that will enable those of that persuasion to worship and witness joyfully and with good conscience within the fellowship of the reunited Church.

Here I would insert the assumption that all would understand that the reunited Church must remain in the ecumenical movement and its councils. It must be no less—it must be even more concerned beyond itself, recognizing that its reunion was but a stage and a step toward that unity which Christ requires His Church to manifest. This means also that the reunited Church must provide that such relationships of fellowship, cooperation, and intercommunion as the several Churches now have will be continued; this despite the difficulty and tension that such ambiguous relationships will continue to cause.

In conclusion I would remind you that precise ways of formulating such a reunion as I have sketched have been worked out in several ways particularly in the sub-continent of India in the several plans of union there. One may ask why they have preceded us in this, and alternatively why we should look to their example for light and inspiration toward union here.

The answer to these questions is a simple one. Christians in India recognize themselves to be a small and beleaguered minority in a pagan and secular world. They have realized full well that they could not afford the luxury of their divisions. I submit that even though our numbers and wealth and prestige may be greater than theirs, we too need to recognize that we cannot afford longer the luxury of our historic divisions. It is because of this conviction that I have felt impelled to preach this sermon.

There are two results that I pray may, under God, come from it. If there is support for what I have said in my own Church, any or all of our presbyteries may, if they will, overture the General Assembly which meets next May asking that Assembly to make an official proposal. I further hope that the Protestant Episcopal Church, by its own processes will also take an early action in this direction so that in your General Convention next fall the invitation to the Methodist Church and the United Church of Christ may be jointly issued to proceed to draw up a plan of union to which any other Churches of Jesus Christ accepting the bases suggested and the plan developed will be warmly invited to join.

Now I have not forgotten that this is a sermon and that it is an unconscionably long time since I announced my text. To you who have patiently listened to my longer than usual exposition, I ask one thing more: that you pray for the reunion of Christ's Church and that as you think about it and examine your own heart and mind, you do it in the spirit of the Apostle Paul when he addressed the saints and bishops and deacons of the church at Philippi.

Paul wrote, "Complete my joy by being of the same mind, having the same love, being in full accord and of one mind." The Apostle continued: "Do nothing from selfishness or conceit, but in humility count others better than yourselves. Let each of you look not only to his own interests but also to the interests of others. Have this mind among yourselves which you have in Christ Jesus, who, though he was in the form of God, did not count equality with God a thing to be grasped, but emptied himself, taking the form of a servant, being born in the likeness of men. And being found in human form, he humbled himself and became obedient unto death, even death on a cross. Therefore God has highly exalted him and bestowed on him the name that is above every name, that at the name of Jesus every knee should bow . . . and every tongue confess that Jesus Christ is Lord to the glory of God the Father."

If you, dear friends, and all others who consider and discuss this proposal do so in this spirit and from this motive, I have no fear but that the eternally recreative God will find His way to renew and reunite His Church.

Ascription: Now the God of hope fill you with all joy and peace in believing, that ye may abound in hope through the power of the Holy Ghost. Amen.

Response

James A. Pike
Grace Cathedral
San Francisco, California
December 4, 1960

I CANNOT PROCEED WITH the liturgy without saying an enthusiastic *Amen* to what this great Christian leader has said, under the Word of God, in this Cathedral Church dedicated in its founding document to the promotion of the unity of Christ's Church. I believe that I speak for you all when I say that the response to this sermon should be the same as that which we sang in response to the Gospel: *Glory be to thee, O Lord: Praise be to thee, O Christ.*

Just as Dr. Blake has not spoken officially for his own Church, I cannot speak officially for mine. But as a Bishop in the historic succession, which the preacher regards as an element in the united Church, I can say that his prophetic proclamation is the most sound and inspiring proposal for the unity of the Church in this country which has ever been made in its history. I hope and pray that his plan will be received by the four Churches—and others—in the Christian spirit in which it has been offered and that definite action toward its fulfillment will soon be forthcoming. I shall certainly labor to this end.

But that I am not alone in what I know will be a warm response throughout my own Church is clear not only from the fact that the Lambeth Conference of 1958 (consisting of 310 Bishops of the Anglican Communion assembling from forty-six countries) gave general approval to participation by our diocese in the area to current unity plans, based on the same principles, in North India, Pakistan and Ceylon; but also from the fact that at Lambeth we said the following, which I quote from the Lambeth Report:

"'Physician, heal thyself'—such is the challenge which comes with ever increasing urgency to the Church today, as the Church seeks, in obedience to Christ, to proclaim the word of reconciliation in the midst of a world torn by divisions and conflicts ...

"We fully recognize that there are other forms of ministry than episcopacy in which have been revealed the gracious activity of God in the life of the universal Church. We believe that other Churches have often borne more effective witness, for example, to the status and vocation of the laity as spiritual persons and to the fellowship and discipline of congregational life than has been done in some of the Churches of our communion. It is our longing that all of the spiritual gifts and insights by which the particular Churches live to His Glory may find their full scope and enrichment in a united Church.

"The unity between Christian Churches ought to be a living unity in the love of Christ which is shown in full Christian fellowship and in mutual service, while also, subject to sufficient agreement in Faith and Order, expressing itself in free interchange of ministries, and fullness of sacramental Communion. Such unity, while marked by the bond of the historic episcopate, should always include congregational fellowship, active participation of both clergy and laity in the mission and government of the Church, and zeal for evangelism.

"Such is the vision we set before ourselves and our own people, calling them to regard the recovery and manifestation of the unity of the whole Church of Christ as a matter of the greatest urgency."

Today the Stated Clerk of The United Presbyterian Church has for Christians in our country made that vision more clear and that urgency more evident. Glory be to thee, O Lord; Praise be to thee, O Christ.

Abbreviations of Church Names

AME	African Methodist Episcopal Church
AMEZ	African Methodist Episcopal Zion Church
CCDC	Christian Church (Disciples of Christ)
CME	Christian Methodist Episcopal Church
EC	Episcopal Church
EUB	Evangelical United Brethren Church
ICCC	International Council of Community Churches
MC	The Methodist Church
NCCC	National Council of Community Churches
PCUS	Presbyterian Church in the United States
PCUSA	Presbyterian Church in the United States of America
UCC	United Church of Christ
UMC	United Methodist Church
UPCUSA	United Presbyterian Church in the United States of America

COCU Timeline of Meetings
(Plenary Assemblies)

First Meeting—April 9-10, 1962—Washington, D.C.

James I. McCord (UPCUSA), Chair
Charles C. Parlin, Secretary
George L. Hunt, General Secretary
Participating churches: EC, MC, UCC, UPCUSA
The Consultation on Church Union established; invitations sent to CCDC, EUB, and Polish National Catholic Church to join

Second Meeting—March 19-21, 1963—Oberlin, Ohio

James I. McCord (UPCUSA), Chair
Charles C. Parlin, Secretary
George L. Hunt, General Secretary
Participating churches: CCDC, EC, EUB, MC, UCC, UPCUSA
Consensus on "Scripture, Tradition, and the Guardians of Tradition"

Third Meeting—April 13-16, 1964—Princeton, New Jersey

James I. McCord (UPCUSA), Chair
Charles C. Parlin, Secretary
George L. Hunt, General Secretary
Paul A. Crow Jr., Associate General Secretary
Participating churches: CCDC, EC, EUB, MC, UCC, UPCUSA
Consensus on Baptism and the Lord's Supper

Fourth Meeting—April 5–8, 1965—Lexington, Kentucky

Robert F. Gibson Jr. (EC), Chair
Eugene Carson Blake, Vice Chair
George L. Hunt, General Secretary
Paul A. Crow Jr., Associate General Secretary
Participating churches: CCDC, EC, EUB, MC, UCC, UPCUSA
Discussion of issues related to the ministry

Fifth Meeting—May 2–5, 1966—Dallas, Texas

Robert F. Gibson Jr. (EC), Chair
Eugene Carson Blake, Vice Chair
George L. Hunt, General Secretary
Paul A. Crow Jr., Associate General Secretary
Participating Churches: AME, CCDC, EC, EUB, MC, UCC, UPCUSA
Principles of Church Union approved

Sixth Meeting—May 1–4, 1967—Cambridge, Massachusetts

David G. Colwell (UCC), Chair
James K. Matthews, Vice Chair
George L. Hunt, General Secretary
Paul A. Crow Jr., Associate General Secretary
Participating Churches: AME, AMEZ, CCDC, CME, EC, EUB, MC,
    PCUS, UCC, UPCUSA
"Guidelines for the Structure of the Church" approved
Decision to develop a plan of union

Seventh Meeting—March 25–28, 1968—Dayton, Ohio

David G. Colwell (UCC), Chair
James K. Mathews, Vice Chair
George L. Hunt, General Secretary
Paul A. Crow Jr., Associate General Secretary
Paul A. Washburn, Acting Associate General Secretary
Participating Churches: AME, AMEZ, CCDC, CME, EC, EUB, MC,
    PCUS, UCC, UPCUSA
Approved *Principles of Church Union* (Preamble and Chapters I–IV) as the
    basis upon which to formulate a plan of union.

An Order of Worship for the Proclamation of the Word of God and the Celebration of the Lord's Supper received

Eighth Meeting—March 17-20, 1969—Atlanta, Georgia

James K. Mathews (UMC), Chair
George G. Beazley Jr., Vice Chair
Paul A. Crow Jr., General Secretary (first full-time person)
W. Clyde Williams (CME) becomes Associate General Secretary (first full-time person)
Participating Churches: AME, AMEZ, CCDC, CME, EC, PCUS, UCC, UMC, UPCUSA
"A Preliminary Outline of a Plan of Union" presented
"Guidelines for Local Interchurch Action" transmitted to the churches

Ninth Meeting—March 9-13, 1970—St. Louis, Missouri

James K. Mathews (UMC), Chair
George G. Beazley Jr., Vice Chair
Paul A. Crow, Jr., General Secretary
W. Clyde Williams, Associate General Secretary
Participating Churches: AME, AMEZ, CCDC, CME, EC, PCUS, UCC, UMC, UPCUSA
"A Plan of Union for the Church of Christ Uniting," commended for study
"Guidelines for Local Interchurch Action" adopted

Tenth Meeting—September 27-30, 1971—Denver, Colorado

George G. Beazley Jr. (CCDC), Chair
Charles S. Spivey Jr., Lois Stair, Vice Chairs
Paul A. Crow Jr., General Secretary
W. Clyde Williams, Associate General Secretary
Participating churches: AME, AMEZ, CCDC, CME, EC, PCUS, UCC, UMC, UPCUSA
Recommendations to churches concerning racial justice, increased interchurch activity, middle judicatory relations, and change of COCU delegations so that they include a more equitable representation of minority groups, women, and persons under twenty-five

Eleventh Meeting—April 2-6, 1973—Memphis, Tennessee

George G. Beazley Jr. (CCDC), Chair
Charles S. Spivey Jr., Vice Chair
Paul A. Crow Jr., General Secretary
William C. Larkin, Associate General Secretary
Participating churches: AME, AMEZ, CCDC, CME, EC, PCUS, UCC,
    UMC
Five priorities listed: Institutional Racism; Faith, Worship, Ministry, Gen-
    erating Communities, Study of the Local Expression of the Church;
    Interim Eucharistic Fellowship
Decision to revise "A Plan of Union"
Proposal to establish Generating Communities
IN COMMUNITY, a newsletter for the Generating Communities Project
    authorized,
Task force to study the forms of the church and the local level and a Com-
    mission on Institutional Racism authorized
"Guidelines for Interim Eucharistic Fellowship"
"Steps to Interim Eucharistic Fellowship"
An Order for the Celebration of Baptism received

Twelfth Meeting—November 4-8, 1974—Cincinnati, Ohio

Frederick D. Jordan (AME), Chair
Rachel Henderlite, Arthur Marshall Jr., Vice Chairs
Gerald F. Moede becomes General Secretary
John H. Satterwhite becomes Associate General Secretary
Participating churches: AME, AMEZ, CCDC, CME, EC, PCUS, UCC,
    UMC, UPCUSA
"Toward the Mutual Recognition of Members" referred to the churches
"Recommendations for Action" made on the issue of racism

Thirteenth Meeting—November 3-6, 1976—Dayton, Ohio

Frederick D. Jordan (AME), Chair
Rachel Henderlite, Arthur Marshall Jr., Vice Chairs
Gerald F. Moede, General Secretary
John H. Satterwhite, Associate General Secretary
Participating churches: AME, AMEZ, CCDC, CME, EC, NCCC, PCUS,
    UCC, UMC, UPCUSA

In Quest of a Church of Christ Uniting sent to the churches as a statement
   of emerging theological consensus for study and response
National Council of Community Churches becomes tenth participating
   church

Fourteenth Meeting (First Session)—March 6-9, 1979—Cincinnati, Ohio

Rachel Henderlite (PCUS), President
Albert M. Pennybacker, Secretary
Gerald F. Moede, General Secretary
John E. Brandon, Associate General Secretary
Participating churches: AME, AMEZ, CCDC, EC, NCCC, PCUS, UCC,
   UMC, UPCUSA
Commission on Governance appointed
WORD BREAD CUP published (1978)

Fourteenth Meeting (Second Session)—January 22-24, 1980—Cincinnati, Ohio

Rachel Henderlite (PCUS), President
Albert M. Pennybacker, Secretary
Gerald F. Moede, General Secretary
John E. Brandon, Associate General Secretary
Participating Churches: AME, AMEZ, CCDC, EC, NCCC, PCUS, UCC,
   UMC, UPCUSA
Chapter VII of *In Quest* sent to the churches
An Order for An Affirmation of the Baptismal Covenant received
An Order for the Birth or Adoption of a Child received

Fifteenth Meeting—March 7-12, 1982—St. Louis, Missouri

Arthur Marshall Jr. (AMEZ), President
Robert W. Huston, Louise Wallace, Vice Presidents
Gerald F. Moede, General Secretary
William D. Watley, Associate General Secretary
Participating Churches: AME, AMEZ, CCDC, CME, EC, ICCC, PCUS,
   UCC, UMC, UPCUSA
Responses from *In Quest* received from churches

Covenanting introduced for discussion

United Presbyterian Church, USA, and Presbyterian Church, US unite,
forming Presbyterian Church (USA)

Sixteenth Meeting—November 26–30, 1984—Baltimore, Maryland

Arthur Marshall Jr. (AMEZ), President

Robert W. Huston and Louise Wallace, Vice Presidents

Gerald F. Moede, General Secretary

William D. Watley, Associate General Secretary

Participating Churches: AME, AMEZ, CCDC, CME, EC, ICCC, PCUSA,
UCC, UMC

The COCU Consensus: In Quest of a Church of Christ Uniting. Approved
and commended to the churches by the Sixteenth Plenary of the
Consultation on Church Union. Edited by Gerald F. Moede (Princeton:
Consultation on Church Union, 1985).

Covenanting concept accepted for study and response by member
churches

The Sacrament of the Lord's Supper: A New Text received

Seventeenth Meeting—December 5–9, 1988—New Orleans, Louisiana

George H. Pike (PCUSA), President

Marshall Gilmore, Donald J. Parsons, Vice Presidents

David W. A. Taylor, General Secretary

Associate General Secretary

Participating Churches: AME, AMEZ, CCDC, CME, EC, ICCC, PCUSA,
UCC, UMC

*The COCU Consensus: In Quest of a Church of Christ Uniting, Second
Edition.* Approved and commended to the churches by the Sixteenth
Plenary of the Consultation on Church Union. (Princeton: Consulta-
tion on Church Union, 1989)

Churches in Covenant Communion: The Church of Christ Uniting. Approved and recommended to the churches by the Seventeenth Plenary
of the Consultation on Church Union. (Princeton: Consultation on
Church Union, 1988).

January 20–24, 1998— Eighteenth Meeting—St. Louis, Missouri

Vivian U. Robinson (CME), President

Vinton R. Anderson, Alice C. Cowan, Vice Presidents

Lewis H. Lancaster Jr., Interim General Secretary

Participating Churches: AME, AMEZ, CCDC, CME, EC, ICCC, PCUSA, UCC, UMC

Churches Uniting in Christ Inauguration—January 18–21, 2002— Memphis, Tennessee

Michael K. Kinnamon, General Secretary

Gordon White, Associate General Secretary

Participating Churches: AME, AMEZ, CCDC, CME, EC, ICCC, PCUSA, UCC, UMC

The Consultation on Church Union is closed and the participating churches create a new ecumenical structure, Churches Uniting in Christ

Bibliography

Digests of Proceedings and Papers of the Plenary Assemblies of the Consultation on Church Union

THROUGHOUT ITS FORTY-YEAR HISTORY, the Consultation on Church Union published digests of the proceedings, essays, papers, and Bible studies presented at the plenary assemblies. These digests included financial reports and rosters of participants. For meetings one through eleven, these materials were published in two forms: in *Mid-Stream*, the quarterly journal of the Council on Christian Unity of the Christian Church (Disciples of Christ), and as separate volumes entitled *Digest of the Proceedings of the . . . Meeting of the Consultation on Church Union*. Beginning with the twelfth plenary assembly, *Mid-Stream* published only the essays, papers, and Bible studies. The Consultation's Princeton office published the *Digest of Proceedings*, including rosters of participants and financial reports. The titles of these publications varied across the years, but libraries tend to use standardized forms for reporting these documents in their catalogs.

In this bibliography, the digests of the Consultation on Church Union are listed in a standardized pattern that includes publication information. An abbreviated title is used in footnotes. Whenever possible, the *Mid-Stream* location is given for addresses, essays, and major reports prepared for COCU plenary assemblies. This journal can be accessed through the database maintained by ATLA (American Theological Library Association).

Digest of the First Meeting of the Consultation on Church Union. Mid-Stream 2:4 (1963).
Digest of the Second Meeting of the Consultation on Church Union. Mid-Stream 2:4 (1963).
Digest of the Third Meeting of the Consultation on Church Union. Mid-Stream 3:4 (1964).
Digest of the Fourth Meeting of the Consultation on Church Union. Mid-Stream 4:4 (1965).
Digest of the Fifth Meeting of the Consultation on Church Union. Mid-Stream 5:3 (1966).

Digest of the Sixth Meeting of the Consultation on Church Union. Mid-Stream 6:4 (1967).

Digest of the Seventh Meeting of the Consultation on Church Union. Mid-Stream 7:3 (1968).

Digest of the Eighth Meeting of the Consultation on Church Union. Mid-Stream 8:1 (1969).

Digest of the Ninth Meeting of the Consultation on Church Union. Mid-Stream 9:1 (1970).

Digest of the Tenth Meeting of the Consultation on Church Union. Mid-Stream 10:2–3 (1971).

Digest of the Eleventh Meeting of the Consultation on Church Union. Mid-Stream 12:1 (1973).

Digest of the Twelfth Meeting of the Consultation on Church Union. Worship, Articles, Essays. *Mid-Stream* 14:2 (1975). *Official Record, Supplement.* Princeton: Consultation on Church Union, 1975.

Digest of the Thirteenth Meeting of the Consultation on Church Union. Addresses and Reports. *Mid-Stream* 16:1 (1977). *Official Record.* Princeton: Consultation on Church Union, 1977.

Digest of the Fourteenth Meeting of the Consultation on Church Union. First Session. Mid-Stream 18:3 (1979). *Proceedings.* Princeton: Consultation on Church Union, 1979.

Digest of the Fourteenth Meeting of the Consultation on Church Union. Second Session. Princeton: Consultation on Church Union, 1980.

Digest of the Fifteenth Meeting of the Consultation on Church Union. Princeton: Consultation on Church Union, 1982.

Digest of the Sixteenth Meeting of the Consultation on Church Union. Articles and Papers. *Mid-Stream* 24:2 (1985). *Proceedings.* Princeton: Consultation on Church Union, 1985.

Digest of the Proceedings of the Seventeenth Meeting of the Consultation on Church Union. Princeton: Consultation on Church Union, 1989.

Digest of the Eighteenth Meeting of the Consultation on Church Union. Preparatory Papers. *Mid-Stream* 37:3–4 (1998). *Proceedings. Mid-Stream* 39:1– 2 (2000).

Inauguration of Churches Uniting in Christ. Addresses. *Mid-Stream* 41:2–3 (2002).

Essays, Articles, and Books

Abraham-Williams, Gethin, et. al. "Survey of Church Union Negotiations, 1994–1996." *The Ecumenical Review* 49/2 (1997) 223–62.

Allen, Horace. "One Visibly Catholic Church." *Theology Today* 18:3 (1961) 321–329.

"Appeal to the Churches 'To Seek God's Beloved Community.'" *Mid-Stream* 41/2–3 (2002) 27-29.

Arndt, Elmer J. F. "The Ministry of the Church: Toward a Limited Ministry in the United Church." *McCormick Quarterly* 20 (1967) 215–22.

Bannister, Kathryn. "There Is Still Room." *Mid-Stream* 41/2–3 (2002) 11-16.

Baptism, Eucharist and Ministry. Faith and Order Paper No. 111. Geneva: World Council of Churches, 1982.

Bayne, Stephen F., Jr. "The Worship of the Church." *McCormick Quarterly* 20/3 (1967) 201–6.

Beazley, George G., Jr. "Editorial Introduction." *Mid-Stream* 3/4 (1964) vii.

————. "Editorial Introduction." *Mid-Stream* 5/3 (1966) i–v.

————. "The Faith of the Church." *McCormick Quarterly* 20/3 (1967) 194–200.

————, ed. *News on Christian Unity.* Indianapolis: Council on Christian Unity, 1970.

————. "A Personal View of the Consultation on Church Union." In *Church Union at Midpoint,* edited by Paul A. Crow Jr. and William Jerry Boney, 13–19. New York: Association Press, 1972.

Berger, Peter L. "A Call for Authority in the Christian Community." *Mid-Stream* 10/2–3 (1971) 113–29.

————. *The Noise of Solemn Assemblies.* Garden City, NY: Doubleday, 1961.

Best, Thomas F., and Theodore J. Nottingham, eds. *The Vision of Christian Unity: Essays in Honor of Paul A. Crow Jr.* Indianapolis: Oikoumene, 1997.

Blake, Eugene Carson. *The Church in the Next Decade.* New York: Macmillan, 1966.

————. "An Interim Report on the Proposal Toward the Reunion of Christ's Church in the United States." *The Ecumenical Review* 14/1 (1961) 82–91.

————. "A Proposal Toward the Reunion of Christ's Church." In *The Challenge to Reunion,* compiled and edited by Robert McAfee Brown and David H. Scott, 271–83. New York: McGraw Hill, 1963. Republshed in *The Ecumenical Review* 38/2 (1986) 140–48.

————. "The Union Proposal Two Years Later." *Christian Century,* March 27, 1963, 394–98.

Brackenridge, R. Douglas. *Eugene Carson Blake: Prophet with Portfolio.* New York: Seabury, 1978.

Brandon, John E. "Three Black Methodist Churches in the Consultation on Church Union: Problems and Prospects for Union." DMin diss., Boston University, 1986.

Brown, Robert McAfee, and David H. Scott, eds. *The Challenge to Reunion.* New York: McGraw-Hill, 1963.

Burnley, Lawrence A. Q. *The Cost of Unity: African-American Agency and Education and the Christian Church, 1865–1914.* Macon, GA: Mercer University Press, 2009.

Burt, John H. "Adventures in Mending the Seamless Robe of Christ." In *Joy in the Struggle,* edited by Edward W. Jones, 1–40. Cincinnati: Forward Movement, 1992.

Cate, William B. *The Ecumenical Scandal on Main Street.* New York: Association Press, 1965.

Church of South India. *The Book of Common Worship.* London: Oxford University Press, 1963.

Coalter, Milton J., et al. *The Diversity of Discipleship: Presbyterians and Twentieth-Century Christian Witness.* Louisville: Westminster/John Knox, 1991.

COCU and Covenant: Austin Seminary Review 96 (1981). Includes "Covenant in Recent Old Testament Studies," by Francisco O. Garcia-Treto; "Because the *Lord* Is Lord: Old Testament Covenant Imagery and Ecumenical Commitment," by W. Eugene March; "Appropriating New Testament Covenant Vocabulary in Ecumenical Commitment," by John F. Jansen; "The Covenant in Church History," by Robert S. Paul; "The Covenant Theme in Ecumenism and Ethics," by Lewis S. Mudge; and "The Covenant as Ecumenical Paradigm," by Paul A. Crow Jr.

Colwell, David. G. "The Sacraments in a United Church." *McCormick Quarterly* 20/3 (1967) 207–14.

Commission on Faith and Order. *"Racism in Theology" and "Theology Against Racism."* Geneva: World Council of Churches, 1975.

Commission on Worship of the Consultation on Church Union. *A Lectionary*. Princeton: Consultation on Church Union, 1979.

———. *An Order for an Affirmation of the Baptismal Covenant*. Princeton: Consultation on Church Union, 1980.

———. *An Order for the Celebration of Holy Baptism with Commentary*. Cincinnati: Forward Movement, 1973.

———. *An Order of Thanksgiving for the Birth or Adoption of a Child*. Princeton: Consultation on Church Union, 1980.

———. *An Order of Worship for The Proclamation of the Word of God and The Celebration of the Lord's Supper With Commentary*. Princeton: Consultation on Church Union, 1968.

———. "Sacrament of the Lord's Supper: A New Text 1984." Princeton: Consultation on Church Union, 1984.

———. *Word, Bread, Cup*. Princeton: Consultation on Church Union, 1978.

Consultation on Church Union. *Churches in Covenant Communion: The Church of Christ Uniting*. Princeton: Consultation on Church Union, 1989.

———. *Churches in Covenant Communion and The COCU Consensus*. Combined edition. Princeton: Consultation on Church Union, 1989.

———. *The COCU Consensus: In Quest of a Church of Christ Uniting*. Princeton: Consultation on Church Union, 1985.

———. *The COCU Consensus: In Quest of a Church of Christ Uniting*. 2nd ed. Princeton: Consultation on Church Union, 1989.

Corney, Richard. "The Reverend Canon Richard A. Norris Jr., 1930–2005." *Anglican Theological Review* 90/3 (2008) 419–23.

Crow, Paul A., Jr. "COCU and the Sparks of the Spirit." Editorial in *Mid-Stream* 18/3 (1979) pages unnumbered.

———. "Commitment for a Pilgrim People." *Mid-Stream* 10/2–3 (1971) 165–76.

———. "Education for Church Union—A Plan for Encounter." *Mid-Stream* 9/2–3 (1970) 82–100.

———. "Living Our Way Toward Union: COCU's Vital Signs." *Mid-Stream* 14/2 (1975) 210–23.

Crow, Paul A., Jr., and William Jerry Boney, eds. *Church Union at Midpoint*. New York: Association Press, 1972.

Day, Peter, ed. *Enter Into This Dialogue: A Resource for Studying a Plan of Union for the Church of Christ Uniting*. New York: Seabury, 1971.

Deschner, John. "COCU at the Turning Point." *Mid-Stream* 24/2 (1985) 138–49.

———. "Ecclesiological Aspects of the Race Problem." *International Review of Mission* 59/235 (1970) 285–95.

———. "A Theological Basis for the Consultation on Church Union." *Mid-Stream* 16/1 (1977) 23–29.

Dillenberger, John. "Theological-Cultural Factors Demanding Union of the Churches." *Mid-Stream* 2/4 (1963) 58–68.

———. "Theological Givens as Theological Orientations." *Mid-Stream* 6/4 (1967) 42–52.

Duba, Arlo D. *Presbyterian Worship in the Twentieth Century: With a Focus on the Book of Common Worship*. White Sulphur Springs, WV: OSL, 2012.

Erickson, Theodore. "Mission or Unity: COCU, The Local Church and the UCC." Privately circulated paper, 1970.

Filson, Floyd V. "The Consultation on Church Union." *McCormick Quarterly* 20/3 (1967) 187–93.

———. "Freedom Within Unity." *Mid-Stream* 4/4 (1965) 143–57.

Fox, William K. "Black and White Together: Challenge to True Ecumenism." *ACS Journal* (February 1967) 6–9.

Gibson, Robert F., Jr. "The Christian Ministry." In *Approaches Toward Unity*, edited by Ivan Lee Holt and Stephen E. Keeler, 63–74. Nashville: Parthenon, 1952.

Gros, Jeffrey. "Eradicating Racism: A Central Agenda for the Faith and Order Movement." *Journal of Ecumenical Studies* 47/1 (1995) 42–51.

———. "The Requirements and Challenges of Full Communion: A Multilateral Evaluation?" *The Ecumenical Review* 42/2 (2007) 217–42.

Guidelines for Interim Eucharistic Fellowship. Princeton: Consultation on Church Union, 1973.

Halberstam, David. *The Fifties.* New York: Fawcett, 1993.

Hall, Douglas John. *The End of Christendom and the Future of Christianity.* Eugene: Wipf & Stock, 2002.

Hamby, Daniell C. "The Winter Is Past! The COCU Vision Becoming a Reality." *Mid-Stream* 34/3 (1995) 51–59.

Handy, Robert T. "For the Record." *Foundations* 9 (1966) 363–74.

———. "The Ministry in American History: A Reflection in the Light of Ecumenical Encounter." *Mid-Stream* 4/4 (1965) 107–32.

Harrison, Paul M. *Authority and Power in the Free Church Tradition.* Princeton: Princeton University Press, 1959.

———. "Sociological Analysis of the Participating Communions." *Mid-Stream* 2/4 (1963) 96–119.

Haselden, Kyle. "Review of *The Challenge to Reunion*." *Theology Today* 20/3 (1963) 439–42.

Hazelton, Roger. "The Diaconate in a United Church." *Mid-Stream* 8/1 (1969) 74–87.

Henderlite, Rachel. "Musings on Christian Education (Upon receiving the Union Medal)." *Austin Seminary Bulletin [Faculty edition]* 99/8 (1984) 5–13.

Hoge, Dean R., and David A. Roozen, eds. *Understanding Church Growth and Decline, 1950–1978.* New York: Pilgrim, 1979.

Holland, DeWitte Talmadge, et al., eds. *Sermons in American History: Selected Issues in the American Pulpit, 1630–1967.* Nashville: Abingdon, 1971.

Hollinger, David A. *After Cloven Tongues of Fire: Protestant Liberalism in Modern American History.* Princeton: Princeton University Press, 2013; a chapter with that title also published in *American History* 98 (2011) 21–48.

Holt, Ivan Lee, and Stephen E. Keeler, eds. *Approaches Toward Unity: Papers Presented for Discussion at Joint Meetings of Protestant Episcopal and Methodist Commissions.* Nashville: Parthenon, 1952.

Hotchkin, John F. "COCU and the Wider Reality of Ecumenism." In *Church Union at Midpoint*, edited by Paul A. Crow Jr. and William Jerry Boney, 215–22. New York: Association Press, 1972.

Houck, Davis W., and David E. Dixon. *Rhetoric, Religion and the Civil Rights Movement, 1954–1965.* Waco: Baylor University Press, 2006.

Hunt, George L., and Paul A. Crow Jr. eds. *Where We Are in Church Union: A Report on the Present Accomplishments of the Consultation on Church Union.* New York: Association Press, 1965.

Indicators of Institutional Racism, Sexism, and Classism: Some Suggested Responses. New York: National Council of the Churches of Christ in the U.S.A., 1994.

Jameson, Vic. *What Does God Require of Us Now? A Resource for Studying a Plan of Union for the Church of Christ Uniting.* Nashville: Abingdon, 1970.

Jeske, Mark W., et al., trans. *Communio Sanctorum: The Church as the Communion of Saints.* Collegeville, MN: Liturgical, 2004.

Jones, E. Stanley. *The Christ of the American Road.* Nashville: Abingdon-Cokesbury, 1944.

Jones, Edward W. "Episcopalians and the Consultation on Church Union: 1985–1995." *Mid-Stream* 34/3 (1995) 61–73.

———, ed. *Joy in the Struggle: Personal Memoirs of Ecumenical Dialogue.* Cincinnati: Forward Movement, 1992.

Karefa-Smart, Rena. "The Ecumenical Challenge of United and Uniting Churches." *The Ecumenical Review* 47/4 (1995) 464–71.

Kavanagh, Aidan. *The Shape of Baptism: The Rite of Christian Initiation.* New York: Pueblo, 1978.

Kearns, Raymond V., Jr. "The Consultation's Unfinished Work on 'The Structure of the Church.'" *McCormick Quarterly* 20/3 (1967) 223–29.

Keller, Adolf. *Five Minutes to Twelve: A Spiritual Interpretation of the Oxford and Edinburgh Conferences.* Nashville: Cokesbury, 1938.

Kinnamon, Michael. "Ecumenical Ecclesiology: One Church of Christ for the Sake of the World." *Journal of Ecumenical Studies* 44/3 (2009) 341–51.

———. "We Have Come This Far By Faith: Reflections on Where We Have Been and Where We are Headed as Churches Uniting in Christ." *Mid-Stream* 41/2–3 (2002) 1–9.

Kinnamon, Michael, and Brian E. Cope, eds. *The Ecumenical Movement: An Anthology of Key Texts and Voices.* Geneva: WCC, 2002.

Lehman, Paul. "The Unity of the Church in the Struggle for Justice." *Mid-Stream* 14/2 (1975) 257–74.

Macquarrie, John, et al., eds. *Realistic Reflections on Church Union.* N.p, 1967.

Maertens, Marlene, ed. *The Challenge to the Church: The Niemöller-Blake Conversations.* Philadelphia: Westminster, 1965.

Mathews, James K. *A Church Truly Catholic.* Nashville: Abingdon, 1969.

———. *A Global Odyssey: The Autobiography of James K. Matthews.* Nashville: Abingdon, 2000.

———. *Set Apart to Serve: The Meaning and Role of Episcopacy in the Wesleyan Tradition.* Nashville: Abingdon, 1985.

"Meditation for Maundy Thursday." *Theology Today* 33/4 (1977) 368.

Moede, Gerald F. "Called Together." *Mid-Stream* 14/2 (1975) 230–31.

———. "The Consultation on Church Union: COCU's Second Era, 1974–1988." Unpublished paper, 1998.

———. "Ecumenical Pressure and the Mutual Recognition of Baptism/Members." *Mid-Stream* 17/3 (1979) 238–66.

———, ed. *God's Power and Our Weakness.* Task Force of Persons with Disabilities. Princeton: Consultation on Church Union, 1982.

———. "Members, Ministers, and Morphe of the One Body." *Mid-Stream* 18/3 (1979) 209–29.

———. *The Office of Bishop in Methodism.* Nashville: Abingdon, 1964.

———. *Toward Unity in Covenant Communion*. Princeton: Consultation on Church Union, 1988.

Mollengen, Albert T. "The Relationship Between the Ministry of the Whole People of God and the Ordained Ministry." *Mid-Stream* 4/4 (1965) 133–42.

Morrison, Charles Clayton. "The Ecumenical Trend in American Protestantism." *The Ecumenical Review* 3/1 (1950) 9–13.

Mudge, Lewis S. *Renewing the Ecumenical Vision: Theology and Worship Occasional Paper No. 7*. Louisville: Presbyterian Church (U.S.A.), [1996].

———. *The Sense of a People: Toward a Church for the Human People*. Philadelphia: Trinity, 1992.

Murray, Peter C. *Methodists and the Crucible of Race, 1930–1975*. Columbia: University of Missouri Press, 2004.

"National Act of Worship Inaugurating Churches Uniting in Christ." *Mid-Stream* 41/2–3 (2002) 42–51.

Nelson, J. Robert. "Pike, Hedley and Otwell." *Christian Century*, March 9, 1960, 279–80.

Norgren, William A., and William G. Rusch, eds. *Toward Full Communion* and *Concordat of Agreement: Lutheran-Episcopal Dialogue, Series II*. Minneapolis: Augsburg, 1991.

Osborn, Ronald E. *A Church for These Times*. Nashville: Abingdon, 1965.

———. "The Meaning of Presbyter in the United Church." *Mid-Stream* 8/1 (1969) 88–105.

———. "Ministry or Ministries." *Mid-Stream* 4/4 (1965) 206–26.

———. "Moving Yet and Never Stopping." *Mid-Stream* 14/2 (1975) 198–209.

———. "Religious Freedom and the Form of the Church." *Lexington Theological Quarterly* 11/3 (1976) 85–106.

———. *The Spirit of American Christianity*. New York: Harper, 1958.

———. "Theology in the Consultation: Commitment, Consensus, Integrity." In *Church Union at Midpoint*, edited by Paul A. Crow Jr. and William Jerry Boney, 64–79. New York: Association Press, 1972.

Outler, Albert C. *The Christian Tradition and the Unity We Seek*. New York: Oxford University Press, 1957.

———. "The Mingling of Ministries." *Mid-Stream* 8/1 (1968) 106–18.

———. "Scripture, Tradition and the Guardians of Tradition." *Mid-Stream* 2/4 (1963) 83–95.

Pastoral Letter on Contemporary Racism and the Role of the Church. Cleveland: The United Church of Christ, 1991.

Paton, David M, ed. *Breaking Barriers: Nairobi 1975*. Grand Rapids: Eerdmans, 1976.

Paul, Robert S. "The Cost of Covenant: Studies in the New Covenant." *Digest of the Fifteenth Meeting*, 12–35.

———. "The Covenant in Church History." *Austin Seminary Bulletin: COCU and Covenant* 96 (1981) 38–50.

Pennybacker, Albert M. "The Possibilities in the Parish." *Mid-Stream* 12/2–4 (1973) 97–104.

———. "Singing from the Heart . . . A Guide for Disciples Studying Churches in Covenant Communion." St. Louis: Christian Board of Publication, [1991].

Pike, James A. "Response: Statement Made after the Sermon on Church Unity." In *The Challenge to Reunion*, compiled and edited by Robert McAfee Brown and David H. Scott, 283–84. New York: McGraw Hill, 1963. The typescript of Pike's remarks following Blake's sermon is housed in his papers at Syracuse University, http://library.syr.edu/digital/guides/p/pike_ja.htm.

———. "That They May Be One: In Reply to Professor Otwell." *Christian Century* January 13, 1960, 46–48.

———. "Three-Pronged Synthesis." *Christian Century*. December 21, 1960, 1496–1500.

Plan of Union for the Church of Christ Uniting. Princeton: Consultation on Church Union, 1970.

Principles of Church Union, Adopted by the Consultation at Its Meeting, 1966. Cincinnati: Forward Movement, [1966]; Revised and expanded edition, *Consultation on Church Union 1967: Principles of Church Union, Guidelines for Structure, and a Study Guide*. Cincinnati: Forward Movement, 1967.

Quillian, James D., Jr., et. al. *The Celebration of the Gospel: A Study in Christian Worship*. Nashville: Abingdon, 1964.

Raiser, Konrad. *For a Culture of Life: Transforming Globalism and Violence*. Geneva: WCC, 2002.

Rasmussen, Larry L., ed. *Reinhold Niebuhr: Theologian of Public Life*. Minneapolis: Fortress, 1991.

Robertson, David M. *A Passionate Pilgrim: A Biography of Bishop James A. Pike*. New York: Knopf, 2004.

Robinson, Vivian U. "Reflections of the President on the Past Ten Years of the Consultation on Church Union." *Mid-Stream* 39/1–2 (2000) 35–39.

Rogers, Cornish R. "Blacks and COCU: A New History." *Christian Century*, December 30, 1970, 1554.

Root, Michael. "Faith and Order in a Postmodern World: A Response." *Journal of Ecumenical Studies* 42/4 (2007) 560–70.

Root, Michael, and Risto Saarinen, eds. *Baptism and the Unity of the Church*. Grand Rapids: Eerdmans, 1998.

Rose, Stephen C. "COCU 1970: A Symposium." *Christian Century*, February 25, 1970, 231–43.

———. "The Coming Confrontation on the Church's War Investments." *Christian Century*, October 14, 1970, 1209–11.

———. *The Grass Roots Church: A Manifesto for Protestant Renewal*. New York: Holt, Rinehart and Winston, 1966.

Rusch, William G., ed. *Justification and the Future of the Ecumenical Movement*. Collegeville, MN: Liturgical, 2003.

Satterwhite, John H. "Church Union for Justice and Liberation." *Mid-Stream* 14/2 (1975) 250–56.

———. "For Authentic Freedom: COCU and Black Churches." *Christian Century*, February 25, 1970, 236.

———, ed. *Liberation and Unity: A Guide for Meditation and Action*. Memphis: Department of Education of the Christian Methodist Episcopal Church, 1977.

Shands, Alfred. *The Liturgical Movement and the Local Church*. Rev. and enlarged ed. New York: Morehouse-Barlow, 1965.

Shenk, Wilbert R. "Lesslie Newbigin's Contribution to the Theology of Mission." *TransMission*, Special Edition (1998) 3–6.

Shepherd, Massey H., Jr. *The Oxford American Prayer Book Commentary*. New York: Oxford University Press, 1950.

———. "Toward a Definition of the Church's Liturgy." *Mid-Stream* 2/4 (1963) 120–34.

————, ed. *Worship in Scripture and Tradition.* New York: Oxford University Press, 1963.

Shriver, Peggy L. *Getting to Know You: Churches Seeking Communion.* Princeton: Consultation on Church Union, 1991.

Significance of the Responses to A Plan of Union for the Church of Christ Uniting. Princeton: Consultation on Church Union, 1973.

Signs of Hope—Promise of Change: In Celebration of the Inauguration of Churches Uniting in Christ. Cincinnati: Forward Movement, 2002.

Silcox, Claris Edwin. "Ten Years of Church Union in Canada." *Christendom* 1 (1935–36) 81–91; 350–61.

Small, Joseph D. "Ecclesial Identity and Ecumenical Decisions in the Presbyterian Church (U.S.A.)." *Journal of Ecumenical Studies* 37/1 (2000) 1–12.

Sommerville, Raymond R., Jr. *An Ex-Colored Church: Social Activism in the CME Church, 1870–1970.* Macon, GA: Mercer University Press, 2006.

Statistical Abstract of the United States: 1972. 93rd ed. Washington, DC: U. S. Bureau of the Census, 1972.

Stauffer, Paul S. "The Parish Concept in a Plan of Union." *Mid-Stream* 12/2–4 (1973) 116–21.

Wagner, C. Peter. "Church Growth Research." In *Understanding Church Growth and Decline, 1950–1978,* edited by Dean R. Hoge and David A. Roozen, 270–87. New York: Pilgrim, 1979.

Watkins, Keith. "Coming Away with Hope: Thoughts about the Inauguration in Memphis of Churches Uniting in Christ." *Mid-Stream* 41/2–3 (2002) 102–6.

————. "Liturgical Challenges for Churches Uniting in Christ." *Doxology* 19 (2002) 1–13.

————. "Twenty Years with the Consultation on Church Union." *Mid-Stream* 34/3 (1975) 93–103.

Watley, William D. "Lambs and Wolves: A Vision of Hope." *Mid-Stream* 24/2 (1985) 150–54.

————. *Singing the Lord's Song in a Strange Land.* Grand Rapids: Eerdmans, 1993.

————, ed. "The Word and Words: Beyond Gender in Theological and Liturgical Language." Princeton: Consultation on Church Union, 1983.

Weaver, James W. "Brethren Response to the Consultation on Church Union." *Brethren Life and Thought* 14 (1969) 227–47.

Wedel, Theodore O. "The Body-Spirit Paradox of the Church." *Mid-Stream* 2/4 (1963) 69–82; also published in *The Ecumenical Review* 4/4 (1952) 345–54; and in *Approaches Toward Unity,* edited by Ivan Lee Holt and Stephen E. Keeler, 133–47. Nashville: Parthenon, 1952.

White, James F. *Protestant Worship: Traditions in Transition.* Louisville: Westminster/John Knox, 1989.

Wilburn, Ralph B. "The One Baptism and the Many Baptisms." *Mid-Stream* 3/4 (1964) 72–107.

Williams, Colin W. "The Structure of the Church." *Mid-Stream* 6/4 (1967) 53–74.

Williams, Preston. "COCU and the Cultural Revolution." *Mid-Stream* 10/2–3 (1971) 131–43.

Winter, Gibson. *The Suburban Captivity of the Churches: An Analysis of Protestant Responsibility in the Expanding Metropolis.* Garden City, NY: Doubleday, 1961.

Wolf, William J. *Documents on Church Unity*. Joint Commission on Approaches to Unity. New York: Seabury, 1962.

———. "The Ordained Ministry in Uniting Churches." *Mid-Stream* 4/4 (1965) 37–106.

Wyatt, Peter. "Exploring New Forms of Co-operation: The Project of 'Mending the World.'" *Journal of Ecumenical Studies* 35/3–4 (1998) 347–52.

Young, Franklin M. "One Table in Contemporary New Testament Studies." *Mid-Stream* 3/4 (1964) 119–42.

Young, McKinley. "An Ecumenical Epiphany," *Mid-Stream* 41/2–3 (2002) 17–22.

Ziegler, Jesse H. "Shall We Go into Consultation and Union? Yes!" *Brethren Life and Thought* 11/1 (1966) 4–13. See other essays in this same volume by Vernard Eller, Raymond R. Peters, Harry M. Gardner, Dale W. Brown, and C. Wayne Zunkel.

Index